Affective Genealogies

Affective Genealogies

Psychoanalysis, Postmodernism,
and the "Jewish Question"
after Auschwitz

ELIZABETH J. BELLAMY

University of Nebraska Press

Lincoln and London

⊚ The paper in this book meets the minimum
requirements of American
National Standard for Information Sciences —
Permanence of Paper for
Printed Library Materials, ANSI z39.48-1984.

Library of Congress
Cataloging in Publication Data
Bellamy, Elizabeth J. (Elizabeth Jane)
Affective genealogies: psychoanalysis,
postmodernism, and the "Jewish question"
after Auschwitz / Elizabeth J. Bellamy.
p. cm. – (Texts and contexts)
Includes bibliographical references and index.
ISBN 0-8032-1249-6 (cloth: alkaline paper)
1. Holocaust, Jewish (1939-1945) – Influence.
2. Holocaust, Jewish (1939-1945) –
Psychological aspects. 3. Pyschoanalysis.
4. Postmodernism. 5. Jews – Politics
and government – 1948- I. Title.
II. Series. D804.3.B444 1998
940.53'18–DC21 97-10838
CIP R97

Contents

Affective Genealogies

I

Mourning and Melancholia in the French Post-Holocaust

Postmodernism and the "Crisis" of Memory

The current debate over the radical divide, the epistemological break, between modernism and postmodernism is lengthy and complex, involving thinkers with agendas as diverse as Habermas's and Lyotard's, and, to be sure, it is a debate that extends far beyond the scope of this book. Regardless of whether one interprets the virgule that separates the binary "modernism/postmodernism" as implying a chronological continuum between the two epochs or as the mark of an epistemic irruption or *coupure,* I am interested in exploring the ways in which many of the discursive practices of postmodernism are fashioning themselves (either consciously or unconsciously) "psychoanalytically." An implicit irony of this study is postmodernism's dismissal of psychoanalysis as an ever-receding (and increasingly irrelevant) chapter in the story of Western modernity, even as it persists (quite "symptomatically," we may add) in using psychoanalytic terms to constitute itself.[1] To phrase it broadly, I argue that the much-debated "slash" between modernism and postmodernism demarcates, among other things, an obscure psychic threshold of repression, disavowal, denegation, or foreclosure of an unresolved modernism—all the psychic defenses against the violence of the divide between modernism and postmodernism, for which a melancholic strain within postmodernism has become the most observable aftereffect. I also argue that this unacknowledged melancholia in turn serves as the ironic backdrop for postmodernism's often contradictory engagement with psychoanalysis as a modernist "grand narrative" that it seeks both to appropriate and to reject.

It was Walter Benjamin's reactions to Fascism that, as much as anything, first prompted a "psychoanalyzing" of modern experience as inherently melancholic. Benjamin's oft-cited depiction of his "angel of history," peering expectantly into the future but with a face turned to

the past as a "pile of debris," the "wreckage" of catastrophe, builds skyward,[2] serves perhaps as the paradigmatic icon of modernism's melancholic view of the catastrophes of the twentieth century. But postmodernism, as a critique of modernity, evinces its own melancholic reaction
to the "debris" of history and thus also, and perhaps inevitably, lends
itself to psychoanalytic considerations. After all, postmodernism can be
summarized as, among other things, a kind of melancholic reaction to
the loss of modernity's narratives of coherence. Thus a current trend in
postmodern discourse is its increasingly "apocalyptic" anxieties that the
exhaustion of modernity means we are hurtling toward some sort of
end, a theme perhaps most prominently interrogated in Derrida's essay
"Of an Apocalyptic Tone Recently Adopted in Philosophy."[3] And in his
recent essay "The Apocalyptic Imagination and the Inability to Mourn,"
Martin Jay has forged a specific link between what he calls postmodernism's "apocalyptic imaginary" and melancholia, as if to argue that
postmodernism inhabits an ambiguous psychic space between an anxiety for an unknown future and a melancholic fixation on an unrecoverable past.[4]

In this context, we can turn also to Jürgen Habermas's criticism of
such diverse philosophers as Heidegger, Adorno, and Derrida and what
he perceives as their persistence in philosophizing in the "shadow of
the 'last' philosopher, as did the first generation of Hegelian disciples.
They still feel the need to battle against those 'strong' concepts of system, totality, truth, and completed theory which belong to the past."[5]
Thus Habermas implies that even as much contemporary philosophy
seeks a break with the past, there exists a melancholic compulsion, like
Benjamin's angel of history, to "worry" the past—to keep the past, as
it were, "encrypted" within philosophy's own anticipation of the future. More recently, Eric Santner has argued compellingly that the postmodern project (as the "death" of modernity) is obsessed with "death,
loss, and impoverishment," manifested as "discourses of bereavement"
whose labor of mourning a lost modernity enact not a true sense of
loss, but rather a kind of bizarrely playful *jouissance* celebrating the discontinuities of the alienated postmodern subject.[6] Here Santner astutely "psychoanalyzes" postmodernism as enacting a kind of *Trauerspiel,* in the process revealing its own repressions of a melancholic
nostalgia for the past.

One lesson of Freud's "Mourning and Melancholia" is that melancholia is a kind of perversion or distortion of memory—a refusal of a

salutary remembrance of loss, a refusal to mourn, that condemns the subject to a futile "acting out." Thus I would argue that what may make any "psychoanalyzing" of a postmodern "unconscious" a particularly overdetermined (and potentially ironic) gesture is that many of the discursive practices of postmodernism are *consciously* engaged with a (pseudo) psychoanalytic critique of memory, even as a postmodern melancholia inadvertently foregrounds memory (and its many unconscious distortions) as constitutive of much contemporary philosophy itself.

We should note that the "apocalyptic imaginary" of much current postmodern discourse seems concerned with the privileged (but, from a postmodern perspective, over-essentialized) Freudian concept of memory and the question of whether there can be such a thing as a postmodern memory. In some circles, postmodernism has become synonymous with *posthistoire*, or the point at which postmodernism threatens to expose, as Saul Friedländer has phrased it, "a growing irrelevance of historical consciousness."[7] If, as an "apocalyptic imaginary" contends, history has indeed "come to an end," then such concepts as collective memory and historical consciousness threaten to become obsolete in a postmodern era.

As a consequence, much current postmodernism is conceiving itself psychoanalytically as a kind of crisis in memory that seeks to deconstruct the traditional opposition between remembrance and forgetting. In this sense, postmodernism is the immediate heir to modernism's own ambivalences about memory. Nietzsche, in the second treatise of his *On the Genealogy of Morals,* was perhaps the first modernist thinker to problematize the operations of memory by hypostatizing an "active forgetfulness." Freud made the further move of positing repression *(Verdrängung)* as the receding of memory into the unconscious. For Freud, memory is always subject to distortion through forgetting (as argued in such works as *Beyond the Pleasure Principle, Studies in Hysteria,* and "Screen Memories") — and in a letter to Fliess (December 1896), he made the provocative claim that even in the best of times *"consciousness and memory are mutually exclusive."*[8] In this context, one can also think of Heidegger (whose own intellectual career, as we shall consider in the next chapter, is overdetermined within the radical divide between modernism and postmodernism) and his configuration of Being not as a concept, but as nothing less than the "forgotten" in modern philosophy. This brief genealogy of modernist memory provides only a few examples of how, as Andreas Huyssen summarizes so eloquently, "the issue of remembrance and forgetting touches the core of Western identity, however multifaceted and diverse."[9]

Could we say, then, that what constitutes the radical divide between modernism and postmodernism is a vast cultural repression of modernism's own anxieties about the erosion of identifiable barriers between memory and forgetting? And if this is the case, then to what extent is any postmodern critique of an "essentializing" memory *itself* a kind of (melancholic) forgetting of the past that constitutes a precarious psychic space for, in particular, a "thinking" of trauma as the absolute shattering of memory? Memory, forgetting, mourning, melancholia, repression—all these profoundly psychoanalytic phenomena converge not coincidentally in trauma, specifically the Holocaust as perhaps the major unresolved trauma lying at "the core of Western identity," a trauma that haunts the divide between modernism and postmodernism and overdetermines any postmodern attempt to proclaim a "crisis" of memory.[10]

No one understood better than the Nazis how fragile memory can be. In his preface to *The Drowned and the Saved,* Primo Levi quotes from Simon Wiesenthal's *The Murderers Are Among Us* and its grim reenactment of the ss's taunting its prisoners: "However the war may end, we have won the war against you; none of you will be left to bear witness, but even if someone were to survive, the world will not believe him . . . because we will destroy the evidence together with you."[11] For Levi, as for so many survivors of Auschwitz, the *Endlösung* (or "Final Solution") is characterized as, among other things, a vast Nazi effort to efface memory itself. Thus, in the wake of the Holocaust, the concept of memory has become an even more inherently Jewish concern such that, as Emil Fackenheim argues, to forget the Holocaust is to grant Hitler yet another victory.[12] Particularly concerned with how easily memory can be distorted, Pierre Vidal-Naquet argues that current "revisionists" like Robert Faurisson threaten to achieve just such a collective forgetting of the Holocaust through their sinister "assassinations" of memory.[13] That the trauma of the Holocaust remains an ongoing crisis in memory—for the perpetrators as well as for the survivors—is vividly demonstrated in Claude Lanzmann's *Shoah,* where Walter Stier, former chief architect of the transport of the Jews to the death camps, struggles to remember: "Like that camp—what was its name? It was in the

Oppeln district. . . . I've got it. Auschwitz."[14] Stier's outrageous "lapse" in memory—constituted within the obscure psychic threshold of a traumatized remembrance and a Nietzschean "active forgetfulness"— enacts a perverse counterpoint to *Zakhor,* the Jewish commandment to remember;[15] and it serves as a disturbing illustration of Huyssen's contention that "the issue of remembrance and forgetting touches the core of Western identity." As I will argue later, the issue of remembrance and forgetting "touches the core" of Western postmodernism when it seeks to "remember" the Holocaust.

Historical Memory "after Auschwitz"; or, Psychoanalyzing Germany

"Repressions that have failed," Freud observes provocatively, "will of course have more claim on our interest than those that may have been successful."[16] For Freud, repression (in particular, the collective repression of cultural memory) is more often a case of *failed* repression, an inconclusive *agon* between consciousness and the unconscious that, in its most acute form, signals the onset of psychic trauma.

In a postmodern era (an era when Walter Stier must struggle to remember "that camp . . . in the Oppeln district"), it is increasingly argued that we now find ourselves positioned within the temporal frame of an "after Auschwitz" as one of the twentieth century's most horrifyingly vivid demonstrations of a Freudian "failed repression." In an oft-cited and resounding judgment, Adorno has warned that "to write poetry after Auschwitz is barbaric."[17] More recently, but no less urgently, Werner Hamacher has argued that "we do not just write 'after Auschwitz.' There is no experiential 'after' to an absolute trauma."[18] Maurice Blanchot, in a moment that seems particularly attuned to the mnemonic overdeterminations of an "after Auschwitz," asks: "How philosophize, how write in the memory of Auschwitz, of those who have said to us sometimes in notes buried near the crematories: 'know what has happened,' 'do not forget,' and, at the same time, 'you will never know'?"[19] The temporal frame of an "after Auschwitz," serving as both the convergence *and* the deconstruction of history, memory, and trauma, has perhaps inevitably been characterized psychoanalytically. And the crucial point I wish to emphasize here is that if Auschwitz can effectively be summarized as the central trauma of European modernity, then psychoanalysis has become increasingly prominent as a means of further investigating the nature of trauma—with Germany becoming the specific site of a psychoanalysis of its Nazi past.

One of the first and most ambitious efforts at "psychoanalyzing" the German national character *(Volkstümlichkeit)* was Alexander and Margarete Mitscherlich's groundbreaking *The Inability to Mourn,* a thorough study of the extent to which postwar German society of the 1950s, through persistent denegation and repression, failed to confront and work through its Nazi past (such that, among other strange psychic developments, the perpetrators tended to view themselves as victims).[20] Their book also provides compelling arguments that the psychic processes of mourning and melancholia are not just interior and private, but also inherently cultural, social, and political in their ramifications. The book is simultaneously a reminder that the attempt to represent trauma is itself traumatic, and a compelling affirmation of Freud's theory that, in matters of trauma, it may be impossible fully to convert into understanding an acting out of the past.

But Adorno has surely been the most influential in configuring recent German history psychoanalytically. In his lecture "What Does Coming to Terms with the Past Mean?" Adorno suggests that a remembrance and "making sense" of the Holocaust in Germany is as much a psychoanalytic as a political imperative.[21] His term *Aufarbeitung* ("coming to terms with") expresses the urgency of Germany's need to assimilate the trauma of the Holocaust into a collective national consciousness, to "remember" and "work through" its past in ways that are explicitly psychoanalytic. In this context, Jürgen Habermas has also offered a version of "after Auschwitz" as a crisis in German memory: "Today the grandchildren of those who at the close of World War II were too young to be able to experience personal guilt are already growing up. Memory . . . has not become correspondingly distantiated. Contemporary history remains fixated on the period between 1933 and 1945. It does not move beyond the horizons of its own life-history; it remains tied up in sensitivities and reactions that . . . still always have the same point of departure: the images of that unloading ramp at Auschwitz."[22] Like Adorno, Habermas points to a crisis in memory—the difficulty of fully accommodating the unloading ramp at Auschwitz within a collective national consciousness—as the most significant psychic obstacle to Germany's refusal to mourn its "unmasterable past." For both Adorno and Habermas, the temporal frame of an "after Auschwitz" enacts the explicitly psychoanalytic (and cultural) allegory of an extended German "melancholia" that refuses to allow for a genuine "mourning."

What it is that German history "remembers" (as well as the question of how the historian enters into an exchange with the past) has never been so problematized as with the Holocaust—what Hamacher has referred to as "a 'history' [that] cannot enter into any history of development."[23] If we view the Nazis' Final Solution as an incinerating effort at eliminating all traces of memory of the Jews *(Vernichtung)*, then how can German history reconstruct, or "re-member," this unutterable project of absolute "forgetting"? "After Auschwitz," a haunting question persists as to whether it is even possible to *do* something like a history (a collective cultural remembrance) of the trauma of the Holocaust.

In recent years, one of the more widely publicized controversies concerning the aims of historiography (and the context of Habermas's observations on German memory) has been the so-called West German *Historikerstreit,* which was initiated in the mid-1980s by certain revisionists seeking a "normalization" of recent German history as a response to what was perceived as an unfair tendency among earlier historians toward moral condemnation of Germany for its Nazi past. As an example of such revisionist "memories," one can cite Andreas Hillgruber's sympathizing with the German troops fighting on the Eastern front at the end of the war, a history that has the bizarre result of transforming Germany into a "victim" of the Allies while ignoring the victims of the extermination camps. Or one can consider Martin Broszat's call for a history of the everyday lives of ordinary Germans, or an *Alltagsgeschichte.* Such a history would be resolutely shaped by nonideological factors, its focus on ordinary experiences in small villages and towns highlighting patterns of social "normality" that would "relativize" the horror of Nazi ideology. Or one can turn to the even more controversial Ernst Nolte (a former student of Heidegger), who contextualizes the Holocaust as only one of many twentieth-century genocides and portrays Hitler's "Final Solution" for the Jews as a kind of defensive reaction to the Bolshevik genocides in the Gulag.[24]

What, one is moved to ask, can history *do* with trauma in a postmodern, post-Holocaust era? Even this briefest of overviews of the *Historikerstreit,* where the ineffable horror of the Holocaust is repeatedly effaced in favor of "larger" contexts, gives rise to a number of questions concerning the relationship between history and psychoanalysis, both of which, in their broadest scope, attempt their own "working through" of trauma. For both history and psychoanalysis, a series of questions emerge: How does one enter into an exchange with the past that can negotiate trauma and, at the same time, locate and preserve historical specificity? In its interactions with the past, what does history "remember" or "repress"? How valid is the concept of a "historical consciousness" when it seeks to write history "after Auschwitz"?

Whether or not history is a genre that can allow for the psychic processes of mourning and working through is the central concern of the recent work of the intellectual historian Dominick LaCapra, who has focused in particular on one of the privileged foundations of psychoanalysis: the concept of transference and the extent to which it deeply informs the pursuit of history, even as the historian disavows transference. As LaCapra interprets it, transference "refers to the manner in which the problems at issue in the object of study reappear (or are repeated with variations) in the work of the historian."[25] Thus, psychoanalysis is always already embedded within the practice of historiography insofar as the relation of the historian to the object of study is often unavoidably transferential.

More specifically, in his recent essay "Representing the Holocaust: Reflections on the Historians' Debate," LaCapra argues that the Holocaust "presents the historian with transference in the most traumatic form conceivable."[26] Picking up where Habermas left off, LaCapra builds his essay around this central question: if we take into account the disavowal of transference that characterizes the *Historikerstreit*, can history ever achieve a genuine "mourning" of the trauma of the Holocaust? Or, as the point at which the unconscious will inevitably impinge on a narrative reconstruction of events, is Holocaust history doomed to serve as the locus of repetition compulsions — of endless compulsions either to try to "remember" ("act out"?) or "forget" ("repress"?) a trauma that always already threatens to deconstruct memory itself? "After Auschwitz," all linguistic or semantic innocence has been lost, such that even simple words like "mourning" cannot be invoked without inadvertent and grim ironies. With uncanny significance for the Holocaust, Jean-Bertrand Pontalis argues vividly that the "teleological purpose [of mourning] has been said to be to 'kill the dead'"[27] — as if to remind us that genuine mourning "after Auschwitz" (whether on the part of victims or perpetrators or bystanders) always threatens to deteriorate into a melancholic repetition compulsion that "kills," but never fully "remembers" the dead.

As if the matter of historical memory had not been made complicated enough by psychoanalysis, positivist historiography in general, even as it attempts to answer the question of whether or not it is possible to *do* something like a history of the Holocaust, now finds itself (like psychoanalysis, as we have seen) challenged by the rigorously nonessentializing discourse of postmodernism that proclaims we are now in an era of *post*-history. And much recent postmodern theoretical discourse threatens to expose the kind of mourning and working through of trauma that the Mitscherlichs' *Inability to Mourn* called for as naively and piously essentializing. Thus, larger questions arise as to whether a genuine mourning for the Holocaust is now even *possible* in a post-Holocaust era that has also become distinctly postmodern.[28] Within postmodernism's project as a radical critique of modernity, what is the "place" of the Holocaust as, in the view of many, the chronological marker of the final failure of the Enlightenment? Can the nonessentializing discourse of postmodernism ever enable a genuine "working through" to an understanding of the horror of the Holocaust? Can a genuine mourning for the Holocaust be conceived as something other than simply a relapse into modernist nostalgia? In the interstices between the psychoanalytic process of mourning and a postmodern *Trauerspiel* lies Auschwitz — or is it rather the temporal space of an "after Auschwitz" as the postmodern marker of a Holocaust that has not been fully "worked through"?

Erinnerung, Verdrängung, Trauerspiel, Aufarbeitung, Vergangenheitsbewältigung (Habermas's term for mastery of the past) — all these terms trace the convergence of historical memory and psyche in postwar Germany, a convergence that is portrayed, from Adorno to Habermas to the Mitscherlichs, as somehow quintessentially (and chronically) "German." As Eric Santner claims, immediately after the war "Germans had to mourn *as Germans* for those whom they had excluded and exterminated in their mad efforts to produce their 'Germanness.'"[29] Thus it is as if, in a postwar era, "Germanness" has become an almost exclusively psychoanalytic phenomenon.

Anti-Semitism, the "Jewish Question," and the "Question" of Psychoanalysis

In response to postmodernism's drift into an era of *posthistoire* and its claims that memory is, in effect, obsolete, it is perhaps imperative "after Auschwitz" that we place postwar Germany's "inability to mourn" in an earlier historical context before Auschwitz. In so doing, we will discover that postmodernism's "inability to mourn" the Holocaust may be viewed historically as an ongoing symptom of modernism's inability to solve the "Jewish Question." In other words, we will come to discover that what gets disavowed in, say, the failure of the *Historikerstreit* to confront the horror of the Holocaust is, specifically, the phenomenon of anti-Semitism; and we will come to discover that the trauma of the Holocaust cannot be fully confronted without considering (however briefly) modernism's struggle with the "Jewish Question" and the specificity of Jewish identity in the Enlightenment. To what extent is Adorno's proclamation that we now inhabit the temporal space of an "after Auschwitz" rendered even more meaningful when we consider his own conflicted identity as a modernist Jew *before* and *during* Auschwitz?

Invoking Adorno in this context can remind us that a "working through" of the Holocaust entails at least a brief consideration of the relationship between the project of the Frankfurt Institute of Social Research and the status of the Jew in modernism. As I have argued earlier, much postmodern discourse seeks to fashion itself "psychoanalytically"; but we might consider the extent to which modernism, particularly as interpreted by the Frankfurt Institute, was also fundamentally shaped by its engagement with psychoanalysis. Indeed, it seems no coincidence that it was in the years leading up to Auschwitz that the Frankfurt Institute undertook to fashion itself the most "psychoanalytically."

Even as it began to disintegrate as a result of the rise of fascism (with more and more of its members, including Horkheimer and Adorno, forced to become émigrés), the Frankfurt Institute chose largely to ignore the "Jewish Question" in Germany.[30] The Institute's interest in the psychology of Nazi authoritarianism did not necessarily lead to an immediate and specific interest in the fate of the Jew under Hitler. Rather, as Martin Jay points out, the Institute was far more concerned with such issues as the relationship between fascism and its bureaucratization of the economy, its bridging of the public and private realm, and so on, than with the issue of anti-Semitism as such. Even as many of its members sought to suppress their Jewish origins, the Institute's analysis of the relationship between fascism and capitalism tended to view anti-Semitism as merely an inevitable result of class conflict under fascism and capitalism, thus (even after the Nazis seized power) ironically recapitulating one of the most notorious anti-Semitic topoi since the rise of Early Modernism: the stereotype of the Jew as the root of all capitalist evil and as thereby reducible to a socioeconomic category. Certainly one of the more strident documents illustrating the complex psychoanalytic phenomenon of "Jewish self-hatred" (and a major influence on the economic theory of the Frankfurt Institute) was Marx's "On the Jewish Question" (1843).[31] And it could be argued that the "Jewish self-hatred" behind Marx's claim that the Jew is to blame for the crisis of capitalism became encrypted, as it were, as a key "symptom" of the social research of the Frankfurt Institute.[32] Through much of the 1930s, then, the Frankfurt School's "psychoanalyzing" of fascist authoritarianism ironically recapitulated its own version of a kind of Jewish self-hatred, with a Marxist critique of capital being used to give economic categories priority over the realities of impending mass victimization defined racially.

In 1939, however, the emphasis began to shift with the publication of Horkheimer's essay "The Jews and Europe" ("Die Juden und Europa"). As Jay has compellingly argued, "the increased integration of psychoanalysis into critical theory coincided very closely with the growing attention they began paying to anti-Semitism during the war."[33] Moreover, a document that may be even more melancholic than Benjamin's "Theses on the Philosophy of History" is Horkheimer and Adorno's *Dialectic of Enlightenment,* a pessimistic view of modernity written against the backdrop of the rise of fascism, and the first analysis of anti-Semitism to come out of the Holocaust.[34] Horkheimer and Adorno were perhaps the first to "psychoanalyze" anti-Semitism by means of their concept of "repressed mimesis": "Anti-Semitism is based on a false projection. It is the counterpart of true mimesis, and fundamentally related to the repressed form; in fact, it is probably the morbid expression of repressed mimesis."[35] Like Sartre's *Anti-Semite and Jew, Dialectic of Enlightenment* suggests paranoia, repression, and a kind of narcissism gone awry as the fundamental psychic underpinnings of an anti-Semitism that always forces the Jew into alterity. Thus, out of the flames and ashes of the Holocaust arose a new linkage between psychoanalysis and the anti-Semite. With their conviction that anti-Semitism is ingrained in the collective (un)consciousness of the Enlightenment, Horkheimer and Adorno, in the temporal frame of "after Auschwitz," relinquished the Frankfurt Institute's earlier repetition compulsion of Jewish self-hatred (that is, complicity with anti-Semitism's stereotype of the "capitalist" Jew) and pointed the way to a newer and more sophisticated understanding of anti-Semitism as a psychic phenomenon.

Psychoanalyzing France and *La Question Juive*

As noted at the end of this chapter's second section, it is as if in a post-war era "Germanness" (or German guilt, trauma, and melancholia—all the psychic processes that have served as the backdrop for German anti-Semitism) has become an almost exclusively psychoanalytic phenomenon. But let us now shift our location to France, which, though not nearly so readily conceived in the popular imagination as suffering from a postwar collective guilt, has its own lengthy, grim, and complex history of anti-Semitism. Indeed, the fact that France has produced no systematic study of the psychic effects of its collaborationist past on its population that could be seen as comparable to the Mitscherlichs' *Inability to Mourn* in Germany would indicate a history of disavowal and denegation of its own scarcely confronted "Jewish Question" even more complex than Germany's. To quote again from Santner, immediately after the war "Germans had to mourn *as Germans* for those whom they had excluded and exterminated in their mad efforts to produce their 'Germanness.'" But a key question to pose in the context of France is: have the French truly mourned *as the French* for those whom they have reviled in their efforts to produce "Frenchness"?

Let us trace briefly some of the key events in the history of French anti-Semitism in order to lay the foundation for a better understanding of France's postwar struggles with the "Jewish Question." As Seth L. Wolitz has observed, "Imagining the Jew is a French intellectual pastime that dates back some two hundred years."[36] As we shall see, implicit in Wolitz's observation is the French Gentile's psychic obsession with "imagining the Jew" to be authentically "French." One of the hopes following the French Revolution in 1791 was that the Jews of France, the first Jewish community in Europe to be emancipated and granted full rights of citizenship, would become "outmoded"; the goal was nothing less than for "Jewishness" (*judéité*) to become obsolete. The emancipatory ideology of *régénération*, which eventually shaped the French Jew of modernity, held that *judéité* was incompatible with French citizenship, and thus the individual Jew became occluded under the broader laws of the State. In short, under the impulse of *régénération,* it was imperative that the Jew be perceived as a *French* citizen, not as a Jew.[37]

The briefest of overviews of French history from the nineteenth century, however, reveals the steady deterioration of the ideology of *régénération* into anti-Semitism. By the late 1800s, a French anti-Semitic *mentalité,* fueled by, among other developments, the racial theory of Gobineau's four-volume *Essai sur l'inégalité des races humaines* (1853–55), had asserted itself to the point that, within a Gentile cultural imaginary, it was no longer possible to perceive the Jew as authentically "French." The French Jew (like the German Jew) was then in the impossible position of being labeled either a Bolshevik or a capitalist financier (in an anticapitalist fervor that would evolve by the 1970s into a bizarre alliance between the right-wing anti-Semitism of the *Nouvelle Droite* and a left-wing anti-Semitism originating with the likes of Proudhon and Toussenel). And in 1886, Edouard Drumont, future founder of the Ligue Antisémite, published his notorious *La France juive,* portraying the Jews of France as wealthy capitalist exploiters.[38] In 1894, the widely chronicled national trauma of *l'affaire Dreyfus* exploded, culminating in cries of *"Mort aux Juifs!"*[39] Decades later, the 1920s and 1930s saw a wave of immigration into France, with the prevailing sentiment becoming *"La France aux Français";* by the Depression, anti-Semitism in France had reached rampant, even obsessive, proportions, as exemplified by the fascist writings of Louis-Ferdinand Céline, Robert Brasillach, and Pierre Drieu La Rochelle in such right-wing journals as *Je Suis Partout.*[40] In 1936, Léon Blum, who had taken office as prime minister, was the subject of an ugly attack by Charles Maurras in the right-wing *Action Française,* and in 1940 Georges Montandon's *Comment reconnaître le Juif?* ominously mirrored France's wartime treatment of the Jew, portraying the Jew as a threat to French national identity.[41]

All of which brings us to World War II and the collaborationist regime of Vichy and, in particular, its lessons in what postwar French history has chosen to "forget" about its own national trauma. The psychic phenomena of memory, forgetting, melancholia, and repression all converge on Vichy as the locus of France's characteristic "inability to mourn," and they serve as a vivid demonstration that France's *Aufarbeitung* has been delayed much longer than Germany's. Since the

1970s, however, studies of Vichy have proliferated, demonstrating an increased willingness to lift the veil of repression around the *collaborateurs,* an increased willingness to abandon France's customary narratives of Resistance heroism and their persistent portrayals of Laval's and Pétain's policies as marginal to the larger French national community, and an increasing disinclination to validate the collective amnesia surrounding France's complicity with fascism—a "forgetting" originating with de Gaulle and perpetuated by his successors.[42] These studies have been instrumental in revealing the horror of Jewish experience in occupied France, exposing, for example, the fact that between 1940 and 1944 close to eighty thousand Jews (mostly foreign Jews who had immigrated to France) were killed. As any number of these studies have emphasized, particularly grim evidence of the alacrity of French involvement in the enacting of the Nazis' Final Solution was the notorious *Statut des Juifs* of October 1940, which, without any prompting from the Germans, redefined the "Jew" to include anyone with two Jewish grandparents and a Jewish spouse—a racial definition far more inclusive than German legal definitions of the Jew.

The very title of Henri Rousso's authoritative 1987 study *Le syndrome de Vichy* gets to the heart of the psychoanalytic implications of France's "inability to mourn" its collaborationist past, for the "Vichy syndrome" has indeed created a France that is, as Freud might have described it in his *Civilization and Its Discontents,* "neurotic." And no doubt because of the country's unresolved memories of Vichy and its willingness to conceal an encrypted Holocaust within its national identity, resurgences of anti-Semitism have continued to characterize French history since World War II. One thinks immediately of the controversies and explosive emotions surrounding the recent trial in France of the German Klaus Barbie, former Gestapo chief in Lyon, perhaps the most recent evidence that a French *Trauerarbeit* for its wartime past has scarcely begun.[43]

In this context, one is also reminded of *l'affaire Faurisson* and Faurisson's insidious revisionist history claiming that the gas chambers never existed (a history that has transformed *la question juive* into "la question des chambres à gaz"). Pockets of Holocaust revisionism are appearing in a number of countries, such as Sweden, Italy, Australia, and the United States—but, as Vidal-Naquet has observed, "it is the French case that seems the most interesting and complex."[44] The particular complexity of French *révisionnisme* as an "assassination of memory" is embodied, as Vidal-Naquet has argued, in the overdetermined figure of Paul Rassinier, who on the one hand was a member of the Resistance and a deportee to Buchenwald and Dora, but on the other hand played a key role in France's revisionist movement—estimating the number of Jewish losses during World War II at around only one million and regarding the Centre de Documentation Juive Contemporaine as an archive of forgeries. Moreover, the eulogy at his Paris funeral was delivered by neo-Nazi Maurice Bardèche. That *l'affaire Faurisson* continues to present a major obstacle to France's "inability to mourn" its collaborationist past is perhaps most vividly demonstrated in *L'Express*'s 1978 interview with Louis Darquier de Pellepoix, Vichy's commissaire général of Jewish affairs during the deportation years of 1942–44. Pellepoix remarked that the only thing gassed at Auschwitz was lice.

It is clear that anti-Semitism has been a constitutive aspect of French culture since the Enlightenment, a phenomenon that has persistently denied that the Jew can ever be authentically "French." Moreover, one can perceive the extent to which the "Jewish Question" in France, perhaps even more than in Germany, is an inherently psychoanalytic phenomenon—a collective (un)consciousness that perpetuates itself by means of disavowal, denegation, and repression. In a compelling essay, Shmuel Trigano has described the resurgence of anti-Semitism in modern France in explicitly psychoanalytic terms. Because, in the ideology of *régénération,* the Jew was to be perceived as a citizen and not as a Jew, "[w]hat served to grant the Jew his emancipation served to deny him his Jewishness."[45] In other words, in order to erect the "myth" of the citizen, the essence of the "Jew" had to be disavowed. But because it was, in Trigano's words, "*a* Jew who was to undermine from within the conceptual clarity of *the* citizen," anti-Semitism made its inevitable (and paradoxical) return: "This irrepressible tendency of the republican system to turn the Jews into the very entity that the system forbade them to become could be likened to the psychoanalytic logic of the return of the repressed."[46]

To further unpack the psychic implications of Trigano's paradox, when the Jew seeks to become "French" through assimilation into the State, he fails all the more to conceal his true "Jewish" essence. The result is that the French Jew is never more "Jewish" (or *enjuivé*) than when he seeks to become "French"—or, phrased psychoanalytically, it is as if efforts at Jewish assimilation into "authentic" French citizenship serve only to exacerbate a fetishizing of the "real Jew" on the part of the French

Gentile. Thus, it is both a disavowal of the Jew *and* a fetishization of the Jew that constitute the weird psychic paradox that traps the figure of the Jew within the cultural imaginary of French anti-Semitism.

In light of this impossible double bind, it is perhaps not surprising, then, that as Wolitz has argued, "[n]ot since the Martin Buber–Franz Rosenzweig debates in Germany of the 1920's has there been anywhere, in the diaspora or in the land of Israel, such intense intellectual debate as in France to define and imagine the Jew."[47] Wolitz's phrase "imagining the Jew" suggests a distinctly psychoanalytic resonance, pointing to the ongoing psychic crisis of French Jewry's efforts to represent itself *for* itself—in effect, to escape the psychic paradox of being trapped between disavowal and fetishization.

It could be argued that the process of "imagining the Jew" in postwar France begins with Sartre, whose humanist existentialism has a long postwar history of standing in opposition to French Heideggerianism and its dismissal of humanism. Given his humanist (and anti-Heideggerian) emphasis, it is not surprising that Sartre, in his essay "What Is a Collaborator?" (originally published in 1945), was perhaps the first postwar intellectual to challenge the fascist intellectual to articulate the bizarre psychology behind French anti-Semitism.[48] But without doubt Sartre's *Anti-Semite and Jew* (written in 1944) is one of the most important documents emerging from postwar France, and is crucial for a fuller understanding of the project of contemporary French Heideggerianism.[49] This melancholic book, not unlike Horkheimer and Adorno's *Dialectic of Enlightenment* in the case of Germany, is one of the first postwar analyses of anti-Semitism as a specifically *French* problem: "for it is the problem of the French Jew that is *our* problem." And thus (as I discuss in chapter 2) even as Heidegger remained silent on the death camps, Sartre called much-needed attention to what he refers to as the French "*idea* of the Jew."[50]

Ironically, despite Sartre's life-long antipathy toward psychoanalysis, *Anti-Semite and Jew* was one of the first studies to frame *la question juive* in what could be viewed as psychoanalytic terms, applying psychological insights not to the Jew but to the anti-Semite. In Sartre's scheme, the Jew and the anti-Semite create a psychic dyad that renders the French perception of the Jew impossibly neurotic and, in his words, "overdetermined" (79). The perverted narcissism in which the Jew, always the "stranger" or the "intruder," is positioned as the specular "Other" for the French anti-Semite prompts Sartre to make the provocative claim that the Jew is virtually a psychic *need* for the anti-Semite: "[i]f the Jew did not exist, the anti-Semite would invent him. . . . It is the anti-Semite who creates the Jew" (13, 143). Indeed, when Sartre writes, "we must ask, not 'What is a Jew?' but *'What have you made of the Jews?'* " (69; italics in original), it is almost as if he is uncannily anticipating French postmodernism's fetishization of the Jew—and its embedded assumption that whatever the Jews are, they are *not* French.

No doubt because of Sartre's influential book, an ongoing preoccupation in contemporary France is to "imagine the Jew" within a post-Holocaust *sensibilité;* as we shall see, these post-Holocaust "imaginings" of the Jew all, in one form or another, pick up on the psychic implications of Sartre's accounts of the French anti-Semite's representation of the Jew as stranger, intruder. *La question juive* is the focus of much of the work of, for example, Edmond Jabès, an Egyptian Jew educated in France. Common threads running throughout virtually all of Jabès's writings are images of nomadism and exile, such that in an interview with André Velter, Jabès confesses, "Never have I known where I was. When I was in Egypt, I was in France. Since I have been in France, I have been somewhere else. . . . The stranger no longer knows what his place is."[51]

Perhaps the most eloquent writer currently seeking to "imagine the Jew" in a postmodern, post-Holocaust France is Alain Finkielkraut. The possibility that memory is in crisis in a post-Holocaust era, and the attendant concern that Jewish memory itself is threatened, is central to Finkielkraut's work. In *The Imaginary Jew,* a reflection on the crisis of Jewish identity in the post-Holocaust, Finkielkraut, though a child of Holocaust survivors, recounts his struggles to be *un Juif engagé* in the post-Holocaust, confessing his fears that he is somehow belated, inauthentic, born too late to experience the suffering of the beleaguered Jews of Sartre's *Anti-Semite and Jew.* Instead of being *un Juif engagé,* Finkielkraut suspects that he is really *un Juif imaginaire,* a post-Holocaust Jew lacking in cultural specificity—lacking, in some sense, in *judéité* itself.[52]

From Sartre to Jabès to Finkielkraut, the ongoing process of "imagining the Jew" in postwar France is a paradoxical process of not just rejecting but also *intro*jecting the anti-Semitic trope of the Jew as the strange and uncanny "other." Consequently, the postwar Jewish imaginary in France has become an extended meditation on the themes of *l'altérité, déracinement, l'étrangeté*—stereotypes left over from an earlier, modernist anti-Semitism, but which have experienced complex psychic metamorphoses in the post-Holocaust. Finkielkraut's figure of the *Juif imaginaire* and his preoccupation with whether or not the Jew of France can be authentically "French" provide a crucial backdrop to understanding the convergences between psychoanalysis and postmodernism in the post-Holocaust.

Cryptonymies: Psychoanalysis and Postmodernism in the Post-Holocaust

The previous two sections of this chapter have discussed the relationship between psychoanalysis and anti-Semitism—that is, the ways in which a specifically psychoanalytic focus on anti-Semitism can increase our understanding of the paradoxical and perverted logic by which the anti-Semite relegates the Jew to the role of psychic "Other." But *la question juive* in France becomes even more complex when we consider not only the (psychic) history of French anti-Semitism in general, but also the encryptedness of the "Jewish Question" within the history of French psychoanalysis in particular—a project that becomes even more overdetermined when we remember that the history of psychoanalysis in France is traversed by the Holocaust. I contend that Shmuel Trigano's characterization of French anti-Semitism (and the process by which the Jew has never been allowed to be authentically "French") as a vivid cultural demonstration of the "return of the repressed" calls for not only a "psychoanalyzing" *of* France, but also a brief "psychoanalyzing" of psychoanalysis itself *in* France.

One naturally and immediately tends to associate French psychoanalysis with the phenomenon of "French Freud"—Jacques Lacan's revolutionary "return to Freud" and its ambitious reconfiguring of French psychoanalysis. But the history of psychoanalysis in prewar France can also be associated with an ongoing French repression of *judéité* and the subsequent struggle (both conscious and unconscious) to make psychoanalysis authentically "French," not "Jewish." The many psychoanalytic resonances of French Jewry's crisis in "imagining the Jew" in the post-Holocaust are reflected in the history of French psychoanalysis before the Holocaust and its ongoing entanglement in the "Jewish Question." The cultural anxieties of prewar French psychoanalysis return us to the central preoccupation of the preceding section: both the French

Gentile's and the French Jew's difficulty with imagining the Jew as authentically "French."

The vexed (and heavily freighted) question of whether or not psychoanalysis is a "Jewish" science has always, since the founding days of Freud, been strangely encrypted within the discipline of psychoanalysis — an encryptedness that has centered on the still widely debated significance for psychoanalysis of Freud's Jewish identity. Despite Freud's well-known attempts at recruiting non-Jews such as Jung to the psychoanalytic movement, there has always been controversy and disagreement among Freud scholars over the question of the "Jewish" origins of psychoanalysis.[53] But rather than press for any kind of definitive answer to this question, it may be more productive to turn our attention to the extent to which the indeterminate nature of the Jewish dimension of psychoanalysis has become embedded within the discipline — a debate that is seldom acknowledged openly, but that nevertheless haunts psychoanalysis like a repressed ghost. In other words, the question of the "Jewish" origins of psychoanalysis is *the* constitutive anxiety not only of psychoanalysis in general but also of French psychoanalysis in particular, where Jews have played such prominent roles, even as this prominence has often been attenuated by the ongoing determination of French psychoanalysis to configure itself as *French,* not "Jewish."

An indispensable source for much of our information about the history of French psychoanalysis is Elisabeth Roudinesco's magisterial two-volume study, *La bataille de cent ans,* the first volume of which, as Jeffrey Mehlman (Roudinesco's English translator) argues, constitutes "a history — or prehistory — of French psychoanalysis concomitant with a history of French anti-Semitism."[54] More specifically, in her first volume Roudinesco provides a detailed account of the circumstances surrounding Lacan's appointment to the Société Psychanalytique de Paris, a narrative strongly suggesting the possibility that Nazism's hostility toward "Freudianism" was already firmly entrenched in the cultural imaginary of French psychoanalysis. In 1938, Édouard Pichon, president (and one of the four founders) of the SPP and opposed to the largely Viennese International Psychoanalytical Association, informed Rudolph Loewenstein (both Lacan's analyst and, ironically, the author of a work on the psychoanalysis of anti-Semitism) that if Loewenstein wanted him to appoint Heinz Hartmann (who was then fleeing from Hitler and seeking refuge in Paris) to the SPP, Loewenstein would have to agree to Pichon's appointment of his protégé Lacan.[55] As Jeffrey

Mehlman observes in his "Translator's Foreword" to Roudinesco's second volume, "Plainly if the conflictual lines of force informing the emergence of a human subjectivity are of the essence in psychoanalysis, the political deal that saw Lacan—in no way an anti-Semite—traded off for a Jewish victim of persecution . . . cannot but be of central importance."[56]

The story of the power politics behind Lacan's appointment to the SPP is, in many ways, a founding parable of the anxiety of French psychoanalysis about *la question juive:* Pichon agrees to "save" the German Jew Hartmann from Nazism, but only if he receives assurances that the SPP can, in effect, become further "Gallicized" through the appointment of the French Gentile Lacan.[57] For further commentary on this episode we can return to Trigano on the impossible double bind of the French Jew: "what served to grant the Jew his emancipation served to deny him his Jewishness." In the case of Lacan's appointment to the SPP, what served to grant Hartmann his emancipation (from Nazism) served also to deny French psychoanalysis a certain "Jewishness": the "Jewishness" of Loewenstein and Hartmann (who would eventually become the founder of American ego psychology) had to be occluded so that a more properly "Gallic" psychoanalysis could emerge.[58]

It is important to bear in mind that the postwar history of French psychoanalysis yields no oversimplifying allegory of anti-Semitism. As Roudinesco argues, the history of French psychoanalysis during World War II reflects no major acts of collaboration. It is true that when German troops arrived in Paris, the SPP closed down, Freud was openly discredited, and Jews were forced either to emigrate or to go into hiding. But it is also true that the SPP rescued virtually all of its members from Nazi concentration camps; and there is no evidence of any kind of "psychoanalytic Vichy" (see Roudinesco, 151–73). After the war, the second generation of French psychoanalysts was well represented by Jews and non-Jews alike—most notably by Lacan; Daniel Lagache, a particularly active rescuer of wartime Jews; and Sacha Nacht, whose open admission of his Jewish identity certainly did not prevent him from becoming head of the SPP in 1949.[59]

At this juncture it may be useful to turn to the career of Nicolas Abraham, surely one of the most important (if, in the shadow of Lacan, often overlooked) figures to emerge from French psychoanalysis in the post-Holocaust. As a Jew who emigrated to France from Hungary in 1938 and who lost his family in the Holocaust, and as at best a marginal figure within the SPP (though a frequent publisher in major psychoanalytic journals), Abraham embodies all the themes of *l'altérité, déracinement,* and *l'étrangeté* that, for the likes of Jabès and Finkielkraut, have become the recurring themes of French Jewry's efforts to "imagine" itself in the post-Holocaust. And it is Abraham's work on trauma, a theory that can begin to provide a discourse adequate to talking about Auschwitz, that moves us closer to the complex convergence of psychoanalysis and postmodernism in the post-Holocaust.

In 1950, Abraham began collaborating with Maria Torok, herself a Jewish émigrée from Budapest. The most extraordinary outcome of the ongoing sharing of their clinical experiences was their ambitious reconfiguration of the nature of psychic trauma (the first significant "return" to trauma since Ferenczi), eventually published in their book on Freud's notorious case history of the Wolf Man, *Le verbier de l'Homme aux loups.*[60] In *Le verbier,* Abraham and Torok, teasing out the complex psycholinguistic network containing the unspoken, repressed words of the multilingual Wolf Man, set forth their concept of "cryptonymy," a reconfiguration of the Freudian unconscious as a psychic "crypt," a kind of tomb or vault harboring the not fully confronted "phantoms" *(fantômes)* or secrets from the analysand's earlier family history. For Abraham and Torok, traumatic symptoms arise not because of the repressive demands of the Oedipus Complex, but because of unspeakable secrets inherited from an earlier generation—secrets the analysand cannot fully repress, but cannot fully confront either. The "crypt," then, constitutes a new kind of psychic topography, an enigmatic site where repression or incorporation fails, even as the psychic content of the crypt never becomes fully conscious. The crypt marks the trace (or *retrait*) of a ghost, or "ghost-effect," within the unconscious where trauma and memory converge and yet fail to produce anything more than a kind of uninterpretable knot of incompletely buried signifiers. Abraham and Torok repeatedly use such terms as *revenance, spectre,* and *fantôme* to explain their theory of cryptonymy—and it is in this sense that they prefer to conceive of psychic trauma not as repressed, but as "encrypted."

It is perhaps not merely coincidental that Abraham and Torok's theory of the crypt (where secrets are neither fully "alive" nor "dead") was conceived in Adorno's temporal and psychic space of an "after Auschwitz"—not merely coincidental that between Ferenczi's research on trauma and Abraham and Torok's "return" to trauma lies the historical event of the Holocaust. The work of Abraham and Torok, themselves

Holocaust survivors, seems uncannily attuned to the complex collective unconsciousness of the generation that survived Auschwitz, a generation that (as Finkielkraut, for one, confesses) is urged to "forget" Auschwitz (and to forget the dead) in order to assume new lives, even as its members persist in keeping the memories of Auschwitz alive—if only in the form of a "crypt"-ic kind of melancholia that must inhabit an obscure threshold between memory and forgetting. When immersed in *les spectres* and *fantômes* of Abraham and Torok's cryptonymy, one can all too readily envision the ghosts of the Holocaust perishing in their own grim crypts: the locked vaults of the gas chambers and the incinerating tombs of Auschwitz-Birkenau's crematoria—real historical cryptonymies that, for the surviving generations (whether they were immediate witnesses of Nazi atrocities or not), were forced to exist all too often as not-fully-repressed memories within the tomb of the survivors' psychic "crypt."

Although Abraham and Torok's theory of the "crypt" was not always well received by their colleagues within the French psychoanalytic community,[61] it enjoyed a much happier reception with Jacques Derrida—and at this point it is relevant to argue for Abraham and Torok's cryptonymy as a significant bridging of the disciplinary (and discursive) gap between psychoanalysis and a French postmodern philosophy that has often fashioned itself as, among other things, a deconstruction of memory. In 1959, Abraham met Derrida at a conference in Cérisy, marking the beginning of a long and close friendship. But beyond the personal dimension of this friendship, their meeting at Cérisy may have marked the "origin" of the complex juncture of psychoanalysis, postmodern philosophy, and the "Jewish Question" that (either consciously or unconsciously) has underwritten so much French intellectual thought in the post-Holocaust. This juncture constitutes its own psychic "crypt," because even as psychoanalysis and postmodern philosophy (or, more synecdochically, "French Heideggerianism") have their discursive differences, we can see that French postmodernism shares with French psychoanalysis an enigmatic and never fully worked through encryptedness of the "Jewish Question."

Perhaps because of his theoretical affinity for the "aporias" and liminal borderlines that have consistently served as the focus of his deconstruction, or perhaps because of his own deracinated identity as a Sephardic Algerian Jew (perhaps the same "strangeness of the Other" experienced by such colonized North African Jews as Jabès and Memmi), it should not be surprising that Derrida was especially receptive to Abraham and Torok's notion of encrypted *fantômes* within the unconscious. Throughout his career, Derrida has deconstructed any theory or concept that has posited "origins" for itself. But the mnemonic effractions of Abraham and Torok's "crypt" render memory an "always-already" experience: in the psychic crypt, memories do not so much "originate" as occur retroactively, or *nachträglich*. Derrida's essay "Fors," whose title is an almost untranslatable term designating a space neither fully interior nor fully exterior, is an extended meditation on Abraham and Torok's cryptonymy in which the author seems particularly attuned to the deconstructive ontology of the crypt as a paradoxical *non-lieu*, or "no place," in which, in Derrida's deceptively simple axiom, "[n]o crypt presents itself."[62] Because the dead (whether family secrets or the victims of mass murder) can be kept alive within the unconscious, the crypt hides, even as it disguises the fact of its own hiding: for Derrida, then, the crypt is a "secret interior" that "speaks only to silence" (68, 72).

A central irony of Derrida's positive reception of Abraham and Torok's cryptonymy is that, in many respects, one could also identify Derrida as a key figure in French postmodernism's ambivalence toward the presumed "metaphysical" assumptions of psychoanalysis. In his essay "The Purveyor of Truth," a critique of Lacan's "Seminar on 'The Purloined Letter,'" Derrida claims that psychoanalysis always suspiciously seems to "find itself" (*"La psychanalyse, à supposer, se trouve"*) in the (logocentric) lack or gap of castration.[63] One of the overarching themes of *Of Grammatology* is a critique of Freudian psychoanalysis as belonging to the history of metaphysics — a critique in which Derrida offers writing (or *grammè* as the deconstruction of the spoken word) as a deconstructive alternative to the still too logocentric concept of the unconscious.[64] And Derrida's essay "Freud and the Scene of Writing" is a densely deconstructive critique of Freudian repression, where Freud's "mystic pad" (from his 1925 "A Note upon the 'Mystic Writing-Pad'") is seen merely as a forerunner of the psyche as a written text, and where the psyche is placed *sous rature* as Derrida deconstructs repression as scarcely little more than a "thinking" of the trace-effect of *différance*.[65] Despite these persistent critiques of psychoanalysis, Freud has been a major cultural influence on Derrida's thought, as evidenced most dramatically in *The Post Card* and its chapter "To 'Speculate'—on Freud," an extended meditation on *Beyond the Pleasure Principle* and Freud's account of how organisms, attempting to shield themselves from trauma, follow their own "proper path" toward death. And it is also in *The Post Card* that Derrida poses perhaps *the* most provocative question for French postmodernism: "What does philosophy *not have to do* with psychoanalytic 'speculation'?"[66]

Because of his distinguished career, Derrida's readers have often been drawn to his ambivalences — and it is perhaps not too speculative to suggest that Derrida's ambivalences toward psychoanalysis are at times reflected in his reluctance to be open about his own Jewish identity, a reluctance that prompts a brief glance at the recent book *Derridabase* (coauthored by Derrida and Geoffrey Bennington) and its unique window into the complexities of the "Jewish Question" in Derrida's philosophy. Even the printed layout of *Derridabase* identifies it immediately as a quintessentially poststructuralist endeavor. Though for bibliographical purposes one is constrained to list the book as "coauthored," it is really two separate, though uncannily interrelated, texts in which Bennington's *Derridabase* — among other things, a valuable summary of Derrida's complex career as a philosopher — shares its pages with Derrida's *Circumfession,* an attempt at a kind of poststructuralist autobiography, such that the disorienting result for the reader is a strangely divided consciousness. At one point in his *Derridabase,* Bennington addresses the subject of Derrida's relationship with psychoanalysis, summarizing it as "complicated, to say the least," and commenting that it "has never taken the form of an alliance."[67] Intriguingly (and, I would argue, not coincidentally), "encrypted" in Derrida's "Derrida-base" in the lines running beneath Bennington's argument is a commentary on the ritual of circumcision and "the circumcised Jew" (perhaps Freud himself?) where Derrida, writing of his childhood experiences in Algeria, announces circumcision as "my theme, foreskin and truth," depicting the aftereffect of circumcision as a "traumatic wound," a "crypt"-ic foreskin that (not unlike Abraham and Torok's crypt) presents itself as a kind of interiority of exteriority (135).

What makes this particular page in *Derridabase* (just one of many books by/about Derrida that one could cite in this context) so significant is its conflation of the overdetermined interrelationship of psychoanalysis, postmodern philosophy, and the "Jewish Question." Even as Bennington speaks of Derrida's ambivalence toward psychoanalysis, Derrida offers a parallel meditation on Jewish circumcision ("my theme, foreskin and truth") and on "the figure of the father (Freud)." And even as Freudian psychoanalysis and its allegory of Oedipal castration become the object of Derrida's often ironic postmodern *jouissance,* the *revenant* of a (forgotten?) Jewish identity comes back to haunt and dictate his writing. If Derrida's relationship with psychoanalysis is, in Bennington's succinct summary, "complicated, to say the least," is it because the subject of psychoanalysis (and its "encrypted" cultural anxiety about its "Jewish" origins) always reminds Derrida of the "traumatic wound" of his own Judaism? Even as postmodern philosophy seeks to deconstruct the Oedipal (and metaphysical) framework of psychoanalysis, it is as if the "Jewish Question" intervenes to remind Derrida that deconstructions of psychoanalysis will always be overdetermined by the political urgencies of an encrypted Jewishness.

All of which can return us to the significance of Derrida's affinity for Abraham and Torok's theory of cryptonymy and its postwar meditation on death, *fantômes,* and crypts. Abraham and Torok's crypt is an inherently (and inherently *melancholic*) post-Holocaust reconfiguration of the psyche, implicitly mapping a new kind of psychoanalysis for a generation not so much *directly* traumatized by the Holocaust as doomed (like Finkielkraut's *Juif imaginaire*) to harbor the not fully confronted *fantômes* of the dead inside a psychic crypt.[68] It is as if Derrida acknowledged Abraham and Torok's cryptonymy as a new configuration of Jewish memory and trauma for the post-Holocaust: the crypt (that "speaks only to silence") "speaks" eloquently to the overdeterminations of the psychic space of "after Auschwitz" where mourning cannot fully represent itself to/for itself. Most resonantly, Derrida may have known that the concept of cryptonymy lies at the juncture of psychoanalysis, postmodernism, and the "Jewish Question." Abraham and Torok, never fully welcomed into the ranks of the SPP, came to be marginalized within French psychoanalysis; but in that marginality, both they and Derrida seemed to understand proleptically that the Holocaust and the Jew will always haunt the discourses of psychoanalysis and postmodernism.

Sémitophilie "after Auschwitz"; or, Can Psychoanalysis Be Postmodern?

Let us now pick up where the first two sections of this chapter left off: with the collective, cultural "inability to mourn" that Adorno has designated "after Auschwitz"—a temporal and psychic space that takes on a particularly "symptomatic" resonance in French postmodernism. In his introduction to *The Imaginary Jew,* David Suchoff perceptively identifies Alain Finkielkraut as "one of the first intellectual figures to argue that what we roughly call postmodernity—with its proliferation of images, identities without substance, and textuality-centered culture—is in fact the post-Holocaust era."[69] Thus it is not merely coincidental that one of the first intellectuals to interpret postmodernism as, more precisely, the post-Holocaust is also the originator of the concept of *le Juif imaginaire,* a kind of cultural *revenant* who, after Auschwitz, hovers uncertainly between "Frenchness" and *judéité.* In this context we can also consider that in an address to the spp in 1984 (four years after the publication of *Le Juif imaginaire*), the Jewish psychoanalyst René Major, seemingly echoing Maurice Blanchot's rhetorical question, "How [do we] philosophize . . . in the memory of Auschwitz?," poses a similar challenge to the French psychoanalytic community: "A Question, How indeed can one psychoanalyze after Auschwitz?, should be in the thoughts of every psychoanalyst."[70] Significantly, Major (perhaps himself a paradigm for Finkielkraut's *Juif imaginaire*) frames the ontology of psychoanalysis "after Auschwitz" as a "Question"—as if consciously echoing the "Jewish Question" that is "encrypted" in French psychoanalysis.

Between Finkielkraut's *Juif imaginaire,* who embodies the psychic fate of the French Jew in a postmodern era, and Major's (Jewish) "Question" concerning the new challenges for French psychoanalysis in a post-Holocaust era lies the subject matter of this book. A particular theme of the following chapters is contemporary French philosophy's recent and increasingly problematic appropriations of psychoanalysis for much of its polemical force as an influential discourse "after Auschwitz." The specters of France's own characteristic "inability to mourn" and the phenomenon of France's ongoing postwar "repression" of *judéité* provide a crucial and long overdue context for a deeper understanding of what is at stake in French Heideggerianism and, in particular, its persistent (almost compulsive) encrypting of the Holocaust and the Jew within its discourse. Moreover, the coordinates of (a repressed?) French ambivalence toward *judéité* in the post-Holocaust can perhaps be most productively plotted by the strange transferences of French postmodern philosophy onto psychoanalysis. The result is the emergence of what we could refer to as a Jewish-French psyche within postmodernism that constitutes an extended melancholia for a not fully remembered Holocaust that continually eludes a genuine mourning. If, after Auschwitz, a tension has arisen in France between "philosophizing" and "psychoanalyzing," it can also be said that we are witnessing the (ironic) "cathecting" of postmodernism onto the discourse of psychoanalysis — a cathexis that occurs whenever French postmodernism's "crisis" of memory undertakes to speak of the Holocaust and the figure of the Jew.

To further historicize this strange transference, let us consider briefly some scattered, though interrelated, events in 1933, a significant year for both philosophy and psychoanalysis — as well as for historical developments leading up to the Holocaust. In 1933 in Berlin, Goebbels organized a public burning of books written by Jews (including the works of Freud). This was also the year that Heidegger embraced Nazism, as well as the year the concentration camps at Buchenwald and Dachau were established. In Paris in 1933, Alexandre Kojève began teaching his seminar on Hegel's *Phenomenology of Spirit* at the École Pratique des Hautes Études (seminars that would continue until 1938). Thus, just a few years before the official operation of the concentration camps, Kojève lectured extensively on violence as the essence of "History" before his packed classes (classes that included, among other prominent French intellectuals, Georges Bataille and Lacan), celebrating *la fin de l'histoire* and Hegel's "philosophy of death" as a philosophical negation that, for Kojève (though not for the future victims of the death camps) paradoxically offered the only true access to freedom. "There is no freedom," he asserted, "without death."[71]

Kojève's "death" seminars can serve as the occasion for pondering the extent to which French postmodernism's encrypting of the Holocaust and the figure of the Jew within its discourse has its roots in the French intellectual's protracted fascination (most especially, and ironically, in the years leading up to and just after Auschwitz) with nihilism, necrophilia, and violent sacrifice. These themes are evidenced perhaps most dramatically in any number of writings by Bataille (as noted earlier, one of Kojève's former students) and Blanchot, both of whom have written extensively on death as a kind of metaphysical "beyond" to human experience. Beginning with his readings of Hegel in the 1940s, Blanchot, for example, celebrates death as a kind of "limit-experience" — death as the Impossible, the Unrepresentable[72] — anticipating, as we shall see, many of the privileged themes of postmodernism's own compulsive *Todestrieb*.

Bataille's and Blanchot's fascination with death is one of the major influences on the concepts of myth, community, and sacrifice that inform much of the work of the French Heideggerians and their preoccupation with the "end of philosophy." Bataille's "thinking" of sacrifice as the representation of our own death to ourselves and the surviving of it (a "thinking" with unsettling ironies for the post-Holocaust), and his claim that the victims of the Nazi death camps remain "outside of sacrifice" (a claim that, like so much discourse "after Auschwitz," is both reassuring and enigmatic),[73] are the primary influence on Jean-Luc Nancy's recent analysis, in his *La communauté désœuvrée*, of the concept of "community" as his own (Heideggerian) attempt to think the "political." Nancy defines "community" as the (Bataillesque) excess in any metaphysics of the subject: it is "the impossibility of a pure, collective totality" within society — a concept without essence or telos. Thus Nancy perceives the *communauté désœuvrée* (or "un-worked" community) as a break or caesura in the West's need for mythic unity. Because, for Nancy, there can be no "absolute immanence" to a community, the concept of the *communauté désœuvrée* is intended as, among other things, a salutary critique of Nazi *Gemeinschaft* as a community he chooses to describe (in a not-so-veiled reference to the Holocaust) as its own "conflagration of community."[74] Thus Nancy's lesson for the post-Holocaust is "the impossibility of making a work out of death" (15) — more specifically, the philosophical claim that "making a work out of death" is metaphysically (though not, as history has grimly demonstrated, *physically*) impossible.[75]

We could argue that somewhere in the chronology between Bataille's configuration of the death camp victims as "outside of sacrifice" and Nancy's postmodern concept of community as an "impossibility," one can locate the "political unconscious" (or, more accurately, the cryptonymy?) of not only *La communauté désœuvrée* in particular, but also French Heideggerianism in general: in the seams of Bataille's necrophilic engagements with the theme of sacrifice and of Nancy's post-Holocaust urge to redefine "community" lies a psychic crypt — a not fully worked through mourning for the Nazis' attempt to "make a work out of death," whose ultimate effect constitutes a kind of postmodern *Trauerspiel*. In his concept of the *communauté désœuvrée* and its depiction of the Jew as a Bataillesque excess that deconstructs the "totality" of community, we are offered not Finkielkraut's *Juif imaginaire* as the paradigm of the psychic crisis of the post-Holocaust Jew, but rather, as it were, Nancy's "*Juif désœuvré*," French *sémitophilie*'s "imagining" of the figure of the Jew as the impossibility of "absolute immanence."[76]

In Nancy's elliptical concept of the *communauté désœuvrée*, we can begin to trace the lineaments of an emergent Jewish-French psyche within recent French intellectual thought, a psychic phenomenon of *sémitophilie* constituted at the juncture of psychoanalysis and postmodernism. In order to understand this phenomenon further, let us for the moment go back in time to Freud himself on what he referred to as the ineffability of the figure of the Jew. In April 1936, Freud wrote a letter of condolence to the British psychoanalyst Barbara Low on the recent death of her brother-in-law, analyst David Eder: "We were both Jews and knew of each other that we carried that miraculous thing in common, which—inaccessible to any analysis thus far—makes the Jew."[77] In recent years, it almost seems as though Freud's claim, conceived at a certain "modernist" moment in history, that the Jew is "inaccessible to any analysis thus far" is serving as a kind of challenge to articulate the "inaccessible" Jew within postmodernism. And postmodernism's strange encounter with the "inaccessible" Jew has specific consequences for psychoanalysis. All of which is to say that French postmodernism is beginning to look more (pseudo)psychoanalytic recently because of an ever-growing discourse on the Jew.

I would argue that French postmodernism's preoccupation with the figure of the Jew has its postwar origins not so much in Sartre as in Blanchot. After the war, as evidenced in his *L'entretien infini*, a series of essays written between 1953 and 1965 (years when the psychic temporality of Adorno's "after Auschwitz" was just emerging), Blanchot's reflections on death as the "Unrepresentable" were transformed into an explicitly philo-Semitic discourse of the "unrepresentable" Jew. In a section entitled "Being Jewish" ("Être Juif"), Blanchot (in an expansively Sartrean moment) critiques the anti-Semitic need to impute a "being-negative" to the Jew. But the more Blanchot deplores anti-Semitism's negative ontology of the Jew, the more his discourse threatens to replicate the very impulse he is rightly reviling. Thus he depicts the Jew as, variously, "the exigency of strangeness," "the exigency of uprooting," a subjectivity of "uneasiness and affliction," and (not unlike Hegel on the Biblical Abraham) "the affirmation of a nomadic truth"—descriptions that, even as they are deployed to accuse the anti-Semite, nevertheless have the unintended effect of constituting a repetition compulsion to rehearse and perpetuate the same anti-Semitic stereotypes that

Sartre claimed inevitably transformed the Jew into the specular "Other" for French anti-Semitism.[78]

More recently, we can detect the philo-Semitic impulse to participate in a "discourse of the Jew" in the work of Julia Kristeva, a discourse that forges some overt links between the Jew and psychoanalysis. In her recent book *Strangers to Ourselves*, Kristeva embraces the Jewish "other" as "my ('own and proper') unconscious"; in describing the figure of the Jew as "the strangeness of the other and of oneself," Kristeva's discourse becomes explicitly psychoanalytic at the point at which she refers to the Jew's "combination of the familiar and the strange" as a kind of cultural enactment of Freud's *Unheimliche*.[79] With her perception of the Jew as the embodiment of the uncanny, one cannot help wondering if Kristeva's philo-Semitism has, nevertheless, encrypted within it traditional French anxieties about the "Jewish" origins of psychoanalysis.

In this context, we can also turn to Slavoj Žižek, whose recent "returns" to Lacan are enjoying a wide readership in psychoanalytic circles in France. In particular, his *Sublime Object of Ideology* constitutes, among other things, perhaps the first explicit attempt at a postmodern psychoanalysis—with the figure of the Jew often serving as its nexus. At one point, Žižek makes an ambitious attempt (almost as a conscious renewal of Sartre's project in *Anti-Semite and Jew*) to explain the psychic origins of anti-Semitism itself by imagining how the fascist must have "reasoned" about the Jew: "at first, 'Jew' appears as a signifier connoting a cluster of supposedly 'effective' properties (intriguing spirit, greedy for gain, and so on), but this is not yet anti-semitism proper. To achieve that, we must *invert* the relation and say: they are like that *because they are Jews*. 'Jew' in 'because they are Jews' refers to that unattainable X (and what Nazism tried to seize)."[80] Amidst this analysis of the psychic origins of anti-Semitism, I would pose the following question: is Žižek's positing of an "unattainable X" as the (psychic) origin of anti-Semitism the flip side of Freud's "miraculous thing . . . which—inaccessible to any analysis thus far—makes the Jew"? Or, to pose the question another way, do modernism and postmodernism negotiate the "unattainable X" of Judaism in homologous ways? Or rather, after Auschwitz is any (philo-Semitic) attempt to (psycho)analyze the "unattainable X" of Judaism fraught with its own psychic overdeterminations? Throughout his book, Žižek makes a point of characterizing the Jew as, variously, a "symptom," the object of the anti-Semite's "fetishistic disavowal," Hitler's *point de capiton,* and the purest embodiment of the anxiety of the Lacanian *"Che vuoi?"* as the demand of the Other. In the process (much like Kristeva), he relies so resolutely on psychoanalytic metaphors to configure anti-Semitism that his discourse of the Jew begins to replicate the Sartrean psychic dyad, this time between *philo*-Semite and Jew—but a dyad no less overdetermined by its insistence on configuring the Jew "psychoanalytically."[81]

Blanchot's, Kristeva's, and Žižek's (almost neo-Hegelian) characterizations of the Jew as, respectively, the "exigency of strangeness," the Freudian *Unheimliche,* and a "symptom" are themselves symptomatic of how, within French postmodernism, real Jews have tended to be transformed into tropes or signifiers for the decentered, destabilized postmodern subject in a theoretical system that persists in defining (or "fetishizing") them from without.[82] In such a scheme, it is unjustly and insufficiently thought through to view the French postmodern preoccupation with the figure of the Jew as "anti-Semitic." Rather, this discourse can be viewed more productively as a new kind of post-Holocaust *sémitophilie* that privileges the very figure of the diaspora Jew anti-Semitism has traditionally scorned. But no less than anti-Semitism, which projects all of society's ills onto a scapegoated Jewish Other, philo-Semitism also fails to negotiate the real Jew, instead trapping the Jew within a (Gentile) social imaginary that obfuscates the precise boundary between mystifying and reviling the Jew.

Perhaps inevitably, this postmodern *sémitophilie* has led to an emerging discourse on the Holocaust as the central trauma to European modernity. For example, Blanchot's almost compulsive "discourse of the Jew" has, in turn, prompted him to write about the Holocaust in ways that are almost certainly the precursor of an increasingly frequent topos in the discourse of French Heideggerianism: the crisis of representing the Holocaust. In *L'écriture du désastre,* an extended "thinking" of history that resumes his earlier, privileged metaphors of rupture *(déchirure)* and of death as a "limit-experience," Blanchot depicts the crisis of representing the Holocaust as the "failure" of history—the Holocaust as a "history in excess," and a history "always already outside history."[83] Blanchot's depiction of the Holocaust as history's "excess" has since inaugurated a philosophical discourse that evokes "Auschwitz" (virtually always cast in quotation marks) as less a real historical event than a metaphor for the "unthought" in the transition from modernism to postmodernism[84]—a discourse perhaps most fully realized in Lacoue-Labarthe's depiction of Auschwitz as a "caesura," a "null event," a "nothingness" *(né-ant)*, and Lyotard's depiction of Auschwitz as a "para-experience."

These characterizations of Auschwitz as a conceptual "limit" get us to the heart of French Heideggerianism's complex and often problematic engagement with psychoanalysis. By placing "Auschwitz" in quotation marks, postmodernism seeks to define history, in essence, psychoanalytically—with "Auschwitz" intended as a kind of deconstruction of conventional psychoanalytic representations of memory and trauma. The move is on to use the Holocaust as, among other things, a way to render psychoanalysis more "properly" postmodern. An overarching theme of my book will be that the urge, after Auschwitz, to make psychoanalysis "postmodern" becomes an ironic disavowal of one of the cornerstones of psychoanalysis, the imperative to work through trauma to a salutary mourning.[85]

In the interstices between a psychoanalytic process of mourning and a postmodern *Trauerspiel* lies the figure of the Jew as a privileged trope for the discourse of the French Heideggerians. Thus, although Derrida is the focus of only one of my chapters, the difficulties of "locating" his postmodern philosophy within French Heideggerianism (and, for that matter, Lévinas's as well, who will be discussed in chapter 5) is an implicit theme throughout this book. On the one hand (even as his deconstruction attempts to move beyond Heidegger's critique of the "forgetting" of Being), Derrida is determined to preserve the integrity of the Heideggerian "moment" for postmodernism. But on the other hand, of all the French Heideggerians, Derrida is the most attuned to Abraham and Torok's cryptonymy and the ways in which the Holocaust may have remained encrypted (that is, simultaneously "mourned" and foreclosed upon) within so much current French intellectual thought. We can consider, for example, a work like *Feu la cendre,* where Derrida's concept of the trace as a sign of linguistic play evolves into the ash or cinder as the residue of an encrypted Holocaust within Western thought. A haunting refrain throughout the book is the not easily translated "Il y a là cendre"; and at one point, Derrida writes: "I now have the impression that the best paradigm of the trace . . . is not . . . the animal's tracks, effraction, the rill in the sand, the wake in the sea, the affinity of a footstep for its imprint, but the ash (that which remains without remaining of the holocaust, the conflagration, incense ablaze)."[86] It is through the mnemic trace of the ash that Derrida's concept of *différance* (or the "trace" as an origin without origin), so often critiqued as an essentially "linguistic" and largely apolitical concept, may have evolved into *the* relevant "trope" for the lost real of the Holocaust within postmodern discourse.

Chapter 2 returns to the by now well trodden paths of *l'affaire Heidegger*, but with some new insights into a phenomenon whose resonances may be as much psychoanalytic as philosophical. In particular, I focus on Derrida's *De l'esprit* as his own highly elliptical "discourse of the Jew" constituted within a "defense" of Heidegger and the haunting refrain of *Il y a là cendre*. In chapter 3 I discuss Lacoue-Labarthe and Nancy's overtly philo-Semitic analysis of the figure of the Jew as a salutary antithesis of Nazi myth-making—but a "discourse of the Jew" that, in the final analysis, may have encrypted within it French anxieties about the "Jewish origins" of psychoanalysis. In the final chapter we turn to Lyotard's lower-case "jews" as perhaps postmodernism's most "symptomatic" outcome of French *sémitophilie,* an enigmatic concept that serves not so much as a memorial to Jewish trauma after Auschwitz as the extreme "limit-case" of philosophy— and of psychoanalysis itself. As anticipated by my book's title, *Affective Genealogies,* the next three chapters are also an investigation of the concept of affect as one of the more readily misunderstood cornerstones of Freudian psychoanalysis that has nevertheless become a recurring theme within French Heideggerianism. To undertake a genealogy of affect in postmodern French thought is, I hope, to shed further light on the complex interrelationship between psychoanalysis and *la question juive* that characterizes the French Heideggerian discourse of philo-Semitism.

I would like to conclude this chapter with a general statement about the overall goal of my book. In the introduction to his *Legacies of Anti-Semitism in France,* which focuses on several key French writers whose careers were shaped prior to the events of World War II, Jeffrey Mehlman describes his book as "exploratory rather than accusatory. . . . [I]t will be perceived that [my] readings are ultimately less dependent on any category of intentionality than on the sustaining effects of a cultural *milieu* that at times seems— or seemed— anti-Jewish in its essence" (3). Mehlman's emphasis on French anti-Semitism as less a product of individual "intentionality" than a constitutive part of a larger "cultural *milieu*" serves to frame his study as not simply "accusatory" of the individual writers he discusses, but as enabling a larger investigation of a complex moment within French cultural and intellectual history. In a similar fashion, I am intent on exploring the ways in which, to echo Mehlman, "the sustaining effects of a cultural *milieu*" of an earlier, pre-war France emerge as the "return of the repressed" in the thought of contemporary French philosophers whose careers were shaped "after Auschwitz." I am interested in exploring the ways in which this earlier "cultural *milieu*" has perhaps resurfaced, after a period of latency, even in a discourse constituted to "atone" for this milieu. The ironic result is that the postmodern discourse of philo-Semitism, even as it actively engages psychoanalysis, continues to act out its own unresolved memories of an earlier era. French postmodernism's ongoing commitment to a Heideggerian framing for its method of philosophical inquiry presents a problem for its newly emergent discourse of philo-Semitism. French philo-Semitism's return to the figure of the Jew as a means of coming to terms with the trauma of the Holocaust (and coming to terms with "the sustaining effects of a cultural *milieu*" that served as the historical foundation of these struggles with memory) is both a salutary call for us not to forget or to repress the Holocaust, *and* a Heideggerian attempt to think the "political" that fails to situate the Holocaust historically. It also persistently links the figure of the Jew almost exclusively with this unhistoricized version of the Holocaust. None of this is to make an "accusatory" gesture. Rather, the emergence of a Jewish-French psyche within postmodernism serves as a reminder that, as a discourse designed to warn us that we do not yet have a discourse adequate to Auschwitz, French philo-Semitism constitutes another chapter in the complexities of France's ongoing engagement with *judéité*.

2

Daseinsanalyse: Derrida, Heidegger's Silence, and the Return of the Repressed

Psychoanalyzing Silence

Conceived psychoanalytically, the recent controversies of Heidegger and Paul de Man (specifically, the extent of their involvement in fascism) are directly implicated in the psychic processes of memory and desire. The issue of cultural memory is, broadly speaking, the issue of our relationship with the past; thus, cultural memory is constitutive of both scandals, involving as they do two figures who, in some sense, "forgot" the past, or forgot to "remember" the past—not just any past, but the historical event of the Holocaust, often described as the central trauma for European modernity itself.

One response to trauma is silence—silence, that is, as symptomatic of a memory in crisis. Silence is itself a profoundly psychoanalytic phenomenon, serving as it does as one of the "privileged" strategies of the analysand seeking to subvert the analyst's probing efforts to "guess the secret" behind the symptom. If we move from a clinical setting to the realm of public discourse (and the realm of cultural, as opposed to personal, memory), the phenomenon of silence can, in turn, elicit our desire—a desire to hear a public confession, a ritual expression of guilt or remorse for a complicity with a traumatic past one has chosen not to "remember." The desire to "hear" the unspoken words behind the silence a cultural memory (or a cultural "repression") can induce *is* the "desire" elicited by the Heidegger and de Man scandals. Heidegger's and de Man's detractors crave an apology, confession, admission—anything that might have broken their protracted silences with public expressions of anguish for the victims of the Holocaust.

But Shoshana Felman, for one, has warned us of the inadequacy of any discourse that attempts to break a silence and "remember." Writing in support of de Man, she argues, "The trouble with excuses (with confessions) is that they are all too *readable:* partaking of the continuity of

35

conscious meaning and of the illusion of the restoration of coherence."[1] Apologies or confessions will always thwart our desire to gain access to what motivated the silence. For Felman, the central problem is "the ethical impossibility of *a confession that, historically and philosophically, cannot take place*" (733; italics in original). Here Felman would seem to be in agreement with Freud's axiom, stated most succinctly in a letter to Fliess (December 1896), that "consciousness and memory are mutually exclusive."[2] The public confession, as the object of our desire in both the Heidegger and de Man scandals, is a fundamental "impossibility" because, in Felman's conception, the real meaning of a silence resides in the unconscious, always the site of an inconclusive *agon* between memory and forgetting. Thus, for Felman, de Man's silence becomes an "eloquent" reminder that spoken confession cannot guarantee any salutary "restoration of coherence" to an unspeakable (and always imperfectly remembered) trauma.

But to what extent could Felman's psychoanalytic interpretation of the impossibility of confession in general, and of de Man's silence in particular, itself be viewed as "symptomatic"? In an extended critique of Felman's defense of de Man's silence, Dominick LaCapra focuses on the psychoanalytic concept of transference, and specifically the ways in which, following the 1987 disclosure of de Man's wartime writings, his supporters have "cathected" onto de Man so fully that they have begun to recapitulate (to "act out") his own refusal to work through the trauma of the Holocaust. As LaCapra argues, "Felman is so intent on establishing de Man's status as a victim and survivor that she pays little, if any, attention to those who were the manifest victims and survivors of the Holocaust."[3] LaCapra's critique of Felman points cogently to the relevance of the psychoanalytic processes of "acting out" and "working through" as a means of understanding more fully the complex emotions surrounding the Heidegger and de Man affairs. For their supporters, Heidegger's and de Man's silence must be acknowledged and preserved as the symptomatic marker of a memory too painful to be remembered—a memory that can only be trivialized through public articulation. But as LaCapra's essay contends, in so doing, their supporters enact a repetition compulsion of Heidegger's and de Man's own refusal to remember the past. Heidegger's and de Man's silence should be critiqued not so much as "evidence" of a guilty role in fascism, but as the symptomatic (and regrettable) displacement of affect—an affect that, if made manifest, could assure us that a trauma

36

was being remembered, an affect that could satisfy our desire for an expression of sympathy for the victims of the Holocaust.

At the core of the Heidegger and de Man controversies as tableaus of a cultural memory in crisis, then, lies the key psychoanalytic concept of affect. As LaCapra's essay can remind us, what Heidegger's and de Man's detractors desire is a Heideggerian or de Manian *Angstbereitschaft,* an open and public willingness to experience anxiety—a confessional anxiety that, though perhaps eluding mnemonic coherence, could nevertheless achieve some kind of affective remembrance or working through of the "unthought" of the Holocaust. In short, the "desire" of Heidegger's and de Man's detractors is for affect as a salutary psychic alternative to the distinctly unaffective, intellectual rigor of their wartime and postwar writings.

In this chapter I contend that also at the core of the Heidegger and de Man controversies lies the figure of Derrida, so many of whose writings are extended cultural "remembrances" of and intellectual engagements with both his former mentor Heidegger and his former colleague de Man—remembrances that inhabit the elusive "difference within" the opposing poles of praise and blame. Not coincidentally, throughout his intellectual career Derrida, as the great theorist of *différance* as a kind of absent presence, has always seemed particularly attuned to the issue of silence and the paradoxical ways in which silence always "speaks." In an essay that ostensibly has nothing to do with the de Man and Heidegger controversies (but, perhaps, for that very reason may have *everything* to do with them), Derrida answers his critics as to whether deconstruction is a kind of negative theology, a philosophical negation (a philosophical "silence," if one prefers) that affirms nothing: "How to avoid saying or speaking? [*Comment ne pas parler?*]. . . . At the moment when the question 'how to avoid speaking?' is raised . . . , it is already, so to speak, *too late.* There is no longer any question of not speaking."[4] In other words, as the avoidance of speaking and the affirmation of nothing, silence always already gives voice to everything. Could it be that Derrida is telling us that Heidegger's and de Man's silence cannot "avoid speaking" of the past? Can a denial (a *dénégation*) of speaking really be an affirmation?

It is possible to argue that no one knows better than Derrida the extent to which Heidegger and de Man both "forgot" the past—even as his own frequently "unaffective" deconstruction has at times obscured any certainty as to when he is supporting or when he is critiquing them. And it may not be too speculative to argue that the issue of Heidegger's and de Man's "silence" (in effect, their refusal of the "talking cure") has consistently engaged Derrida. The specter of Derrida, himself a Jew (and, as much of his recent work suggests, deeply involved in his own mourning of the Holocaust), frequently—though, from a public perspective, often enigmatically—writing in support of two figures implicated, however remotely, in Nazism is perhaps one of the most psychically overdetermined events within contemporary French postmodernism. And one can surmise that long before the public disclosures of Heidegger's and de Man's wartime pasts, Derrida may have already been struggling to come to terms with the extent to which the Holocaust haunted so many of their writings. Moreover, I am concerned here with the extent to which Derrida may have known all along that, perhaps even more than the Holocaust, the real issue at stake in Heidegger's and de Man's silence is the unacknowledged figure of the Jew. Derrida may have known all along that behind the absence of a Heideggerian and de Manian affect, behind the now infamous silences, was an anxiety connected to the Jew of the Holocaust—an anxiety that accounts for the distinctly psychoanalytic resonances of the two controversies, and an anxiety that, almost by definition, can never be "spoken" but must be displaced within an anxious silence accessible to no one.

In my chapter, I will focus mainly on *De l'esprit,* Derrida's attempt, following the controversial 1987 publication in France of Victor Farias's *Heidegger et le nazisme,* to rehabilitate Heidegger and to give a more benign "voice" not only to Heidegger's prolonged and infamous silence concerning his affiliation with German National Socialism, but also to his refusal to acknowledge the Nazi persecution of Jews. But as a means of providing a fuller context for his treatment of *l'affaire Heidegger,* I begin with a brief consideration of Derrida's *Mémoires: For Paul de Man* (1986), a poignant epitaph following de Man's death, published just one year prior to the disclosures of de Man's wartime journalism. As I eventually show, even though a radical temporal divide (inasmuch as *Mémoires* predates the de Man controversy, while *De l'esprit* was published in response to the Heidegger controversy) makes any conjunction of these two works problematic, nevertheless both books are deeply informed by psychoanalytic concerns in ways that, despite (because of?) the temporal divide, can add to an understanding of how Derridean deconstruction inhabits an obscure threshold between, on the one hand, enacting a *Trauerspiel* that eludes a genuine mourning after Auschwitz, and on the other, critiquing de Man's and Heidegger's own *Trauerspiel* in the post-Holocaust.

"Caution! (Anxious) Reader at Work"

Surely one of the more complexly ironic trajectories traced by a psychic laboring under the double "post" of postmodernism and the post-Holocaust is the career of Paul de Man. A starting point for an analysis of his "silence" under the double "post" could be, as it is for so much postmodern discourse, the concept of anamnesis. It almost seems as though, for postmodernism, the problem of forgetting serves as nothing less than the condition of the possibility of the subject; this would surely be the contention of de Man, much of whose theory (particularly in his essays in *Blindness and Insight* and *The Resistance to Theory*) seems predicated on the unrecoverability of history and a resistance to memory (a memory "blind" to its own rhetoricity) as a recuperation of the past. In his now classic essay "Literary History and Literary Modernity," for example, de Man alludes (enigmatically, in a post-Holocaust era) to Nietzsche's conception of "a past that . . . is so threatening that it has to be forgotten."[5]

These are the central de Manian themes Derrida enlarges upon in his *Mémoires: For Paul de Man*. Ambitiously opening with a quasi-epic invocation to Mnemosyne, Derrida's book can be summarized not only as an extended mourning for his deceased colleague, but also as a significant demonstration of how postmodernism has often been drawn to a kind of *danse macabre* between mourning and memory in order to fashion itself "psychoanalytically." Derrida writes, "It will not surprise you when I say that all I have recently read and reread by Paul de Man seems to be traversed by an insistent reflection on mourning, a meditation in which bereaved memory is deeply engraved."[6] Constituting its own kind of *ars memorativa,* Derrida's *Mémoires* attempts, among other things, to probe the lineaments of a genuinely postmodern memory — a memory without anteriority or origin. Enlarging on de Man's topos of the "unreadability" of mourning, Derrida, seeking to "locate" mourning within postmodernism, identifies de Man's own death as the occasion for an "impossible mourning" that can be conceived as something other than a relapse into modernist nostalgia: "Is the most distressing, or even the most deadly infidelity that of a possible mourning which would interiorize within us the image, idol, or ideal of the other who is dead and lives only in us? Or is it that of the impossible mourning, which, leaving the other his alterity, respecting thus his infinite remove, either refuses to take or is incapable of taking the other within oneself, as in the tomb or vault of some narcissism?" (6). For Derrida, there is no "true mourning" that can definitively convert trauma (in this case, the death of an esteemed friend) into a "narcissistic" epitaph. If there can be such a thing as "true mourning," then for Derrida it is a mourning that must evacuate memory of any narcissistic attachment to the past: mourning must become aware of its own impossibility.

Perhaps picking up where de Man's suspicion of history and his resistance to memory as a recuperation of the past leaves off, Derrida's concept of an "impossible mourning" deploys a self-consciously psychoanalytic framework—and is, at the same time, a quintessentially postmodern endeavor. Thus, this observation might be an appropriate occasion to go back to Walter Benjamin's ruminations on memory and our relationship to the past in his essay "On Some Motifs in Baudelaire";[7] for if Derrida's meditations on memory in *Mémoires* are constituted within the space of postmodernism and psychoanalysis, Benjamin's essay on memory is constituted within the space of modernism and psychoanalysis, making, as it does, conspicuous use of Freud's *Beyond the Pleasure Principle* and its account of the incompatibility of consciousness and memory.

Whereas Derrida expands on the theme of a de Manian "forgetting," Benjamin speaks of his admiration for figures like Proust who allow themselves to be accosted by memory—that is, *Erfahrung* as "aura," or remembrance as a state of privileged inwardness. As the trace of an "involuntary memory" (Proust's *mémoire involontaire*), it is *Erfahrung* that, for Benjamin, makes true experience (as opposed to the direct consciousness of "shock" or *Erlebnis*) possible. Both Benjamin and Derrida are suspicious of modernist nostalgia; thus Benjamin privileges "aura" as a mode of remembrance that, as Derrida would have phrased it, resists "the tomb or vault of some narcissism." But whereas Derrida configures an "impossible mourning" that resists a "narcissistic" attachment to the past, Benjamin seeks to define what makes true experience *possible*—and what makes experience possible is memory.

Benjamin is, of course, a particularly poignant figure to bring to bear on any discussion of memory in the post-Holocaust. His suicide in early 1940 at the Franco-Spanish border after fleeing Nazi Germany renders

his meditation on memory an especially ironic background for a discussion of a de Manian "resistance to memory." (In this context we can
also note that de Man himself wrote an essay on Benjamin.) Situated
chronologically between Benjamin's positing of *Erfahrung* as the making possible of "true experience" and Derrida's theorizing of an "impossible mourning" that seeks to eliminate any narcissistic attachment
to the past lies the young Paul de Man's early wartime writings for the
Belgian collaborationist journals *Le Soir* and the Flemish-language *Het
Vlaamsche Land*. To describe the phenomenon in Benjaminian terms,
de Man's wartime journalism, in the process of filtering (though not
directly reporting on) the direct, lived experience of wartime events,
constitutes a kind of "shock" that, as seen through the lens of de Man's
later post-Holocaust career, eventually became a "forgetting" of the
past's claims on us. Intriguingly, Benjamin (who himself contributed
to the literary sections of newspapers) refers to newspapers as the "atrophy of experience," the atrophy of memory as that which makes true
experience possible — as if anticipating how de Man's journalism (and
its preoccupation with such topics as the overall "health" of the Western literary tradition) protected him from being haunted later by, say,
memories of the deportations of Belgian Jews that were occurring
amidst de Man's journalistic activities. As Benjamin writes, "The more
readily consciousness registers these shocks, the less likely are they to
have a traumatic effect" (161). Thus, in a Benjaminian framework, de
Man's wartime journalism (in its most benign light) is a paradigm of
how *Erlebnis* and its direct consciousness of "shock" can have the effect
of warding off trauma and inducing a "resistance to memory."

In the midst of this discussion of the absence of a de Manian
"trauma," it is pertinent to consider de Man's later writings on the subject of death. In *The Rhetoric of Romanticism,* for example, de Man writes,
"Death is a displaced name for a linguistic predicament."[8] Death, in
other words, is less a real, material condition than de Man's privileged
trope for displacement (as the impossibility of "naming"). In his perceptive analysis of the persistent melancholia informing de Man's methodology of reading, Eric Santner has noted that the work of de Man,
though continually deploying metaphors of elegy and mourning, is
itself curiously "depleted of affect" — thereby constituting, under the
"post" of the post-Holocaust, an inadequate response to the occurrence
of real death: "By turning death into a purely linguistic operation, de
Man precludes the possibility of distinguishing one victim from an-

other. Furthermore, the historical victim . . . is overshadowed by an impersonal and apathetic 'dismemberment' at the violent hands of the signifier; to be a victim of history is, in the end, to be a victim of a 'purely . . . linguistic operation.'"[9] Santner's depiction of de Man's unaffective death that "forgets" the real victims of history is well perceived, because even had there been no discovery of his wartime journalism, we can still sense the extent to which de Man's "tropic" death is overdetermined within the double "post" of postmodernism and the post-Holocaust. In this context, de Man's occluded victim of history is (inadvertently) far more resonant psychoanalytically than Derrida's self-consciously psychoanalytic "impossible mourning," for de Man's "tropic" death is the psychoanalytic "symptom" *par excellence*—the "symptom" of the psychic dangers (the "silences") that accrue when real death is "forgotten" in a post-Holocaust era.

De Man/Derrida/Freud: The "X" of Anxiety

Up to this point we have looked at the ways in which de Man's later (post-Holocaust) career and its resistance to memory can be broadly diagnosed as "symptomatic." But if we take the time to delve even more deeply into the nature of de Man's writings, we can uncover the complexly ironic nature of de Man's "symptomatic" refusal to mourn the Holocaust not so much in what he *does* say (about death, about the unrecoverability of history, and so on) as in what he does not say—and it is in what he does not say that we can perhaps "locate" a de Manian anxiety that can never be "spoken" but must be displaced within a silence accessible to no one. In this section I explore the extent to which de Man's work is as much a resistance to the discipline of psychoanalysis as it is to memory. Specifically, to what extent is it Freudian psychoanalysis that serves as the "political unconscious" of de Man's intellectual career—and a crucial absent presence that contributes to the cultural complexities of de Man's career within what we have come to call the "post-Holocaust"?

In an intriguing essay now over twenty years old (and one predating the de Man controversy), Richard Klein focuses on the conspicuous absence of Freud in de Man's work: "one cannot help but be struck by the almost total absence of any reference to Freud in all of de Man's published work, an absence all the more surprising in a critic who is elaborating the necessity of some inherent opacity of consciousness."[10]

Klein then invites his readers to consider another central irony in the writings of perhaps the greatest modern theorist of irony: though de Man effaced Freud, he was consistently and overtly engaged with the work of his colleague Derrida, much of which constitutes, as discussed in the first chapter, an intimate encounter with the "question of psychoanalysis."[11] It is at this point that we can speak meaningfully of the phenomenon of "Derrida–in–de Man" and of the ways in which the intersections between the two can be seen, within a psychoanalytic framework, as vastly overdetermined. In an extensive reading of de Man's attempt to "correct" Derrida's reading of Rousseau,[12] Klein deduces perceptively that "it is in the guise of Derrida that de Man encounters Freud."[13] In other words, though de Man "represses" Freudian repression itself, Freud ironically emerges as de Man's "return of the repressed"—but only as a repression *displaced* through the mediating figure of Derrida. For Klein, this process of displacement traces the following psycho-critical narrative: "The work of the son manipulates the proto-Freudian categories of blindness and insight, all the while systematically refusing to read Freud, the father's text. He can only encounter Freud, read the Father, in the guise of Derrida" (43).

At this point in his analysis of the mutual interplay of filiation and foreclosure of the father that characterizes de Man's relationship to Derrida and Freud, Klein also brings in the work of Paul de Man's uncle, Hendrik de Man—a prominent socialist leader in Belgium before the war who, as Zeev Sternhell writes, dissolved his own party in 1940 to welcome the new Nazi regime as the model for a new authoritarian socialism.[14] Klein is especially intrigued by Hendrik de Man because, in his account, the elder de Man "appears to be the first serious Marxist thinker to apply explicitly Freudian categories to the analysis of alienation" (42). In other words, Klein enjoys the irony of Hendrik de Man's openly embracing the very Freudian psychoanalysis that Paul de Man implicitly disavowed. But of further interest here is the fact that Klein refers to Hendrik de Man not as the uncle, but as the *father* of Paul de Man—a (mistaken) paternity that enables Klein to underscore the irony of a father incorporating into his work the Freudian psychoanalysis the son disavowed. (It is worth noting in this context that in a 1955 letter to Harvard's Harry Levin and Renato Poggioli, written to defend himself against charges about his life under Nazi occupation, Paul de Man oddly refers to Hendrik de Man as his father.) In 1973, Paul de Man wrote to Klein, informing the latter of his mistake in re-

43

ferring to Hendrik de Man as his father. But in making it a point to correct Klein—that is, in making it a point to, in effect, disavow Hendrik as the (fascist? or rather, Freudian?) father—once again, de Man inadvertently calls up the figure of Freud as the "return of the repressed" in his career.

What makes a return to Klein's cogent essay its own richly ironic exercise in "blindness and insight" is, of course, a reading of this essay against the grain of the disclosures, some fourteen years after the essay's publication, of the young de Man's wartime writings. I suggest that this most recent and highly controversial "insight" into the career of de Man serves as the occasion for a necessary return to some of the questions raised by Klein's essay: what is at stake in de Man's "repression" of Freud? Or, more simply, what exactly is de Man "repressing"? Is it the discipline of psychoanalysis (such that de Man prefers to deploy the more broadly metaphoric concept of "blindness" rather than the "unconscious")? Or is there a more far-reaching process at work? Is it rather (and now we might be at the heart of the issue of a de Manian "silence") the figure of the Jew—or of Freud *as* the Jew—that de Man "represses"? We should note that the young de Man was far more direct about what Europe perceived as the "Jewish Question" and, in particular, its relationship to Western culture. In his now notorious article (which Derrida himself would eventually refer to as "the most unbearable article" in his wartime journalism),[15] "Les Juifs dans la littérature actuelle," published in *Le Soir* on March 4, 1941, de Man celebrates the Western literary tradition and its strength in resisting certain "foreign" influences (a kind of *force étrangère*) such as Jewish writing. Here, the young journalist de Man *consciously* excludes the figure of the Jew (except for the widely celebrated Proust) from the cultural triumphs of the West.[16] But in de Man's later published work, more unconscious forces seem to be operating in an effort to "preserve" his own thought from becoming *enjuivé*, such that it seems to be psychoanalysis itself (or psychoanalysis and its possible threat to de Man as, in some sense, a "Jewish science"?) that de Man must repress in order to fashion his own concepts of "blindness" and "insight."[17]

De Man's (Oedipal) effacing of psychoanalysis and its importance for Western cultural history, then, is itself transformed into a psychoanalytic "symptom." But we somehow fail to get to the heart of the matter if we speak merely of de Man's "repression" of Freud. It is almost as if the *conspicuous* absence of Freud, as noted by Klein, marks a place of

44

"danger" for de Man—a danger that must not be so much repressed as *contained* and displaced. Should we name the relevant "symptom" of de Man's effacing of Freud "repression"? Or is de Man's later work (and his later "silence") constitutive of that far more elusive psychoanalytic concept, anxiety? If repression entails keeping something away from consciousness, then anxiety, from a Freudian perspective, is the (often uninterpretable) *failure* of repression, a trauma that can be experienced only in displacement *(entstellung)*.[18] For Freud, an absence of affect does not necessarily mean that the affect has somehow "disappeared." Rather, presuming it does not get repressed, the affect is "transformed into a qualitatively different quota of affect [*Affektbetrag*], above all into anxiety."[19] In short, for Freud anxiety is a psychic reaction that is a response to danger—but anxiety (not unlike de Man's "linguistic" death) does not always "know" the danger it is a reaction against. Freud hypothesizes an anxiety "appearing without the subject knowing what he is afraid of" (182). Thus, in Samuel Weber's helpful gloss, anxiety *"calls the very process of cathexis itself into question."*[20] Repression, at least, cathects onto a "thing-representation" *(Sachvorstellung);* but anxiety is the neurosis of displacement. As Weber suggests provocatively, the trauma of anxiety "is always in excess of its recognition or representation, and hence danger is only present, or presentable, as the approach of something else" (54). Anxiety, in other words, does not always know what it is afraid of.

A brief digression is in order here. In *Beyond the Pleasure Principle,* Freud reveals his concern for the interpretive deferrals that all too often characterize psychoanalysis: "The indeterminacy of all our discussions that we call 'metapsychological' is of course due to the fact that we know nothing of the nature of the excitatory process that takes place in the elements of the psychic systems, and that we do not feel justified in framing any hypothesis on the subject. We are consequently operating all the time with a large unknown factor—a capital X—that we are obliged to carry over into every new formula."[21] In this, his most speculative work, Freud worries that psychoanalysis may inevitably be "indeterminate," a concern he locates in "a capital X" that eludes understanding. Furthermore, we could contend that Freud's most indeterminate and uninterpretable neurosis is anxiety.

Freud, never fully succeeding in pinpointing the "danger" to which anxiety reacts, designated its quantum of affect (its "excitatory process") as a kind of "X," marking the spot of the displacement of anxiety. As

Weber suggests, "This 'X' marks the spot to which psychoanalytical thinking is constrained . . . to return, a spot that is impossible to occupy because it is impossible to locate."[22] To be sure, throughout Freud's writings the relationship between anxiety and affect is complex, at times inadequately theorized. But certainly one result of anxiety is "silence" as the constitutive symptom of an absence of affect. Freudian psychoanalysis is "constrained to return" to the enigma of anxiety, what I would argue as the constitutive (and ironic) symptom of de Man's displacement away from Freud. The Jewish Freud is a figure about whom de Man was virtually "silent"; in other words, the Jewish Freud can scarcely be found in de Man's published work. But is it possible that the figure of the Jew can be "found" in the "X" of de Man's anxiety, the unlocatable e*X*cess of his displacement (from Freud to a Derrida who has often been circumspect about his own Jewish identity)? If anxiety is structured on an excess (on the "X" of excess) that is beyond representation, then we could say de Man's anxiety is "located" in a Freud that can be experienced only in displacement onto Derrida.

The unlocatable "place" of anxiety (the unlocatable e*X*cess of anxious displacement) in the work of the later de Man resides somewhere in an uncathected network of floating signifiers: "psychoanalysis," "Freud," the figure of the Jew — avoided as a danger and displaced onto the figure of Derrida. Freud's "Jewish" psychoanalysis becomes metamorphosed (or re-cathected) as Derridean deconstruction, with "Derrida" serving as the locus for de Man's anxiety about Freud (about psychoanalysis? about the "Jewish Question" in Western cultural history?). Insofar as the work of de Man obliquely hints at the very Freudian "danger" he seeks to avoid, one suspects that de Man's postwar silence can be "diagnosed" as a comprehensive symptom of anxious disavowal *(Verwerfung)*.

Before concluding this section, I want to return to Derrida and to the specific issue of a *Derridean* anxiety, in the form of a possible encryptedness of a de Manian disavowal of the "Jewish Question" in Western modernity. After all, the possibility that Derrida plays a key role in a de Manian allegory of anxiety can prompt a discussion not only of the psychoanalytic phenomenon of "Derrida–in–de Man," but also of "de Man–in–Derrida."

As discussed earlier in this chapter, the concept of an "impossible mourning" set forth in Derrida's *Mémoires* is a sustained defense of de Man's resistance to memory, a critique of memory's narcissistic and acquisitive impulses to recuperate an otherwise unrecoverable past. Derrida's "impossible mourning" is a scrupulous effort to maintain the alterity of the Other such that, in the wake of the Other's death, he urges that any process of mourning must respect the Other's "infinite remove." Mourning, in short, must become aware of its own impossibility.

But in "Like the Sound of the Sea," his detailed (and decidedly anxious) defense of de Man's wartime journalism, Derrida inadvertently demonstrates that even for the architect of a postmodern memory, a "narcissistic" identification with the dead, an urge to bridge the Other's "infinite remove," may nonetheless persist. As Derrida ironically demonstrates, it is not always so easy to resist, as he phrases it in *Mémoires*, "the tomb or vault of some narcissism"; it is not always so easy to resist a narcissistic attachment to the past—in this case, a "narcissistic" investment in his and de Man's past efforts at shaping deconstruction as one of the most influential philosophical and critical discourses in the postwar era. Thus, to speak of the psychoanalytic phenomenon of "de Man–in–Derrida" is to speak of the complex process by which de Man's "resistance to memory"—his silence, his refusal to come to terms with his past—becomes encrypted in Derrida's own refusal to come to terms with de Man's refusal of the past. De Man's foreclosure of a mourning of the implications of his wartime past becomes, in turn, its own Derridean crisis in *Trauerarbeit*.

As noted earlier, Derrida, in "Like the Sound of the Sea," readily admits that de Man's "Les Juifs dans la littérature actuelle," his most explicit engagement with the "Jewish Question," is, for Derrida, the "most unbearable article" in the wartime journalism—an article that inflicted a painful psychic "wound" (621) upon his first reading it. In "Les Juifs," the young de Man's commitment to a fascist nationalism—not to mention his specific desire that Belgium have a place in the "New Europe"—is underscored by means of his support of an aesthetic modernism that he claims has maintained its vitality despite lingering perceptions that this tradition has for too long been dominated by Jews. In order to emphasize the cultural triumphs of this "vital" aesthetic modernism, de Man chooses to attack what was commonly referred to at the time as a "vulgar anti-Semitism" that interpreted literary modernism as "degenerate" and *enjuivé;* he makes the further claim that it is the Jews themselves who have been most responsible for perpetuating this misconception of literary modernism. For de Man, then, it is the "vulgar anti-Semite" who is ironically most susceptible to "Jewish propaganda" about the significance of Jewish contributions to literature.

47

In his celebration of literary modernism, de Man carefully dissociates himself from "vulgar anti-Semitism." But the question lingers: does this careful dissociation signal a complete break from subtler forms of anti-Semitism? A definitive answer to this question is, of course, not possible, but as David Carroll argues in his "Open Letter" to Derrida on the subject of de Man's wartime journalism, "De Man, to my knowledge, never questions or distances himself from Brasillach's anti-Semitism in any of the articles in which he refers to him (or from the anti-Semitism of any of the other French fascist writers he discusses)."[23] And in the case of "Les Juifs" in particular, Carroll contends that de Man "replaces 'vulgar anti-Semitism' with a more sophisticated version of anti-Semitism that is rooted in exactly the same myths as the vulgar version. The lethal mythology of the Jew that supports all forms of anti-Semitism remains intact in this article. . . . At bottom, de Man's text . . . uses the worst, the most vulgar, anti-Semitic clichés of our time, for it claims that Jews have made no essential contributions to culture or politics, only negative ones" (64, 66). Without question, de Man was not a practitioner of a visceral anti-Semitism (as was, say, Céline); but, as Carroll suggests, neither did he entirely distance himself from the more "rational" anti-Semitism of the likes of Brasillach or Drieu la Rochelle.

However, the complex issue of Derrida's avoidance of the specter of a de Manian anti-Semitism is more relevant to my argument here than whether de Man was in fact anti-Semitic. Carroll's "Open Letter" interprets Derrida's "Like the Sound of the Sea" as constituting, among other things, a sustained avoidance of the anti-Semitic implications of what he himself refers to as this "most unbearable article." And what we come to discover is that Derrida's thesis in *Mémoires* that mourning must become aware of its own impossibility becomes transformed in "Like the Sound of the Sea" into a never fully articulated anxiety over the issue of whether or not the young de Man was anti-Semitic. Thus Derrida's own "narcissistic" attachment to the memory of his former colleague results in the following apology for de Man: "to condemn 'vulgar anti-Semitism,' especially if one makes no mention of the other kind, is to condemn anti-Semitism itself *inasmuch* as it is vulgar, always and essentially vulgar" (625; italics in original). In other words, de Man's refusal to "speak the name" of a "rational" anti-Semitism offers proof that he was repelled by anti-Semitism in any form.[24]

Carroll interprets Derrida's "Like the Sound of the Sea" as, in the final analysis, a kind of exercise in psychic displacement. Addressing Derrida directly, Carroll argues, "The problem, as I see it, is that you begin quickly . . . to put feelings of sorrow, disappointment, and shock behind you and to displace them, by means of the details, length, and focus of your analysis, onto a secondary level of *your* text—and thus to displace de Man's ideological involvement onto a secondary level of his articles as well."[25] Picking up where Carroll leaves off, I suggest that the essay offers compelling evidence of a Derridean anxiety—an anxiety that, in the process of clinging to de Man's critique of "vulgar anti-Semitism" as definitive "proof" that he rejected anti-Semitism as a whole, forecloses on the possibility that the young de Man may have harbored a more "sophisticated" version of anti-Semitism. Just as the conspicuous absence of the Jewish Freud may have marked a place of "danger" for the later de Man—a danger that had to be not so much re-pressed as contained and displaced—so also could we argue that the possibility of a more "refined" de Manian anti-Semitism marks a simi-lar place of "danger" for Derrida, a danger that results in a displacement of, in Carroll's words, Derrida's own "feelings of sorrow, disappoint-ment, and shock." In this process of displacement onto the secondary level of his own text, a Derridean affect gets contained and displaced, and the traumatic "wound" Derrida early in his essay admitted suffering on first reading de Man's article goes unremembered by the essay's conclusion.

As discussed earlier, anxiety is a trauma that can only be experienced in displacement—in the case of "Like the Sound of the Sea," a dis-placement from the specter of a de Manian anti-Semitism that can be "located" in Derrida's own anxious claim that de Man in fact *critiques* anti-Semitism. Derrida's anxiety (an anxiety perhaps generated by his own Jewish identity?) constitutes itself as the avoidance of the problem of anti-Semitism, a refusal to work through de Man's own refusal to work through the past. To speak, then, of the psychoanalytic phenom-enon of "de Man–in–Derrida" is to speak of how a Derridean anxiety concerning the figure of the Jew (in the young de Man's Belgium, in wartime Europe as a whole) becomes its own "impossible mourning" of the Jew in the post-Holocaust. To echo the terms of Abraham and Torok's cryptonymy, a Derridean anxiety resides in the *non-lieu* of tex-tual and (psychic) displacement; a Derridean anxiety about the "Paul de Man affair" becomes the site of deconstruction's inheritance of de Man's encrypted wartime secrets.

Daseinsanalyse: Freud and Heideggerian Anxiety

Picking up where Klein's discussion of a de Manian foreclosure of Freud left off, one is tempted to ask: Is it the prewar Freud who (ironically) gets us closer to the Holocaust than any "speaking" of a silence in the post-Holocaust? As we ponder the implications of this question, let us turn to the figure of Heidegger, who, like de Man, also maintained a silence after Auschwitz, and from whose work also Freud is conspicuously absent. Before confronting the issue of Heidegger's infamous silence, however, we would do well to reassess what many would perceive as the *non*issue of Freud and Heidegger.

Can there be any logic in speaking of Freud *and* Heidegger? And if so, how would such a linkage be possible (or, for that matter, desirable)? Perhaps not surprisingly, it is Derrida who accepts the challenge, for it is in *La carte postale* that Derrida poses the provocative question: "What does philosophy *not have to do* with psychoanalytic 'speculation'?"[26] But elsewhere in *La carte postale,* Derrida admits that he can approach such a conjunction only tentatively, alluding to two figures who, "according to all appearances and all usual criteria, never read each other, and even less encountered each other. Freud and Heidegger, Heidegger and Freud" (357). For that matter, it is as if Derrida realized that he could only imagine what he refers to as a *Daseinsanalyse* through the odd discursive option of the "Jewish joke." Early in his often quasi-autobiographical *La carte postale,* Derrida recounts the eeriness of his visit to Heidegger's native city of Freiburg: "On the subject of Jewish stories [*histoire* as "joke"]: you can imagine the extent to which I am haunted by Heidegger's ghost in this city" (189). Derrida enters a bookstore and buys two photograph albums—one of Heidegger and one of Freud. But where is the Jewish joke? Leafing through the albums, Derrida narrates that he "burst out laughing when I found that Martin [Heidegger] has the face of an old Jew from Algiers" (189). An intriguing gloss on Derrida's Freiburg anecdote has been offered by Ned Lukacher: "Isn't the joke finally that Heidegger is a kind of father; that in this old photograph of Heidegger, Derrida sees the head of his father?"[27] It is the implicitly Oedipal (and hence inherently Freudian) similarity between Heidegger and Derrida's father as the "old Jew from Algiers"—an unanticipated and strange conjoining of Freud and Heidegger, even after buying photograph albums of the two men—that elicits Derrida's laughter. Even as de Man, as we have earlier seen, plays the son to the Freudian father (disguised as "Derrida"), so also does Derrida play the son to the Heideggerian father (disguised as, in effect, Derrida's father).[28]

But if the reader will permit a brief digression, we could say that "old Jews" are not always such a laughing matter in psychoanalysis. Despite Lacan's celebrated "return to Freud," we could say that contemporary psychoanalysis does not necessarily favor "old Jews"—especially if we shift our location from Freiburg to Hamburg. In his essay "The Suture of an Allusion," Jeffrey Mehlman cites Lacan's strangely intrusive allusion in his *Four Fundamental Concepts* to Léon Bloy's *Le salut par les juifs* as just such an example of how readily "old Jews" become associated with Freudian psychoanalysis (or, more explicitly, with Freud himself).[29] As Mehlman makes clear, Lacan's elliptical allusion to Bloy is, in fact, the latter's registering of his revulsion toward three old merchants, imagined as Abraham, Isaac, and Jacob, whom he encounters in the Jewish marketplace at Hamburg: "I will long remember, nevertheless, those three incomparable wretches [*crapules*] that I still see in their rotting smocks, leaning forehead to forehead over the orifice of a fetid sack that would have frightened the stars and in which were heaped up, for the exportation of typhus, the unspeakable objects of some arch-Semitic transaction" (24). However cryptically, indirectly, or inadvertently, "it is to these Jews," argues Mehlman, "that Lacan compares Freud" (24).

In this context, where Hamburg's "old Jews" become the *locus classicus* of Bloy's anti-Semitism (and, as Mehlman has argued, implicitly become compared by Lacan to Freud), how are we to interpret the reincarnation, in *La carte postale,* of Freiburg's Heidegger as an "old Jew from Algiers"? And again, what is Derrida's (Jewish) joke? Is psychoanalysis merely a "Jewish" science (to carry the implications of Bloy's anti-Semitism to its logical extreme)? Is it based on a merely cultural, nontheoretical paradigm of young sons struggling with their "old" Jewish fathers? Or is Derrida ironically suggesting that Heideggerian philosophy too can be nuanced as the philosophy of a kind of "old Jew" (like the one from Algiers)? Is the "joke," after all, on Freud—or is it on Heidegger?

Under the "post" of the post-Holocaust, as well as on the heels of Derrida's Freiburg anecdote, it seems appropriate to ponder the extent to which Freud is encrypted in Heidegger's work. And to pursue this encryptedness further is to try to understand more fully the extent to which Heidegger, like de Man, may have experienced his own version of (Freudian) anxiety after Auschwitz. If anxiety is the "X" to which psychoanalysis is, in Samuel Weber's words, "constrained to return"—and if indeed Freud is a kind of phantom within Heidegger—then we can perhaps "locate" the primal scene of a *Daseinsanalyse* in *Sein und Zeit* where, under the rubric of "Care as the Being of *Dasein*," Heidegger considers the enigma that is *Angst*, or anxiety: "How far is anxiety a state-of-mind which is distinctive?"[30] Not unlike Freud (though with no acknowledgment of him), Heidegger configures anxiety as a trauma that can be experienced only in displacement away from a perceived "danger": "In anxiety one does not encounter this thing or that thing which, as something threatening, must have an involvement" (231). For Heidegger, anxiety, as an affective response to danger, is its own kind of (anxious) tautology: "That which anxiety is profoundly anxious about is not a *definite* kind of Being for Dasein or a *definite* possibility for it. Indeed the threat itself is indefinite, and therefore cannot penetrate threateningly to this or that factically concrete potentiality-for-Being. That which anxiety is anxious about is Being-in-the-world itself" (232).

In an interview about Heidegger with Lévinas (who, as both a loyal interpreter of Heidegger and a former prisoner of the Germans during the war, is as complex a figure within French postmodernism as Derrida), Philippe Nemo asks Lévinas what, throughout the years, has particularly affected him in Heidegger's phenomenological method. Without hesitation, Lévinas answers, "the passages on anxiety. When superficially investigated, anxiety would seem to be an affective movement without cause or, put more precisely, 'without object'. . . . Anxiety appears to be the authentic and appropriate access to nothing."[31] Lévinas is impressed most by Heidegger's version of anxiety, an "affective movement" which, like Freudian anxiety, does not always "know" the danger it is a reaction against.

If de Man's anxiety is evinced by a Freudian "danger" he seeks to avoid, Heidegger would appear to confront the "danger" of anxiety directly. But the figure of Freud himself remains encrypted within Heideggerian anxiety, a phenomenon Heidegger may have acknowledged, if only tacitly. "In anxiety," Heidegger concludes, "one feels *uncanny*" (232). "Uncanny," that is, as in Freud's *Unheimliche* as the return of the repressed? Or, in this case, an uncanny Freud as the return of the repressed in Heidegger's configuration of anxiety?

All of which is to suggest that we *can* "psychoanalyze" Heidegger under the "post" of the post-Holocaust. But the goal of the rest of this chapter is not so much the topic of Heidegger himself as the mediation of Heidegger through French postmodernism, particularly Derridean deconstruction—and, more specifically, the psychoanalytic implications of such a mediation. We will return to the issue of Heidegger's (Freudian) anxiety later. But for now, such a "psychoanalyzing," a *Daseinsanalyse*, of Heidegger (and his seeming lack of anxiety about his Nazi past) should perhaps begin not in his native Germany, but rather with a "psychoanalyzing" of France (and the philosophical phenomenon that has come to be known as "French Heideggerianism") as the primal scene of *l'affaire Heidegger*. In Lyotard's succinct summary, "The Heidegger affair is a 'French' affair,"[32] the reasons for which resonate with psychoanalytic implications. After all, to quote Derrida, "What does philosophy *not have to do* with psychoanalytic 'speculation'?"— especially French philosophy.

Heidegger's "Silence": "The Authentic Access to Nothing"

Let us begin our "psychoanalyzing" of France in 1947 with a brief glance at the French philosopher Jean Beaufret, who served willingly as the addressee of Heidegger's famous "Letter on Humanism,"[33] a rebuttal of Sartre's "humanist" existentialism—and who thus, in some sense, inaugurated the era of what has come to be called "French Heideggerianism." Interestingly, Beaufret also played a major role in forging a link between psychoanalysis and Heideggerian philosophy. In 1950, five years after he introduced Heidegger's thought into France, Beaufret entered into analysis with Lacan, who at the time was also interested in Heidegger's philosophy. It could be argued that Beaufret's analysis with Lacan forged its own version of a *Daseinsanalyse* when we consider that it was Beaufret who helped Lacan understand the importance of Heidegger's thought for the analyst's own work. As we have seen, throughout his intellectual career Heidegger never acknowledged the work of Freud (a perhaps more synecdochal way of stating that philosophy never acknowledged psychoanalysis); yet it is worth noting that because of Beaufret, in effect (Lacanian) psychoanalysis was granted an "audience" with (Heideggerian) philosophy.[34] But Beaufret, who died in 1982, proved to be a highly contradictory figure in postwar France, as evidenced by the fact that he was both an ex-*Résistant* and, years later, also a sympathetic supporter of Robert Faurisson and his notorious

53

Holocaust *révisionnisme*, particularly his perverse claim that the gas chambers never existed. Thus we are left with the ironic result that both Beaufret and the influential philosopher he introduced into France would, at different points in their careers, come to disavow the Holocaust.

Let us now turn to the phenomenon of French Heideggerianism, an intellectual moment that one could argue is perhaps better understood psychoanalytically than philosophically. Ever since the end of the second world war, it has been not Germany but France that has experienced a near "obsession" (hysteria?) with Heidegger and his past associations with German National Socialism, such that the Heidegger controversy came into being, as it were, only as a (Freudian) *displacement* from Germany to France. It is not insignificant that, as early as 1946, Heidegger's student Karl Löwith observed, "The fact that Heidegger found during the last war a wide audience among French intellectuals, in contrast to the situation of Germany at that time, is a symptom that merits received attention."[35] The French introjection of Heidegger is indeed a "symptom," for the disclosures of Heidegger's Nazi past have constituted a kind of *coupure* that has become nothing less than a source of trauma for many of France's postwar intellectuals — a much-discussed and widely publicized phenomenon that merits its own psychoanalytic speculation. It should be emphasized that *l'affaire Heidegger* did not occur as one central event; rather, it has unfolded over time as a kind of "return of the repressed." Thus we discover that *l'affaire Heidegger* did not "originate" with the 1987 French publication of Victor Farias's *Heidegger et le nazisme*.[36] Rather, the origin occurred much earlier, in 1946, with Sartre's *Les temps modernes*, which published an interview between the two philosophers that took place in Heidegger's Freiburg — an exchange that, after Auschwitz, can perhaps best be rendered as an opposition between a Heidegger who, after the war, persistently refused to speak of his anti-Semitic policies as Rector of Freiburg University, and a Sartre who freely spoke out against anti-Semitism. And perhaps it is in this sense not merely coincidental that also in 1946, in *Les temps modernes*, Löwith was already alluding to Heidegger's French reception as a "symptom."[37]

In addition to its status as French philosophy's "return of the repressed," another major reason why *l'affaire Heidegger* lends itself so richly to psychoanalytic speculation has been the ongoing controversy of a Heideggerian "silence" — the philosopher's persistent refusal to comment either on his Nazi past or on the role of German National Socialism in the genocide of the Holocaust. As early as 1978, prior to the Heidegger controversy, George Steiner wrote, "It is [Heidegger's] complete silence on Hitlerism and the holocaust after 1945 which is very nearly intolerable."[38] But again, it is in France where, under the "post" of the post-Holocaust, this extended Heideggerian "silence" has served as the occasion for an ongoing *Trauerspiel* on the part of those who had hoped Heidegger would say more — that he might openly admit that, in effect, one of the cornerstones of his ontology, *Sein-zum-Tode* (or "Being-toward-Death"), may itself have served as a kind of metaphysical disavowal of any future knowledge of the "Final Solution." To cite a few prominent examples, in 1988, in *Le Nouvel Observateur,* Blanchot depicts Heidegger's silence as a perversely "willful" or "determined" response to the now silent void of Auschwitz. In the same issue, Lévinas, who was one of the first intellectuals in France to write about Heidegger, asks, "But doesn't this silence . . . on the gas chambers and death camps . . . reveal a soul completely cut off from any sensitivity [*sensibilité*], in which can be perceived a kind of consent to the horror?"[39] And in his 1986 book *La poésie comme expérience,* an extended meditation on the poetry of Paul Celan, Philippe Lacoue-Labarthe gives special prominence to Celan's "Todtnauberg," a poem relating the poet's 1967 meeting with Heidegger in the philosopher's mountain hut in the Black Forest, during which Heidegger refused to speak to Celan of the Holocaust. Lacoue-Labarthe judges that Heidegger's refusal to speak of Nazi atrocities to someone who had himself once been imprisoned by the Nazis was particularly unforgivable.

Because of Blanchot's, Lévinas's, Lacoue-Labarthe's, and many others' expressions of outrage, Heidegger's silence has, after Auschwitz, almost come to possess its own essence — as if it has itself acceded to the status of a metaphysical concept. In the minds of his critics, in other words, Heidegger's silence exists where compassion and pathos are *not.* Since Lévinas was himself a survivor of the Holocaust, his depiction of a Heideggerian soul impervious to compassion seems especially resonant. Given that one of the cornerstones of Lévinasian philosophy is the concept of the ethical *response* to the Other, the issue of Heidegger's silence must have been particularly repugnant to Lévinas. As he argues in *Ethics and Infinity,* "The authentic relationship with the Other . . . is discourse and, more exactly, response or responsibility. . . . The *saying* is the fact that before the face I do not simply remain there contemplating it, I respond to it. . . . It is difficult to be silent in someone's presence."[40] In "As If Consenting to Horror," Lévinas even more directly deplores Heidegger's withholding of an ethical response to the Other: the philosopher's antihumanism, claims Lévinas, prevented him from "pronouncing the name of the Jews" (487). In effect, what Lévinas wanted (and never received) from Heidegger was a demonstration of some sort of Freudian "quota of affect" (an *Affektbetrag*), a *sensibilité* that could satisfy his felt need for an elegiac expression of remorse.

For that matter, the impulse to interpret Heidegger's silence (that is, the wish for a Heideggerian "affect") can remind us at this point of our earlier discussion of anxiety. As we came to realize in our earlier analysis of de Man, anxiety was Freud's most uninterpretable neurosis; in his *Sein und Zeit*, Heidegger too attempted to "locate" anxiety's uninterpretability. As we have seen earlier, Heidegger observes, "In anxiety one does not encounter this thing or that thing which, as something threatening, must have an involvement." Like Freud's anxiety, Heidegger's anxiety does not cathect onto (or have an "involvement" with) any object. Or, in Lévinas's gloss, "Anxiety appears to be the authentic and appropriate access to nothing." It is not without irony that it is Lévinas who, on separate occasions, has provided commentary on both Heidegger's discourse on anxiety and his outrageous, nondiscursive silence on Auschwitz. Had Lévinas taken the further step of linking the issue of a Heideggerian (and Freudian) anxiety and the issue of a Heideggerian silence, the logic might have unfolded thus: if Heideggerian anxiety is the "authentic . . . access to nothing" (that is, if anxiety [about a Nazi past?] cannot, in Heidegger's words, "penetrate" to the "factically concrete" [the historical event known as the Holocaust?]), or if, as in Freud's conception, anxiety is the failure of repression (the failure of cathexis itself), then one result of anxiety would indeed be silence — a willful silence that would treat Auschwitz as a "danger" that must be contained and displaced by that silence, an anxious silence that would stubbornly resist cathexis onto what Heidegger evidently (and perversely) judged as the excessive pathos of others' discourse about the Holocaust. Heidegger's silence (like his configuration of anxiety) will yield (to echo Lévinas on Heideggerian anxiety) only the "authentic access to nothing"; it is in this sense that the uninterpretability of (Freudian) anxiety now leads not so indirectly to, say, Blanchot's and Lévinas's struggles with the uninterpretability of Heidegger's notorious post-Auschwitz silence.

The psychic valence of these struggles has not gone unnoticed by Derrida, who, like Blanchot, Lévinas, and others, has also publicly deplored Heidegger's silence about Auschwitz. In light of his earlier *Mémoires: For Paul de Man,* Derrida came to the Heidegger controversy as no stranger to the phenomenon of a post-Holocaust anxious silence. But in his most sustained analyses of Heidegger's silence, he attempts to push further than the others, as if inducing Heidegger's detractors to ask themselves the very simple, yet resonant question, What would we want Heidegger to have said? It is as if Derrida is asking them to analyze their own "desire" behind Heidegger's silence. Derrida poses the following hypothetical situation in which Heidegger offers the much-anticipated apology: "Let us assume that Heidegger had not only said about 1933 'I have made a very stupid mistake' but also 'Auschwitz is the absolute horror; it is what I fundamentally condemn.'"[41] Here Derrida is suggesting the possibility that our "desire" to have the silence broken abuts a Heideggerian "anxiety" to preserve the silence in ways that are (psychically) incommensurable: if anxiety encounters, in Heidegger's own words, "this thing or that thing which, as something threatening, must have an involvement," then to speak of "involvement" is no longer to speak of Heideggerian anxiety, but rather open confession, which, had Heidegger been forthcoming with one, would have signaled for Derrida a regression back to the "metaphysics of the subject." But Heidegger's anxiety means that Auschwitz, for him a "danger" that must be contained and displaced (as if it were, in de Man's words, a Nietzschean past that is "so threatening that it has to be forgotten"?), cannot be discursively "contained" in confession: Heideggerian anxiety will persistently deny his interlocutors easy access to an affective display of Heideggerian remorse, guilt, or *sensibilité.* For Derrida, had Heidegger broken his notorious silence with an "affective" confession, "it would not be necessary for us to ask today what affinities, . . . what common roots Heidegger's thinking could have with National Socialism" (147). In other words, for Derrida, Heidegger's infamous silence is less an occasion for rhetorical displays of public censure than a philosophical opportunity, after Auschwitz, to "think" the "unthought" behind Heidegger's involvement with National Socialism in a way unencumbered by the "metaphysics of the subject."

In such a scheme, Heidegger emerges as a kind of "hero" of anxiety—as if, for Derrida, Heidegger's anxious silence stands as a memorial to the "unthought" of Nazi atrocities. But let us for the moment return to the more relevant issue, raised earlier in this chapter, of a *Derridean* anxiety and of the possible psychoanalytic phenomenon of "Heidegger-in-Derrida." Despite Derrida's warning in *Mémoires* that an "impossible mourning" must resist "the tomb or vault of some narcissism," it may not be so easy for a Derridean memory of Heidegger's prewar and wartime past to resist being transformed into its own Derridean crisis in *Trauerarbeit*. In this context, let us think back to Derrida's affective burst of laughter in Freiburg on seeing the photo of Heidegger, and pose the question: what, precisely, does that burst of laughter reveal? The fact that Heidegger resembles an "old Jew from Algiers" is, for Derrida, an obvious occasion for humor. But can we also discern, embedded in the affective laughter, an anxiety over the vexed issue of "Heidegger and the Jews"? If anxiety is a trauma that can only be experienced in displacement, is Derrida's burst of laughter its own anxious displacement of the "Jewish Question" in Heidegger? Is Derrida's laughter constituted as a refusal to work through Heidegger's own refusal to work through the past? Derrida laughs at the prospect of envisioning Heidegger as "an old Jew from Algiers"—but to what extent does his laughter signal his unwillingness to acknowledge the fact that despite Heidegger's uncanny resemblance to, say, Derrida's father, Heidegger would not, to echo Lévinas, "pronounc[e] the name of the Jews"? I examine these questions in more detail in the next section.

Heidegger and the (Jewish) Question

A densely deconstructive "thinking" of Heidegger's involvement with National Socialism is, of course, the project of Derrida's *De l'esprit*,[42] a work so elaborately complex, so obscure as to when, precisely, it is praising and when it is subverting Heidegger that it has served, in the judgment of many of its readers, as a prime example of the inadequacies of deconstruction as a discursive framework for confronting the highly charged issue of Heidegger's politics. In short, *De l'esprit* has been attacked as an example of the worst impulses of French Heideggerianism itself. Phrased broadly, ever since the Heidegger controversy became widely public in France, French Heideggerianism has constituted itself as an extended warning about the intellectual difficulties of attempting premature separations of the philosophical and the political in Heidegger's writings. In his recent book on Heidegger, Pierre Bourdieu has configured French Heideggerianism as one of his characteristic "fields of production," constituted within the difficult, indeed incommensurable opposition between a political and a philosophical reading of Heidegger—what Bourdieu refers to as "two mental spaces" that cannot converge.[43] And in a recent book on what could best be summarized as "postmodernism and its discontents," Christopher Norris has outlined precisely why French Heideggerianism has been so frustrating for those who want to penetrate the deconstructive layers of rehabilitation (the rigorously intellectual, but often highly elliptical maneuvers of damage control) to accuse Heidegger directly of political atrocities. Norris deplores the fact that for Derrida, Lacoue-Labarthe, and other French postmodernists "any *authentic* discussion of Heidegger must take the form of an immanent critique, or a reading conducted on terms laid down by that same Heideggerian project."[44] Norris's objection is that the "rules" of a deconstructive immanent critique disallow from the outset such overtly political questions as, Why did Heidegger maintain his perverse silence? Or, again to echo Lévinas, Why did Heidegger refuse to "pronounce the name of the Jews"? From the point of view of so much of French postmodernism, these questions are too directly posed. For the French Heideggerians, it is only by means of an immanent critique of Heidegger that one can demonstrate that a Heideggerian "anxiety" may (always already) be constitutive of his "thinking" of German National Socialism.

Norris's frustration with French Heideggerianism gets to the (psychoanalytic) core of the "desire" of Heidegger's detractors: their desire to hear the silence broken with a confession. The desire to hear a confession, however, forces what the French Heideggerians would call the premature intervention of externally posed questions about Heidegger's politics that are discursively incommensurate with Heidegger's own immanent critique of his involvement with Nazism—an immanent critique that, if carefully unpacked, could, in the judgment of Heidegger's defenders, serve as a far more eloquent discourse on Heidegger's politics than any response to a direct interrogation. For Heidegger's critics, Derrida's deconstructive "rules" of immanent critique simply recapitulate the distinctly unaffective nature of Heidegger's silence (serving as a kind of philosophical "repetition compulsion" of Heidegger's own absence of affect). But for Derrida, a Heideggerian affect *is* latent within his philosophy—but accessible only to the reader who "listens" carefully to the silence being "spoken."

All of which returns us specifically to *De l'esprit*, which could be summarized as, among other things, Derrida's return, after the Heidegger and de Man controversies, to his earlier concept of an "impossible mourning." The book has been widely analyzed as Derrida's most elaborate (and most densely argued) "defense" of Heidegger. The book's principal *leitmotif* is Derrida's analysis of Heidegger's use of *Geist* (and a renewal, of sorts, of his earlier consideration of a Hegelian *Geist* in *Glas*), structured on what Derrida calls four "guiding threads": the question (privileged by Heidegger as *the* mode of thinking), technology, animality, and epochality. What we eventually (after much interpretive struggle) discover is that these "guiding threads" tracing Heidegger's ongoing engagement with the "question" of Being have their complex convergence in modernity's most vexing question — the "Jewish Question." As I discuss later, *De l'esprit,* though never making explicit the figure of the Jew or the specter of a Heideggerian avoidance of the problem of anti-Semitism, is at all times haunted by a Heideggerian silence. Moreover, I trace how Derrida's "listening" to the ways in which Heidegger's own immanent critique of his involvement with Nazism not only supposedly "gives voice" to the philosopher's public refusal to acknowledge Nazi persecution of the Jews, but also "gives voice" to Derrida's own anxiety about Heidegger's inability to work through his past. But what we eventually discover is that despite the charge that he might be taking rhetorical cover behind the rigors of immanent critique as a means of "acting out" his own refusal to work through Heidegger's past, by the end of the book Derrida's deconstruction begins to speak more openly about the "unspoken" in Heidegger's politics.

Despite *De l'esprit*'s overtly deconstructive methodology, a careful "listening" to Derrida's argument is intimately bound up with psychoanalysis, particularly with the notion of philosophical ghosts that constitute a return of the repressed for Heidegger's thought, a repressed return that Derrida claims we can perhaps understand better in French than in German. In other words, it is as if Derrida, picking up where Lacan's axiom that the unconscious is structured like a language leaves off, seeks to demonstrate that the story of Heidegger's involvement with Nazism is so (psychically) complex that his silence must, to echo Benjamin, involve "the task of the translator": it must, in effect, be "listened to" in French as well as in German. Arguing that the enigmatic concept of *Geist* in Heidegger deserves as much attention as his *Dasein,* Derrida claims by the end of his book that we can best understand the meaning of Heidegger's silence by reading his German *Geist* against the grain of a French *esprit*.[45]

Derrida opens his study with an enigmatic intention: "I shall speak of ghost [*revenant*], of flame, and of ashes" (1). In other words, counterposed against a Heideggerian silence, we are offered Derrida's "speaking" of ghosts. (We are well reminded here that in *La carte postale*, Derrida also "speaks" of ghosts—specifically how Heidegger's ghost haunted his visit to Freiburg.) Of the "ghostly" mysteries of this opening sentence more will be said later. In the meantime, suffice to say that Derrida's treatment of *Geist* more formally begins with the year 1927, when Heidegger, as part of his interrogation of the "Being" of *Dasein* in his *Sein und Zeit,* places *Geist* in quotation marks in order to deny it any metaphysical, oppositional status to Being. But Derrida argues that once we make a point of submitting Heidegger's *"Geist"* (in quotation marks) to a deconstructive analysis, we will realize that, because of these very quotation marks, the term *Geist* is haunted by a "metaphysical ghost" *(le fantôme métaphysique),* a spectrality that foreshadows (psychoanalytically) the process by which, for Derrida, metaphysics always constitutes itself as the return of the repressed. Although a "ghost" can never be incorporated into metaphysics, it is nevertheless the *geistlich* "ghost" of metaphysics that haunts the quotation marks in *"Geist."*

Perhaps not surprisingly, then, when he moves from 1927 to 1933 and to Heidegger's *Rektoratsrede* (or "The Self-Affirmation of the German University"), delivered when he became Rector of Freiburg University (and often identified as the *locus classicus* of his commitment to German National Socialism), Derrida points out that Heidegger deploys *Geist,* this time without quotation marks, as a concept that is quintessentially German, or, more specifically, *Geist* as the spiritual foundation of the German university. Thus, despite his earlier use of *"Geist"* in quotation marks in *Sein und Zeit,* Heidegger ends up, in the *Rektoratsrede,* with a metaphysical (even a humanistic) *Geist.* Derrida's most polemical point in *De l'esprit*—and the argument that draws us closest to his position on the "essence" of Heidegger's silence—is that Heidegger's *Geist* makes its return (as a metaphysical return of the repressed) as the most compelling evidence of the philosopher's refusal of Nazi biologism. In other words, Derrida argues that Heidegger's *Geist* without quotation marks (*Geist* as "spirit") has been set up in metaphysical opposition to biologism as part of Heidegger's conscious effort to avoid compliance with any politics founded on a perverse myth of racial purity. As we saw earlier in this chapter, Derrida once argued in another context that it is as if those who are most scandalized by Heidegger's silence wanted him to state publicly and openly that "'Auschwitz is the absolute horror.'" But in Heidegger's *Geist* without quotation marks, Derrida argues that we can "listen" to Heidegger speak, in 1933, the words he would later withhold as part of his prolonged silence: for Derrida, the *Geist* without quotation marks becomes Heidegger's proleptic warning that, without a cultural renewal of this concept, the racist policies of Nazi biologism could conceivably lead to an Auschwitz as "the absolute horror." In other words, Derrida implies that Heidegger's infamous silence is less outrageous when we view his *Geist* "before Auschwitz" as far more discursively powerful than any affective remorse or guilt he might have openly expressed "after Auschwitz."

It is as if, for Derrida, Heidegger's *Geist* without quotation marks, despite its manifestly Germanic resonances, is an attempt to anticipate, to "think," the "unthought" of a mass extermination enabled by a nightmarish alliance of biologism and technology. But at this point (even presuming we do find ourselves convinced that Heidegger's removal of the scare quotes around *Geist* constitutes a rigorous "thinking" of the failures of German National Socialism), it should be noted that a Heideggerian critique of biologism does not necessarily imply a critique of Nazism in general. Thus we should move to a consideration of a question Derrida does not ask (not explicitly, at least) in his book on Heidegger and the "question": what is the precise relationship between Heidegger's *Geist* without quotation marks and the "Jewish Question"?

The figure of the Jew is never made manifest in *De l'esprit*; so, before moving to the final stage of Derrida's deconstruction of a Heideggerian *Geist*, we must turn to the subject of technology as one of the four "guiding threads" that structure *De l'esprit*, specifically the way in which technology serves as a key "question" in Heidegger's "thinking" of *Geist*. Derrida alludes to Heidegger's claim that "the essence of technology is nothing technological," often interpreted as Heidegger's attempt to keep philosophical thought "uncontaminated" by technology as one of the cornerstones of modernity. Heidegger's claim comes from one of his unpublished lectures, "The Enframing" *(Das Gestell),* part of a 1949 lecture series at Bremen, "The Question Concerning Technology."[46] In this highly complex and ambiguous lecture, Heidegger attempts to "think" the Being, the essence *(Wesen)*, the very "presencing" of technology *(technik)* itself; and certainly the topic of the Bremen lecture series served, for Heidegger, as an occasion to return to an earlier theme from his writings in the mid-1930s on the relationship between *Geist* and modern technology. Thus, after Auschwitz, it could be said that Heidegger viewed the lecture series as a timely forum for renewing his critique of the "contaminating" influence of modern technology.

Derrida appropriates Heidegger's critique of technology to anticipate his argument, later in *De l'esprit,* that Heidegger wanted to save *Geist* from Nazi biologism. However, amidst this discussion of the "question" of Heidegger's "Question Concerning Technology," an intriguing "question" that can occur to us here is why, at the very moment of this consideration of a Heideggerian ambivalence toward technology, Derrida chose not to acknowledge the one written occasion (in the very same essay) when it could be said that Heidegger *did* break his silence to speak of the Holocaust. In a page that has since been deleted from the original unpublished manuscript (a page that many followers of the Heidegger controversy such as Blanchot, Lacoue-Labarthe, and Lévinas have made a point of noting, but that elicits an odd moment of Derridean "silence" in *De l'esprit*), the following passage appears: "Agriculture is now a motorized food industry — in essence, the same as the manufacturing of corpses in gas chambers and the extermination camps, the same as the blockading and starving of nations, the same as the manufacture of atom bombs."[47] In this astounding passage after Auschwitz, delivered as he was being investigated by Germany's de-Nazification board, Heidegger "speaks" the "unspoken" of his infamous silence, but in a passage that incredibly forges what has struck so many readers as a too casually conceived analogy between modern agricultural technology and the gas chambers — between, say, chemicals of artificial fertilization and pellets of Zyklon B, or tractors and the gas exhaust vans of Chelmno. Thus, in Heidegger's breaking of his silence, a new scandal is born.[48]

In a sustained and detailed analysis of Heidegger's difficult lecture, an analysis that "listens" patiently to Heidegger's thinking of the Being of technology (of *techne* as the essence of knowledge), Richard J. Bernstein accepts the challenge of addressing the unemotional coldness of this passage. Given Heidegger's contention throughout his essay that an emphasis on technology has deluded humankind into thinking that it is destined to control the earth, Bernstein understands the passage to be saying, "Unless we fully acknowledge and confront the essence of technology, even in 'manufacturing of corpses in gas chambers,' unless we realize that *all* its manifestations are 'in essence the same,' we will never confront the supreme danger and the possible upsurgence of the saving power."[49] In other words, Bernstein unpacks Heidegger's enigmatic statement as a warning that if we continue our failure to "think" the "unthought" of *technik,* modern technology can and will lead to mass extermination.

But which is more chillingly cryptic—Heidegger's infamous silence about Auschwitz, or his *spoken* analogy between a "motorized food industry" and the "manufacturing" of corpses? In the end, does it require too many interpretive twists and turns to construe Heidegger's warning that the ambiguous "essence" of technology can harbor, in Bernstein's gloss, both a "supreme danger" and a "saving power" as tantamount to a display of remorse or guilt? Once again, as was the case with his infamous silence, Heidegger leaves his interlocutors demanding something more explicitly sympathetic. Once again, what is conspicuously absent is the salutary display of an affective sympathy (what Lévinas called a *sensibilité*) that could serve not only as evidence of the philosopher's regret for his own role in National Socialism, but also—and now we are at the heart of why *l'affaire Heidegger* lingers in a post-Holocaust era—as evidence of his sympathy for the specific fate of Jews during the war. Whether the issue is Heidegger's infamous silence or his equally notorious spoken analogy between a "motorized food industry" and the "manufacturing" of corpses, his critics claim that what remains unspoken is a sympathetic "thinking" of the plight of the *victim.* As John D. Caputo eloquently argues, Heidegger's discourse on the thinking of Being almost by definition cannot allow for a "thinking" of the victim: "The victim never comes to presence, never makes an appearance on the scene of the history of Being. . . . The victim is invisible in the history of Being, is not a matter of concern, is not what is at issue. The victim does not come toward us and concern us *(an-wesen, an-gehen)* in the history of Being."[50] In other words, because Heidegger's philosophy is concerned not with "beings" but rather with Being itself, the victim necessarily becomes occluded within his critique of technology. When, in his essay "Heidegger's Silence," Derrida poses the question of what we would want Heidegger to have said, we can imagine Lévinas, for one, answering that what he wants is an expression of sorrow for the victim, specifically the Jewish victim.

The central project of *De l'esprit* is to show how deconstruction and its discursive rules of immanent critique disallow any easy or premature access to the issue of Heidegger's avoidance of the problem of anti-Semitism. Because its goal is to confront an argument with its own (il)logic, immanent critique disallows any conclusion deduced by an ego entering the text from the outside. As we have seen, the case of Heidegger's enigmatic analogy prompts the externally posed question: does the conspicuous absence of the Jewish victim reveal a Heideggerian refusal to work through the past? But in *De l'esprit,* which makes no explicit allusion to the controversy of Heidegger's analogy, Derrida claims that his method of immanent critique has already answered the "question" of Heidegger's refusal to work through by means of his analysis of the *Rektoratsrede* as a proleptic anticipation of Nazi biologism's creation of the Jewish victim; Heidegger's *Geist* without quotation marks embodies the philosopher's desire to "save" it from the scandal of a racial politics. In his reading of the *Rektoratsrede,* Derrida believes he is responding to the immediate "question" of Heidegger's politics by portraying, in his subtly deconstructive way, a Heidegger deeply disturbed by the sinister direction of German National Socialism.[51]

Thus, in the face of claims that the essence of Heideggerian philosophy can find no place for the victim, Derrida would remind us of the Heidegger who asserted that technology is the enemy of modernity because, instead of an authentic "thinking" of Being, technology represents nothing more than a disappointing "fall" into metaphysics, the worst manifestation of which would eventually be Auschwitz as a systematic elimination of the Jewish victim. Derrida counterposes Heidegger's *Geist* (without quotation marks) against Nazi biologism as Heidegger's rigorous critique of a modernity defined by a racial eugenics, a perverse "science" that, perhaps even more than technology, had become *the* constitutive feature of modernity.

For Derrida, the *Rektoratsrede,* where *Geist* is presumably formulated as Heidegger's eloquent rejection of biologism, presents a rigorous critique of anti-Semitism itself. But has Derridean deconstruction indeed saved Heidegger from the accusations of his detractors? There is a way of digging more deeply to the elusive core of Derrida's judgment of an unspoken Heideggerian avoidance of the "Jewish Question" (and one that is embedded in *De l'esprit* itself), but we will first have to travel down a more difficult path of interrogation. Before asking if Derrida has indeed successfully rehabilitated Heidegger's politics, let us pose a different question, seemingly uninvolved with the "Jewish Question": how accurate is Derrida's "thinking" of Heidegger's ambivalence toward modernity? What are the implications of the possibility that Heidegger's philosophy in the mid-1930s may be less a rejection of biologism than of modernity itself? In other words, we should consider the possibility that the real *angst* in Heidegger's *Rektoratsrede* is not that technology might, in its worst manifestation, transform racial theory into praxis, leading unimaginably to mass extermination, but rather that technology had become such a constitutive feature of modernity that modernity itself had become merely a renewal of a "metaphysics of subjectivity."

As Luc Ferry and Alain Renaut have discussed at length, a recurrent theme in Heidegger is his ambivalent relationship to modernity; throughout their book, they identify technology as the "real" anxiety in Heidegger.[52] Moreover, we could speculate that given Heidegger's frequent interpretation of modernity as the reign of technology, both of these Heideggerian themes could be seen as constituting their own "affective" concern for the Jew. This is the Heidegger that Derrida fashions — a Heidegger concerned that Nazism's implementation of the technological "logic" of modernity, its misuse of the essence of technology, had begun to constitute such a large-scale "forgetting of Being" that German National Socialism could not possibly become an authentic actualization of modernity.

But what precisely is at stake in Heidegger's critique of modernity? Does a Heideggerian critique of modernist technology lead us logically to a critique of anti-Semitism? When Heidegger implies that Nazism, technology, and metaphysics all, in effect, deserve one another, his reaction can be construed not so much as a total rejection of German National Socialism, but rather as a new embracing of its *anti*modern impulses — a new turn toward antimodernism as a reaction against Nazism's "forgetting of Being." The point I wish to emphasize here is that Heidegger's ambivalence toward modernity, in other words, threatens to recapitulate one of the more common *topoi* of twentieth-century anti-Semitism: a rejection of modernity as, in essence, a rejection of the Jew. In the elusive and ambivalent divide between Heidegger's embracing of German National Socialism and his rejection of modernity lies the space of the "political unconscious" of Heidegger's philosophy in the mid-1930s. The "political unconscious," the *non-dit* of Heidegger's *Geist* and its ambivalence toward modernity (as, among its other faults, too "cosmopolitan"), may be the figure of the Jew, specifically the Jew of modernity, the "alien" Jew, the "socialist" Jew, the "capitalist" Jew, the "parasitic" Jew — in short, all the manifestations of a *Judentum* that had been a "problem" for Germany since (to set the most arbitrary of dates) 1843, the publication date of Bruno Bauer's essay, *The Jewish Question.*

In this context, much of Heidegger's rejection of modernity may be viewed psychoanalytically as a kind of extended melancholia for a new German era free of the "Jewish Question," an era that did not have to concern itself with *Verjudung,* or a German "redemption" of the Jew. And it is in this sense, then, that one might argue that the "Jewish Question" in Heidegger is not, as Derrida, Lacoue-Labarthe, and others have maintained, merely "extrinsic to thought." From a slightly different point of view, Dieter Thomä has asserted that Heidegger is guilty not so much of *anti*-Semitism as what he calls "*a*-Semitism": "That is, Heidegger does not philosophize *against* the Jews, but rather simply *without* them. He is not expressly concerned with the Jewish Question — *he simply pretends that the Jews do not even exist.*"[53] Picking up where Thomä leaves off, we could argue that at the core of Heidegger's judging of Nazism as the forgetfulness of Being (or racism as a new "metaphysics of subjectivity") is the Jew of German modernity, foreclosed within Heidegger's "thinking" of Being, foreclosed within Heidegger's antimodernist turn back to a pre-Socratic Greece as his unacknowledged way of keeping the thinking of Being, in effect, *Judenrein.* Heidegger's "solution" to the "Jewish Question" is to foreclose on the figure of the Jew, to exile the Jew to the "political unconscious" of his own ambivalence toward modernity. It may be because of the anxious displacements of a Heideggerian *a*-Semitism that the philosopher could not, to echo Lévinas, "pronounce the name of the Jews" after the war.

"L'Esprit Revient"

As if Derrida's intentions in writing *De l'esprit* were not complex enough, one can begin to suspect that for Derrida too Heidegger's *Geist* may be a thoroughly a-Semitic concept. Indeed, ever since his opening

67

line, "I shall speak of ghost, of flame, and of ashes," one wonders if Derrida has not been urging us all along to consider the foreclosed Jew within Heideggerian philosophy. As we now move to the third and final phase of Derrida's analysis of a Heideggerian *Geist*, we can begin to understand the embedded irony in Derrida's subtitle — as if it were really meant to read "Heidegger et la Question [Juive]." That Derrida may have already had a prior understanding of the full implications for the "Jewish Question" of Heidegger's antimodernist rejection of a technological modernity is implicit in Derrida's own turn to "epochality" as the last of the four "guiding threads" that structure *De l'esprit's* consideration of Heidegger's *Geist*.

In order to locate the "Jewish Question" encrypted in *De l'esprit*, we must make the linguistic move from German to French. We will remember that *De l'esprit* begins with Derrida's enigmatic speaking of ghosts *(revenants)*; eventually, we will see that for Derrida the "real" ghost that haunts metaphysics as the return of the repressed can only be confronted in French.[54] In the final stage of *De l'esprit*, Derrida advances ("after Auschwitz") to 1953 and to Heidegger's tracing (from his essay "Language in the Poem") of the connotative differences between *geistlig* and *geistlich* in the poetry of Georg Trakl. In this essay, Heidegger approves of Trakl's avoidance of the "Platonic-Christian" *geistig* in favor of *geistlich*, a word which, for Heidegger, leaves no trace of the "Christian-metaphysical."[55] As Derrida observes, Heidegger, in trying to "think" the *geistliche* in Trakl, rejects the "Platonic-Christian" meaning of *Geist* (as the Greek *pneuma* or the Latin *spiritus*), preferring its old Germanic (that is, more "originary" or "authentic") meaning of *Geist* as *Flamme*, "fire" or "flame" (or what Derrida interprets as a kind of "spirit *in-flames*"). Derrida implies that within this "epochal" *agon*, an antimodern Heidegger (the Heidegger who rejected a contemporary German modernity) envisions an old Germanic return to *geistlich* as a more authentic manifestation of the German "spirit." But within Heidegger's return to the old Germanic resonances of the *geistliche*, Derrida suggests that the only "return" occurring here is a "return of the repressed." He perceives a spectral haunting (an *esprit*) that is more "French" than "German," and asserts that a translation of *Geist* as mediated through the French *esprit* may better capture the conflagrational meaning of a "spirit *in-flames*" than does Heidegger's German.[56] "*L'esprit revient*," writes Derrida enigmatically. For Derrida, the French *esprit* is a *revenant* (like the one with which he opens *De l'esprit*), a ghost that haunts Heidegger's return to an old Germanic (or pre-Socratic) epochality. It is as if Derrida is implying that the French *esprit* is a better "answer" to the question Heidegger chose never to pose explicitly in his thought—the "Jewish Question."

Nevertheless . . . *l'esprit revient.* Derrida relentlessly deconstructs his own deconstruction of "spirit" by arguing that the French *esprit*, as the return of the repressed for a German *Geist*, is *itself* haunted by the "return of the repressed." The *revenant* that returns to haunt Heidegger—and here we have reached the core of Derrida's argument, the point at which an immanent critique of *Geist* may have finally reached its limit—is the possibility that the "essence" or "presencing" of *Geist* may have (always already) occurred neither in old German, nor in French, but in ancient Hebrew. For Derrida, it is the Hebrew *ruah,* as a kind of "holy spirit," that serves as the "originary" word that had to be translated in turn by a Greek *pneuma,* a Latin *spiritus,* and a German *Geist.* In this intriguing etymological move, in which Heidegger's commentary on Trakl is inserted into an ancient Judaic "epochality," Derrida has found the "political unconscious" of a Heideggerian *Geist* that, even as it rejects Nazism, can nevertheless find no place for the Jew.[57] For Derrida, what returns *(ce qui revient)* to haunt Heidegger is his insistence that the "presencing" of a *geistlich* knowledge can be "thought" most rigorously in the Greco-German tradition (as opposed to the "Platonic-Christian"). What returns to haunt Heidegger is the Hebrew *ruah* as the originary conflagration that inaugurates an entire tradition of Jewish thought on "fire"—or what Derrida characterizes as "an inexhaustible thinking about *fire*" (101). If, in the post-Holocaust, Derrida indeed suspects that Heidegger could only view the Jew as culturally antithetical to the Greco-German tradition, then the *ruah* is intended to serve as the "return of the repressed" for any "thinking" of spirit that would overlook the Judaic roots of the *geistliche.*

And why does Derrida insist on referring to *l'esprit* as a *revenant* haunting *Geist?* Perhaps thinking of the encryptedness of Freud within Heideggerian anxiety, he readily confesses, "'*Revenant*' is not a word of Heidegger's and no doubt he would not like having it imposed on him because of the negative connotations, metaphysical or parapsychic, that he would be at pains to denounce in it" (91). *Revenant* is a word Heidegger would not have liked because of its "parapsychic," or psychoanalytic connotations—and now we are at the heart of what is so profoundly psychoanalytic about Derrida's interrogation of a Heideggerian *Geist* in *De l'esprit*. Repression, the unconscious, the return of the re-pressed—all of these inherently psychic phenomena are incommensu-rate with Heidegger's "thinking" of Being. And yet Derrida offers the possibility that it is the return of the repressed (the *revenant*)—indeed, psychoanalysis itself—that lies at the core of any articulation between politics and philosophy in the post-Holocaust. In *De l'esprit*, Derrida quotes from Heidegger's *What Is Called Thinking?*: "What is un-thought in a thinker's thought is not a lack inherent in his thought. What is *un*-thought is there in each case only as the un-*thought*" (117 n.5). In this elusive claim, to what extent can we discern a Freudian un-conscious inhabiting Heidegger's critique of the un-*thought*, of the for-getfulness of Being? In this context, it is not merely coincidental that Derrida describes Heidegger's foreclosure of the *ruah* as a "symptom" (100). Somewhere between a Freudian "return of the repressed" and a Heideggerian un-*thought* is the Hebrew *ruah* as a reminder that any discussion of an "epochal" *Geist* must involve the Jew. In order to "think" the "unthought" of Heidegger's association with German Na-tional Socialism—and in response to Heidegger's own rejection (anx-ious avoidance?) of psychoanalysis—Derrida reintroduces the *revenant* as the repressed Jew of Heidegger's (un)thought before the war and of Heidegger's anxious silence after Auschwitz.

We should pause here to consider the implications of Derrida's quot-ing from Aristotle's *De Spiritu* and its association of *pneuma* with vapor or gas as one of its effects (137 n.2). Aristotle's *pneuma* also reminds Derrida of Hegel's depiction of *Geist* as gas *(le gaz)*—and it is at this point that the etymological path from *ruah* to *Geist* leads us directly to the threshold of Auschwitz-Birkenau and the unimaginable genocide of the Jews, forced to perish by the *Geist* as *gas,* and denied, in the cre-matoria of Auschwitz, a truly sacrificial fire.[58] Heidegger, claims Der-rida, would have preferred not to speak in terms of the "parapsychic" *revenant*. But the *revenant* (as the foreclosed Jew of modernity) will al-ways return to haunt the "un-thought" of a Heideggerian *Geist*. After all, to echo Derrida from *La carte postale,* "What does philosophy *not have to do* with psychoanalytic 'speculation'?"—or, put another way, in the post-Holocaust, what does Heideggerian philosophy *not have to do* with the Jew as the *revenant* of philosophy's un-*thought*?

This analysis of *De l'esprit* can remind us of a topic broached earlier: Benjamin's privileging of *Erfahrung* as a kind of "involuntary memory."

It is in his "Theses on the Philosophy of History," an extended meditation on the claims of the past on us, that Benjamin describes his now
oft-cited "angel of history": "Where we perceive a chain of events, he
sees one single catastrophe which keeps piling wreckage upon wreckage and hurls it in front of his feet."[59] A "storm from paradise" (the
storm of progress) propels the angel of history into the future—but
the angel, whose face is turned toward the past, can only watch as a pile
of debris "grows skyward" (258). As I conclude this chapter, I would
like to suggest Benjamin's angel of history (and its viewing of "one single catastrophe") as a way of making a useful connection between Derrida's *Mémoires* (as a "mourning" for de Man prior to the disclosure of
his wartime journalism) and *De l'esprit* (as a "mourning" for Heidegger's involvement in German National Socialism). In these two works,
Derridean deconstruction may be viewed as just such a version of Benjamin's undialectical angel of history that hovers on an obscure threshold between past and future. Even as it is propelled toward the future
(the "future" as the *Mémoires'* theorizing of a new, "postmodern" memory that can resist "the tomb or vault of some narcissism"), the face of
Derridean deconstruction in *De l'esprit* (as well as in his essay "Like the
Sound of the Sea") is turned toward the past—specifically, the event of
the Holocaust (and the "tombs and vaults" not of "some narcissism" but
of the Auschwitz-Birkenau crematoria) as a "single catastrophe which
keeps piling wreckage upon wreckage." A genuinely deconstructive,
postmodern memory (an "impossible memory") cannot be achieved
because a Derridean melancholia cannot turn away from the "wreckage" of de Man's early journalism or works like Heidegger's "Question
Concerning Technology"—textual "piles of debris" that accrue because the trauma of the historical "single catastrophe" of the Holocaust
remains unconfronted.

In *De l'esprit,* then, we could say that the "impossible mourning" of
the *Mémoires* becomes the *impossibility* of an "impossible mourning"—
a melancholic encrypting of a Heideggerian silence about the Holocaust. But if we briefly shift our focus from *De l'esprit* to Derrida's *Feu
la cendre* (both of which were published in 1987), we can see Derrida
moving from a melancholic obsession with the concept of *Geist* to the
concept of *la cendre,* or the "ash" as both the residue of the Nazis' "Final
Solution" for the "Jewish Question" and an undialectical emblem of an
uncertain future in the post-Holocaust. In the post-Holocaust, warns
Derrida, *"Il y a là cendre."* It is difficult to state exactly what the concept

of *la cendre* signifies for Derrida; nor can we be certain what is required in moving from an acting out to a successful process of working through in the post-Holocaust. But Derrida does imply that as long as the "Jewish Question" remains encrypted within any analysis of a Hegelian/Heideggerian *Geist* (or *gaz*), the ash awaits us.

3

L'Histoire Juive: Caesura, Affect, and the "Jewish Question" in Psychoanalysis

Derrida's Jewgreek and "Unconscious Philosophy"

In chapter 2 we looked at the ways in which the labyrinths of Derridean deconstruction will entangle anyone who seeks a premature intervention into the matter of Heidegger and the "Jewish Question." The same entanglements ironically await anyone who seeks an immediate solution to the enigmas of Derrida's Jewish identity. In *The Slayers of Moses,* Susan Handelman seeks just such a direct path to Derrida's Jewish identity, portraying him as a "new Moses," a kind of Jewish prophet exiled within postmodernity.[1] But Derrida himself does not encourage such easy speculation. In an interview with Richard Kearney, he remarks, "I was born a Jew, I do not work or think within a living Jewish tradition. So that if there is a Judaic dimension to my thinking . . . this has never assumed the form of an explicit fidelity or debt to that culture."[2] Perhaps not surprisingly, then, Derrida concludes his essay "Ellipsis" with the signature "Reb Derissa"—that is, the laughable, "risible" Rabbi (himself laughing in Freiburg at a photo of Heidegger resembling an "old Jew from Algiers") who will always playfully and enigmatically deny any "explicit fidelity" to a Jewish identity.

But in an essay on Lévinas, "Violence and Metaphysics," the risible "Reb Derissa" poses a far more serious (almost melancholic) question concerning the issue of a Jewish identity—and a question that, as we will eventually see, has enormous implications for a fuller understanding of the enigmatic philosophy of French Heideggerianism. For although Derrida refuses any direct access to the question of his own Jewish identity, the "Judaic dimension" in his thought experiences a distinctly postmodern transformation by means of his concept of the "jewgreek." Derrida's question concerning the "essence" of a Jewish identity is a conscious play on Paul's claim, in his Epistle to the Galatians (3:28), that "[t]here is neither Jew nor Greek": "Are we Jews? Are

73

we Greeks? We live in the difference between the Jew and the Greek, which is perhaps the unity of what is called history. . . . Are we Greeks? Are we Jews? But who, we? Are we (not a chronological, but a pre-logical question) *first* Jews or *first* Greeks? . . . From whence does it draw the energy of its question? Can it account for the historical *coupling* of Judaism and Hellenism?"[3] The complexities of this oft-cited passage require a careful unpacking that will serve as an indispensable background for what I intend to discuss in this chapter. We can begin the difficult process of interpretation by noting the passage's psychoanalytic resonances, specifically the analogies between Derrida's cultural concept of the "jewgreek" and the enigmas of the unconscious. Like the Freudian unconscious, Derrida's jewgreek knows neither temporality nor logic: the jewgreek is not "chronological," but "pre-logical." If, for Hegel, the "extremes" of Greek and Jew achieve their dialectical reconciliation in the Christian (that is, Christianity as the *Aufhebung* of Judaism), for Derrida the Jew *and* the Greek do not "equal" the Christian (just as, as we saw in chapter 2, the Hebrew *ruah* and the Greek *pneuma* do not necessarily "equal" a German *Geist*); rather, they make up the jewgreek as a kind of psychic "remainder" (the *difference between* the Jew and the Greek) such that the path to a "thinking" of the jewgreek may lie in the unconscious itself.

We will return later to the significance of Derrida's insistence on the jewgreek (and on cultural identity) as not a "chronological" but a "pre-logical" concept. For the present, let us ponder the psychoanalytic significance of Derrida's consideration in the above passage of "the historical *coupling* of Judaism and Hellenism." In his essay "Interpretation at War: Kant, the Jew, the German," Derrida discusses, among other topics, the work of the neo-Kantian Hermann Cohen, in particular his 1915 essay *Deutschtum und Judentum* and its attempt to forge a Jewish-German identity as a response to *the* obsessive question of German modernity, *"Was ist deutsch?"*[4] Beginning with the very kind of "historical *coupling* of Judaism and Hellenism" that Derrida ponders in "Violence and Metaphysics," Cohen suggests a Jewish-German identity as originating in antiquity with Philo Judaeus of Alexandria. Thus Philo inaugurates a Judeo-Hellenic heritage that Cohen interprets as a meaningful cultural link between the German and the Jew. It is as if Cohen is anticipating that if Derrida's question, "Are we Jews? Are we Greeks?," were posed to German modernity, the answer would first have to cede place to yet another question: *"Was ist deutsch?"* Cohen, in response to the German quest for a direct cultural linkage to the Greek (and in, no doubt, an anxious moment about assimilation into German culture), suggests the Jew (specifically the Hellenic Jew) as a comprehensive embodiment of all three cultural identities.[5] In answer to the question *"Was ist deutsch?,"* Cohen offers the figure of Philo (a precursor of Derrida's jewgreek?) as the "forgotten" link in Germany's search for a cultural identity in antiquity. Moreover, in this context it is not insignificant that Derrida chooses to read Cohen's "epochal" fashioning of a Jewish-German identity psychoanalytically: it is as if for Cohen "there is in the German unconscious . . . a proposition which cannot be uprooted, destroyed, or denied, a German *cogito — 'ergo sumus'* all German Jews'" (50). Derrida suggests that for Cohen, the German-in-the-Jew and the Jew-in-the-German are deeply embedded in the German social and cultural imaginary, creating a Jewish-German *psyche* as nothing less than, in Derrida's phrase, "the mirror or reflexive consciousness of modernity" itself (65).

At one point Derrida wonders "whether Cohen takes his story seriously or not" (52) — that is, whether or not Cohen really believed in his Judeo-Graeco-German continuum of cultural identity. Serving as the voice of Cohen, Derrida writes:

> Whether I, a German Jew, believe in it or not, is an uninteresting or irrelevant question. . . . You [the German Gentile] have the right to consider my discourse as a symptom of the madness it describes — this makes no difference for its value, its relevance as a *true symptom,* in some sense. If it is a symptom of what it describes, it is perhaps all the more revealing of the unconscious truth of which it speaks or — and this amounts to the same thing — which speaks through it. In this region, the symptom is knowledge, knowledge is a symptom. (52)

Derrida imagines Cohen arguing from a psychoanalytic perspective that if his account of a Jewish-German genealogy strikes the German Gentiles of modernity as "madness," then it is because there *is* such a thing as a Jewish-German psyche, or "the symptom as knowledge" and "the knowledge as symptom." For Cohen, the "unconscious truth" of his discourse is Philo the jewgreek as the psychic "remainder" of a Jewish-German psyche: in short, somewhere between the jewgreek of antiquity and the Jewish-German of modernity lies the "true symptom" of a German "unconscious."

Derrida's subject matter in "Interpretation at War," the concept of a

Jewish-German psyche as constitutive of modernity itself, seems temporally and geographically distant from France and French postmodernism. But how far removed is it really? Let us now move to another of Derrida's essays, "Onto-Theology of National-Humanism," an extended meditation on the concept of a "philosophical nationality"—that is, the ways in which nationality is "encrypted" within philosophy.[6] Though he never makes it explicit, one suspects that throughout this elliptical essay the phenomenon of French Heideggerianism is foremost in Derrida's mind, and specifically the overdetermined ways in which French postmodern philosophy has absorbed (introjected?) a Heideggerian philosophy that was itself intimately (and disturbingly) involved with a "thinking" of Germanness. As a "philosophical nationality," in other words, French Heideggerianism is in the odd position of serving as the inheritor of German philosophy's own unfinished engagement with an "encrypted" Graeco-Germanness. But the matter of nationality as a *philosopheme* becomes even more (psychically) complicated. As Derrida emphasizes (in a lesson we have already learned from *De l'esprit*), "There is no nationalism without some ghost" (15). If there is such a thing as an "encrypted" philosophy within nationality—if, in Derrida's words, "the German national principle is an essentially philosophical principle" (11)—then the result is, significantly, the phenomenon of French Heideggerianism as an "unconscious philosophy" (12), a philosophy haunted by a "ghost," a "return of the repressed." One implication of Derrida's essay is that French Heideggerianism must struggle as a philosophy not fully Greek (as the never fully attainable "ego ideal" of German philosophy), but not fully "French," or not fully "German"—and, for that matter, not fully "Jewish" or "Gentile."

When French Heideggerianism "returns" to Heidegger, then, it necessarily inherits a ghost. Is the "ghost," we may ask, the specter of Derrida's jewgreek that "knows the truth" of the extent to which French Heideggerianism has become an "unconscious philosophy"? And if French Heideggerianism is (when viewed retroactively) an "unconscious philosophy," then is it because the figure of the Jew is doubly encrypted within its theoretical bounds? When a Jewish-German psyche, only partially acknowledged within a German *cogito* (that perhaps has itself already foreclosed on the jewgreek of antiquity), is imported into France via a French Heideggerianism, is this the point at which the Jew becomes impossibly overdetermined within "philosophical nationality"? If Derrida's assumption of a Jewish-German psyche as "the reflexive consciousness of modernity" is valid, then to what extent is he suggesting to us that French Heideggerianism has inadvertently served to create a Jewish-*French* psyche as "the reflexive [un]consciousness of [*post*]modernity"?

Let us seek to draw some connections between Derrida's essay on Cohen and his essay on a national philosophy, for the purpose of further understanding the psychoanalytic significance of his enigmatic concept of the jewgreek. If, for Cohen, the foundation of philosophy itself is Greek, then an "authentic" Jewish-German identity may be sought in antiquity in the figure of Philo Judaeus. But if, for Heidegger, nationality is encrypted within philosophy (if, in other words, a "pure" Greek beginning in antiquity is necessary for the attainment of an "authentic Germanness"), then the "Germanness" of philosophy can find no place for the jewgreek in philosophy. Cohen's interpretation of antiquity as *Judeo*-Hellenic must be foreclosed (and Philo must be "repressed"). The Jew of antiquity must be denegated; philosophy must become — literally — anti-*Semitic*. In answer to the question, "Are we *first* Jews or *first* Greeks?," Derrida cautions that we respond to such a question not chronologically, but rather "pre-logically." Like the unconscious itself, which knows neither temporality nor logic, Derrida's jewgreek, unlike Cohen's Philo (who was easily enough excised from German philosophy's cultural *renovatio* of a Greek antiquity), serves as philosophy's nonchronological "return of the repressed." In this context, it is worth noting that in *Glas* (amidst, not insignificantly, a number of enigmatic and characteristically veiled allusions to Hegel and the "Jewish Question"), Derrida indulges in a brief moment of what he describes as "bad wordplay" involving the name of Noah: "Noah" suggests the "little gallicism" of "Noé" — and between the ancient Hebrew name "Noah" and the "little gallicism" of "Noé" lies "noesis" (or *Noé*-sis), or logos.[7] Thus Derrida's "Noah-Noé," not unlike Cohen's Philo Judaeus, embodies a kind of jewgreek logos — but a logos that, by implication, is encrypted within French philosophy only as a ghostly "return of the repressed."

Derrida's "noetic" wordplay in French brings us to the central question of this chapter: as the "difference" between the Jew and the Greek, can Derrida's concept of the jewgreek be best articulated and understood within (Gentile) French postmodernism? Is it in France that we are currently and most dramatically "liv[ing] the difference between the Jew and the Greek"? If, as Derrida has suggested, French Heideggerianism is indeed the inheritor of German philosophy's own unfinished engagement with an encrypted Graeco-Germanness—and if, indeed, French Heideggerianism *has* inadvertently created a Jewish-French psyche as "the reflexive [un]consciousness of [*post*]modernity" (a Jewish-French psyche already emergent in *De l'esprit*'s own etymological relationship between the Hebrew *ruah* and the French *esprit*), then we could argue that this Jewish-French psyche manifests itself most ironically and most symptomatically at the site of French postmodernism's *conscious* impulses toward philo-Semitism—that is, its many recurring appropriations of the figure of the Jew as a means of "mourning" the atrocities of the Holocaust. If much of Heideggerian philosophy was constituted as the "unthought" of Heidegger's often subtly encrypted refusal, in Lévinas's words, to "pronounce the name of the Jews," then we could argue that one of the constitutive features of French postmodern philosophy is an encrypted philo-Semitism. I insist on describing this philo-Semitism as "encrypted" (and therefore fraught with psychic implications) because although French postmodernism's figurations of the Jew are overtly positive (almost as if it were seeking to fashion itself, after Auschwitz, as a conscious "working through" of German anti-Semitism), the *a*-Semitic (and, at the same time, distinctly *phil*hellenic) "ghost" it has inherited from Heideggerian philosophy makes its unpredictable returns in ways of which French philosophy (positioned, as it is, precariously and contradictorily on the temporal divide between a prewar Heideggerian philosophy and a post-Holocaust hypostasizing of the decentered subject—in some sense, the temporal divide traced by Derrida's own figure of the jewgreek) cannot always be fully conscious, and over which it cannot always exert full control.

In the philo-Semitic discourse of much French postmodernism, the real Jew is transformed into a privileged trope or signifier for the decentered, destabilized postmodern subject in a philosophical and theoretical system that nevertheless persists in defining the Jew from without. This chapter demonstrates some of the unsettling ways in which a seeming philo-Semitism (which, as we will also see, consciously engages with psychoanalysis and, at the same time, constitutes its own unconscious "symptom") threatens to converge ironically with anti-Semitism. The philo-Semitism of French postmodernism recurs as if it were a kind of ritual atonement for postmodernism's encrypting of Heideggerianism. But what we discover is that no less than anti-Semitism, which projects all of society's ills onto a scapegoated Jewish "other," the seemingly benign and, in a post-Holocaust era, overtly salutary impulse of philo-Semitism fails to negotiate the real Jew, instead deconstructing the Jew within a (Gentile) social imaginary that renders elusive the precise boundary between a mystification and a reviling of the Jew. What we discover is that the philo-Semitism of French postmodernism is a phenomenon so psychically overdetermined that the figure of the Jew becomes encrypted within an impossible double bind: in its most positive manifestation, the post-Auschwitz Jew serves to embody the decenteredness so widely celebrated in postmodernism; but in its worst manifestation, it recapitulates depictions of the nomadic "Wandering Jew," a common anti-Semitic topos dating as far back as the Middle Ages.

In the first half of this chapter, we consider some of the recent work of Philippe Lacoue-Labarthe, and in particular the extent to which his privileged concept of mimesis renders much of French postmodernism an ambiguous return to the figure of the jewgreek—an "ambiguous" return, I should emphasize, because the ostensibly philo-Semitic impulse behind Lacoue-Labarthe's rigorous critique of the "onto-mimetology" of German National Socialism returns to Auschwitz by means of a Graeco-German tragic aesthetics that, almost by definition, exiles the Jew from tragic suffering. In the second half we turn to some of the recent coauthored work of Lacoue-Labarthe and his colleague Jean-Luc Nancy. In particular, we investigate their "return" to Freudian affect and the extent to which the figure of the Jew has become the overdetermined focus of French postmodernism's attempts at a post-Freudian and post-Lacanian psychoanalysis—a "return" to Freud that also constitutes a (repetition) compulsion to "return" to the question, Is psychoanalysis a "Jewish" science? In the final analysis, amidst Lacoue-Labarthe and Nancy's contention that philosophy and psychoanalysis have "exhausted" their possibilities, lies the figure of the Jew—not, however, Derrida's jewgreek (who, in some sense, "knows the truth" of an encrypted French philo-Semitism), but a deconstructed Jew that knows no essence. Even in the years prior to the publication of Lyotard's controversial *Heidegger and "the jews,"* we see that French postmodernism's philo-Semitic impulses are already well under way toward configuring French Heideggerianism as an "unconscious philosophy."

Deconstructing German National Socialism

In 1980, a major conference was held in Cérisy, France, entitled "The Ends of Man: Spinoffs of the Work of Jacques Derrida."[8] A primary topic of the conference was whether or not there could be such a thing as a deconstructionist politics at "the end of metaphysics" (a topic directly implicated in Derrida's concept of an "encrypted" nationality within philosophy). Two participants in the conference, the so-called French Heideggerians Philippe Lacoue-Labarthe and Jean-Luc Nancy, were particularly engaged in "thinking" the political implications of deconstruction within a Heideggerian framework. Deploying Heideggerian critique as a means of rigorously pushing against the "limit" of the political, Lacoue-Labarthe and Nancy conceived of their project as nothing less than an interrogation of the philosophical essence of the political itself (or *le politique*), as opposed to "mere" politics *(la politique).*

In his essay "Transcendence Ends in Politics," Lacoue-Labarthe asks whether or not the political overdetermines the philosophical: "What does the political [*le politique*], in its essence, consist of?"[9] If, within a Heideggerian framework, philosophy has in fact exhausted its possibilities, then for Lacoue-Labarthe the "limit" of philosophy, the political overdetermination of the philosophical, begins with a "thinking" of the concept of mimesis — specifically, the relationship between mimesis and cultural (or political) identity. For Lacoue-Labarthe, the "logic" of mimesis points to an instability (a *désistement*) in any positing of identity, such that, as a concept, mimesis does not exist, but rather *desists* and defers any philosophical or metaphysical essence. Lacoue-Labarthe's use of mimesis to interrogate "limits" — specifically, the political overdetermination of the philosophical — eventually leads us to the figure of the Jew as the "limit" of philosophy itself. But we must patiently trace a number of discursive twists and turns before we are in a position to understand fully the implications of this preoccupation in Lacoue-Labarthe's theory.

First, let us examine the crucial role Lacoue-Labarthe's concept of mimesis plays in his ongoing critique of German National Socialism (and, implicitly, its exclusion of the Jew). He argues that German national identity has historically (and mistakenly) centered on the concept of mimesis. His book *Heidegger, Art and Politics* and his essay "Hölderlin and the Greeks" investigate, among other things, the (mimetic) role of ancient Greece within the constituting of a German cultural "imaginary." Lacoue-Labarthe knows that such a consideration must begin with Johann Winckelmann's *Thoughts on the Imitation of Greek Art in Painting and Sculpture* (1755) and *History of Ancient Art* (1764) and their ambitious appropriation of "Greekness" *(Greichentum)* for an aesthetic discourse that could become inherently "German": "The only way we can become great, and, if this is possible, inimitable," argues Winckelmann, "is by imitating the Greeks."[10] But Lacoue-Labarthe interprets Winckelmann's celebration of a German "return" to a Greek "essence" as acting out the flaw inherent in mimesis. Rigorously pursuing Winckelmann's own paradox of creating a German "inimitability" through a mimetic appropriation of Greece, Lacoue-Labarthe argues that ever since Winckelmann, a "specter" has haunted Germany—the German Idealist "specter" of imitation and the belief that an "originary" Greek identity exists to be appropriated for a rebirth of Germany. Thus, under the "post" of the post-Holocaust, Lacoue-Labarthe offers the political trap of an "onto-mimetology" as a significant link between Winckelmann and Heidegger, whose disastrous embracing of German National Socialism (as "the *truth* of the political")[11] was overdetermined by an unacknowledged mimetology based on the chimera of a recuperable Greek essence. But as Lacoue-Labarthe argues, "Greece *itself* does not exist. . . . *The Greeks' proper is inimitable because it never took place.*"[12] What German National Socialism never came to realize was that as long as it remained committed to a cultural renewal of Greece, Germany could only be belated—in short, that mimesis (a mimetic identification with Greece) marks the "limit" of the political.

Hölderlin's "Caesura" and the Victims of Auschwitz

As if in anticipation of this charge, Heidegger's thought had, by the mid-1930s, turned from National Socialism (which he earlier believed would truly bring about a renewal of *Dasein*) to what Lacoue-Labarthe refers to as a "national aestheticism" *(national-ésthetisme),* as he began to conceive of Western history by means of aesthetic categories derived specifically from Greek tragedy, as opposed to Winckelmann's Greek models of clarity, art, and harmony taken from painting and sculpture. In such works as *An Introduction to Metaphysics* (1935) and his lectures that make up "The Origin of the Work of Art" (1936), Heidegger, inspired by Hölderlin's translations of Sophocles' *Antigone* and *Oedipus Tyrannus* (both published in 1804 as *Die Trauerspiele des Sophokles*), seeks an aesthetics that could go beyond mimesis.[13] He argues that an "authentic" people required an authentic work of art—not something merely mimetic, or representational (not art as *techne,* or art as depicted in the aesthetic language of Plato and Aristotle), but an ontological work of art that could reveal the *being* of entities, a work of art *(poiesis)* that could disclose, make manifest, *reveal* the German *volk* as they seek to situate themselves within a possibility of a historial (not merely "historical") *Dasein.* For Heidegger, such an "authentic" work of art as a revelatory "truth-event" was Greek tragedy, specifically Hölderlin's aesthetic theory of tragedy. For Heidegger, the tragic poet could embody the renewal of *Dasein;* and it was Hölderlin who truly understood the full essence *(Wesen)* of a tragic Greece. Thus Heidegger appropriates Hölderlin's theory of tragedy to anticipate a time when Germany will accede to History (the *geschichtlich*) through an authentic "thinking" of Greece. For Heidegger, a Hölderlinian aesthetics does not merely represent, but actually *embodies* the primal rift *(Riss)* that constitutes a truth-event. It was Hölderlin, in short, who could rescue Germany from "mere" mimesis (bad artistic representation) and restore to it a Platonic *aletheia* (an authentic, revealed truth). In Michael Zimmerman's apt summary, "Hölderlin's poetry could enable the Germans to become accessible to the *pain* involved in the horror of modernity."[14] For Heidegger, the German *volk* must experience great suffering (as a tragic "truth-event") in order to become truly heroic. Hölderlinian tragedy could serve as Germany's aesthetic guide through a tragic suffering of the "pain" of modernity (and, as we saw in the last chapter, the pain of modern technology) as the necessary first step toward a mythic rebirth.

But in both *Heidegger, Art and Politics* and his essay "Hölderlin and the Greeks," the crucial question Lacoue-Labarthe poses to Heidegger is: to what extent did the German *volk* succeed in fulfilling the aesthetic requirements of the Hölderlinian tragic hero? Before answering this question directly, Lacoue-Labarthe describes a Hölderlin who, unlike Winckelmann or Schiller, had perceived the *désistement* that haunts any attempt at an onto-mimetology. Lacoue-Labarthe suspects that Hölderlin may have always known that "Greece, as such, Greece *itself,* does not exist, that it is at least double, divided—even torn."[15] Thus if Hölderlin did understand the full "essence" of a more authentically tragic Greece, it is because he knew that tragedy begins with the "ruin of the inimitable" (247). For Lacoue-Labarthe, it is this very "inimitability" that calls for a reassessment of Heidegger's appropriation of Hölderlinian tragedy as a model for Germany's quest for the "pure emergence" of a Greek essence.

Specifically, Lacoue-Labarthe urges a return to Hölderlin's reconfiguration of the Sophoclean tragic "caesura" as a key juncture between aesthetics and history (indeed as nothing less than what Lacoue-Labarthe refers to as *"the* concept of historicity")[16] that can free us from the trap of an "onto-mimetology." Hölderlin depicts Sophocles' tragic "caesura" as a hiatus, a nullity, a fractured temporality representing the catastrophic and "categorical turning away" of the divine. This "caesura" presents itself as a "counter-rhythmic interruption" (Hölderlin's *antirhythmische Unterbrechung*) — a withdrawal, a nothingness (what Lacoue-Labarthe describes as a *né-ant*), a rupture (a "disarticulation") of history itself such that, because of the resulting divide between God and man, the end can never represent the beginning. For Hölderlin, the Sophoclean tragic conflict is the nullity of the immediate: it is, in Lacoue-Labarthe's words, the "appearance of God at the abyss and the chaos of his withdrawal."[17] The withdrawal of God is the "tragic cut, the advent of nothingness, the pure event" (44), where beginning and end can no longer coincide. The caesura is the moment at which tragic conflict transcends representation and appears "in itself." Thus, in Lacoue-Labarthe's summary, tragedy begins with the "ruin of the inimitable."

Under the "post" of the post-Holocaust, and in direct opposition to Heidegger's appropriation of Hölderlinian tragedy as a model for a German rebirth, Lacoue-Labarthe then makes the extraordinary move of appropriating the Hölderlinian "caesura" as a metaphor for Auschwitz itself. Like Hölderlin's "caesura," Auschwitz, writes Lacoue-Labarthe, "opens up, or closes, a quite other history than the one we have known up until now" (45). It is important at this point (at the point of this "quite other history") that we pause to ponder further what, precisely, is at stake in Lacoue-Labarthe's configuration of Auschwitz as a Hölderlinian "caesura." In Heidegger's assessment of contemporary German history, Auschwitz becomes the primal rift, "the truth-event" where the Germans accede to the true horror and pain of modernity. For Heidegger, it is (perversely) the Germans who are the Hölderlinian tragic heroes, forced to suffer the tragic consequences of their *hubris* — a technological modernity that precipitated a calamitous and "categorical turning away" of the divine from the Germans. But in an overtly

philo-Semitic moment, Lacoue-Labarthe appropriates the Hölderlinian "caesura" in order to remind any of his readers who might find
themselves seduced by Heidegger's reasoning that it was, of course, not
the Germans but the Jews who were the real victims of the technological nightmare that was Auschwitz. As Lacoue-Labarthe argues, "those
who suffer the 'categorical turning away' in the unprecedented figure
not even of death, but of a mere purging (an unutterable degradation
of catharsis)—are not those who desired immediacy or committed a
crime, but those upon whom those who did do these things literally
discharged themselves. . . . making of Auschwitz, no less literally, the
discharge of Germany (and of Europe)" (45–46). Among other things,
what Lacoue-Labarthe is reacting against here is the strange psychic
phenomenon of Heidegger's post-Auschwitz disavowal of the plight of
the Jews, as evidenced in his lecture "Question Concerning Technology," where "the manufacturing of corpses in gas chambers" becomes
analogous merely to a "motorized food industry." Lacoue-Labarthe
has astutely perceived that Heidegger's symptomatic refusal to allow
for a "thinking" of the Jewish victim is thus recapitulated in his aesthetic theory that (even after Auschwitz) only the Germans can be authentically tragic.

We must not underestimate the significance of Lacoue-Labarthe's
constituting the unspeakability of Auschwitz within the framework of
a Graeco-German tragic aesthetics. In response to Heidegger's persistent postwar refusal to blame Germany for the Holocaust (and his implied claim that wartime Germans had acceded to the status of the "authentic" Hölderlinian tragic hero), Lacoue-Labarthe views Auschwitz
as a Hölderlinian "caesura" that confers genuine tragic suffering not on
the hubristic German perpetrators, but on their Jewish victims as the
authentic sufferers of the pain of technological modernity. At this point
it is tempting to speculate even further on the extent to which Lacoue-
Labarthe is fully aware that through his linking of the Hölderlinian
"caesura" and Auschwitz, he has attempted nothing less than a philo-
Semitic overturning of German Idealism's denial of authentic "aesthetic," or tragic, status to the Jew.

Let us indulge this impulse for further speculation by means of a
brief overview of a few key anti-Semitic topoi Heidegger would have
inherited from German Idealism's hypostasizing of Greek tragedy. For
only through such an overview can we fully understand the cultural
significance of Lacoue-Labarthe's philo-Semitic configuration of Ausch-

witz as a Hölderlinian "caesura"—as well as, eventually, the significance of how Lacoue-Labarthe's philo-Semitism unwittingly doubles back onto some of the traditional assumptions of anti-Semitism.

Heidegger's refusal to view the victims of Auschwitz as authentically tragic could be viewed as the culmination not of Hölderlin's but of Hegel's theory of tragedy and its explicit rejection of the figure of the Jew as anachronistic. In Hegel's vision, the Jew had fulfilled his historical purpose and now found himself stranded outside of world history. In his *Early Theological Writings,* for example, Hegel accused Noah, Abraham (the philosopher's paradigmatic figure of Jewish exile), Joseph, and Moses of being responsible for what he perceived as the Jew's removal from history and community. Because he has been superseded by world history, the Jew is inherently "unaesthetic," such that within the Hegelian dialectic the Jew can only represent loss of union and reconciliation.[18] In contrast to Hellenic harmony, the Jew embodies "the insurmountable cleavage [*Kluft*] between the being of God and the being of men."[19] In perhaps the most virulent of his anti-Semitic impulses, Hegel writes, "The Jewish multitude was bound to wreck His [Jesus'] attempt to give them a consciousness of something divine, for faith in something divine, something great, cannot make its home in feces [*im kote*]."[20]

For Hegel, it follows logically that the Jew, because of his inherently "unaesthetic" nature, cannot be authentically "tragic." At this point, a brief overview of the importance of the figure of Oedipus for the formation of a German cultural imaginary can provide further insight into Heidegger's perverse exclusion of the Jew from the "tragic pain" of German modernity—an overview that, in many ways, is haunted by and anticipates Derrida's question, "Are we Jews? Are we Greeks?" In the first section of *Beyond Good and Evil,* Nietzsche poses a simple but resonant question: "Who of us is Oedipus here? Who the Sphinx?"—a question that also echoes a central Hegelian preoccupation with the essence of an "Oedipal" identity.[21] In his *Aesthetics,* at the end of a chapter titled "Unconscious Symbolism," Hegel writes: "The works of Egyptian art in their mysterious symbolism are therefore riddles; the objective riddle *par excellence.* As a symbol for this proper meaning of the Egyptian spirit we may mention the Sphinx."[22] And in his *Philosophy of History,* Hegel writes, "Whereas the spirit of the Egyptians presented itself to their consciousness in the form of a *problem* [the riddle of the Sphinx], the Greek Apollo is its solution; his utterance is *'Man, know thyself.'*"[23]

If, for Freud, the story of Oedipus is the fulfillment of the archetypal destiny of patricide, for Hegel it is the overcoming of the enigmatic Sphinx (an overcoming of Egypt as an "unconscious symbolics," or *Die unbewusste Symbolik*) and the raising of humanity to self-consciousness itself. Put another way, for Hegel, Oedipus defeats Egypt (the "Oriental spirit" of the Sphinx) and thereby inaugurates the cultural superiority of Greece.[24] For Hegel, then, what is at stake in the Oedipus myth is nothing less than the formation of cultural identity. But one also suspects that what is even more at stake in this myth is the appropriation of a "Greek" Oedipus as superior to the Jew specifically. It is as if the myth of Oedipus also becomes, for Hegel, the basis of another potentially sinister question for the formation of cultural identity: "Who of us is the ('Graeco') German here? Who the Jew?"—or, even more fundamentally, *"Was ist Deutsch?"*

The answer depends on German perceptions of what constitutes the essence of Sophoclean tragedy. We can investigate this matter further by formulating the following question: for German Idealism, how inherently "Jewish" is the fate of Oedipus, his abandonment by the gods? In *The Spirit of Christianity*, Hegel, positing tragedy as the highest expression of the human condition (as evidenced by Oedipus's embodiment of self-consciousness itself) seeks a sublime for tragedy that would separate it from the ethical (and, by extension, from the "Judaic"). At one point, Hegel, with grim irony for a post-Holocaust era, argues: "The great tragedy [*Trauerspiel*] of the Jewish people is no Greek tragedy; it can rouse neither terror nor pity, for both of these arise only out of the fate which follows from the inevitable slip of a beautiful being [*schönen Wesens*] . . . it can arouse horror [*Abscheu*] alone. . . . [F]ate has a more extended domain than punishment has."[25] Fate, as the heroic fulfillment of self-consciousness itself (even when that fulfillment must later manifest itself in the form of a nonrecognition of the father), is, unlike the "Judaic" dimension of punishment, sublimely tragic—or, more to the point, sublimely "Greek." Much later, Heidegger too will come to identify "Greek" tragic fate as the apotheosis of an "ontic" authenticity. In his *Introduction to Metaphysics* Heidegger argues that it was through Sophoclean tragedy that the *Dasein* (or "being-there") of the Greeks "was in the truest sense created."[26] And Heidegger insists that "we cannot regard Oedipus only as the man who meets his downfall; we must see him as the *Gestalt* of Greek *Dasein* . . . the passion for unveiling being, i.e., the struggle for being itself" (107). The tragedy of the

Greek Oedipus, then, is the ultimate distillation of the Aristotelian catharsis of terror and pity, the apotheosis of "being-there," in opposition to what Hegel viewed as the nontragic "horror" of the Judaic narrative of punishment.

At this point, to paraphrase Nietzsche (and, later, Derrida), a new question arises: "Who of us is Oedipus here? Who the Jew?" Heidegger's attempt to locate a German *Dasein* in the Greek Oedipus might be interpreted as its own kind of implicit insistence on an answer to the question, "Who of us is the German here? Who the Jew?" If we remember that for Hegel the Jew is not properly "cathartic," not properly *Greek,* then it would follow logically that for Heidegger, the "beautiful being" (in whom a Hegelian *Geist der Schönheit* is made manifest) can only be the German, whose tragic suffering as a result of his *hubris* is much more sublime than the narrative of Jewish *Abscheu* (or horror).

Thus, when Lacoue-Labarthe refers to the Hölderlinian "caesura" as "*the* concept of historicity," we must pause to consider its complex resonance within this brief overview of German Idealism's "thinking" of Greek tragedy. Heidegger, echoing Hegel's contention that the Jew is removed from history, offers the tragic German an authentic accession to his privileged concept of the "historial," while the "nontragic" horror of the Jewish victims of Auschwitz (always left unacknowledged by Heidegger) is implicitly relegated to the merely "historical." But for Lacoue-Labarthe, the Hölderlinian "caesura," when brought to bear as a commentary on Auschwitz, becomes "*the* concept of historicity" that can render Jewish experience authentically tragic. It is in this sense that Lacoue-Labarthe's "thinking" of Auschwitz through Hölderlin becomes an openly philo-Semitic refutation of Hegel's blunt judgment that "the great tragedy of the Jewish people is no Greek tragedy." For Hegel, the Jew has no "tragic" authenticity, no *Dasein.* For Lacoue-Labarthe, however, Hölderlin's "caesura" (not unlike Derrida's concept of the jewgreek) becomes a much-needed Sophoclean alternative to Hegel's contention that the West is Oedipal (that is, not "Jewish").

At this point, however, Lacoue-Labarthe's philo-Semitic discourse begins to reveal itself as a "symptom"—what we have earlier described as philo-Semitism's "symptomatic" tendency to double back on and recapitulate, or "act out," some of the negative impulses never fully "worked through" in anti-Semitism. Despite Lacoue-Labarthe's carefully calculated deployment of the Hölderlinian "caesura" to overturn German Idealism's denial of a tragic essence to the figure of the Jew, his configuration of the Hölderlinian "caesura" itself becomes an inadvertent encrypting of German Idealism's refusal to incorporate the Jew within a tragic *Dasein;* for embedded in Lacoue-Labarthe's renewal of the Hölderlinian "caesura" for an understanding of the horror of Auschwitz are several traditionally anti-Semitic topoi.

One interpretive ambiguity embedded in Lacoue-Labarthe's philo-Semitic "caesura" is his account of the tragic victims of Auschwitz as suffering "an unutterable degradation of catharsis." Lacoue-Labarthe is to be commended for seeking, in effect, to refute Hegel's claim that "the great tragedy of the Jewish people is no Greek tragedy." But when viewed in the context of Hegel's charge that the drama of the Jews "can arouse neither terror nor pity"—that is, that the Jews can provide no access to an "authentic" catharsis, but only to a horrible *Abscheu*—then how should we judge the cultural resonances of Lacoue-Labarthe's otherwise philo-Semitic depiction of Auschwitz as "an unutterable degradation of catharsis"?[27] In such a scheme, to what extent do the Jews of Auschwitz end up merely recapitulating the formless, "unaesthetic" Jews barred from a Hegelian aesthetics?

Another interpretive difficulty in evaluating the effect of Lacoue-Labarthe's philo-Semitic discourse is determining precisely what is entailed in his depiction of Auschwitz as a "pure event." For Hegel and Heidegger, when the divine catastrophically turns away from humanity, the resulting primal rift *(Riss)* constitutes a "truth-event" (Heidegger's *Ereignis*) that confers upon the hero an authentically tragic status; the primal rift is a "truth-event" that allows for a true revelation of *Being,* and a "presencing" of temporality itself. But Lacoue-Labarthe's version of the Hölderlinian "caesura" embodies, for lack of a better term, a kind of *anti*-"truth-event"—a "hiatus," a "nullity," a "nothingness" *(né-ant):* it is the "truth-event" not as a "historial" *Dasein,* but rather the "pure event" as a rupture that *deconstructs* the tragic sufferer within a "disarticulation" of history. In such a scheme, the Jewish victim of Auschwitz is indeed accorded a tragic "essence"—but one that precariously (dis)appears as the "nullity of the immediate." As a "quite other history," Lacoue-Labarthe's configuration of Auschwitz becomes, as we have seen, a vivid illustration of the impulse (currently *de rigueur* within French postmodernism) toward *posthistoire* itself: Auschwitz is a trauma, a rupture within history such that "the end can never represent the beginning." But embedded within this postmodern configuration of historical rupture (in which a Heideggerian *Dasein* is replaced by a "counter-rhythmic interruption"), can we not still discern Hegel's Jew, the Jew who is left stranded outside of world history? In the caesura that is opposed to "total history," in the caesura that represents "the advent of nothingness," can we not still detect the ghost of Hegel's Jew as embodying "the insurmountable cleavage [*Kluft*] between the being of God and the being of men"?

In the final analysis, can Lacoue-Labarthe's configuration of a postmodern philo-Semitism escape the repetition compulsions of a modernist anti-Semitism? Has Lacoue-Labarthe's critique of Heidegger by means of a return to the Hölderlinian caesura really restored a "tragic essence" to the Jew of Auschwitz? In order to answer this question as fully as it deserves, let us briefly consider the relationship between tragedy and temporality, returning to Lacoue-Labarthe's own privileged concept of mimesis as a temporal phenomenon. In his essay "The Echo of the Subject," Lacoue-Labarthe appropriates the Lacanian concept of *après-coup* (itself adapted from Freud's *Nachträglichkeit*) to elucidate further the temporal instability of mimetic "logic." Amidst an allusion to the Lacanian *après-coup,* the delay that constitutes the enigmatic temporality of the imaginary (indeed, the privileged term for psychoanalytic temporality itself), Lacoue-Labarthe writes: "the imago has no fixity or proper being. There is no 'proper image' with which to identify totally, no essence of the imaginary."[28] In the temporal logic of the *après-coup,* there is no essence of the imaginary—only a kind of Lacanian "missed encounter" that fixates on an ego ideal "too late" (such that, as we saw Lacoue-Labarthe argue earlier, "the Greeks' proper is inimitable because it never took place").[29] For Lacoue-Labarthe, the Hölderlinian caesura, in which the end will never represent the beginning, embodies yet another kind of failed, delayed mimesis that cannot recover an originary Greece for German Idealism to "cathect" onto. But with even more significance for the post-Holocaust, the caesura, as the delaying effect of *après-coup* itself, *deconstructs* the Jew at an Auschwitz that, for Lacoue-Labarthe, is "not the essence of tragedy: it is more and less than tragedy."[30] Thus we are left with the implication that insofar as the Jewish victim of Auschwitz *can* be reinserted into tragedy, such a process can occur only as a kind of "counter-rhythmic" *démesure*[31]— an ineffable "more and less than tragedy" (the Lacanian "missed encounter") that prevents tragedy (not to mention the figure of the Jew) from coinciding with itself.

It is perhaps appropriate here to return to the concept with which this chapter opened: Derrida's jewgreek. Bridging, as it does, the gap between Greek (Sophoclean) tragedy and Jewish victimage at Auschwitz, Lacoue-Labarthe's postmodern "caesura" is its own version of a Derridean jewgreek. But whereas the jewgreek is described by Derrida in "Violence and Metaphysics" as "the unity of what is called history," Lacoue-Labarthe's "caesura" is a kind of "disarticulation" of history, whose logical outcome is the disappearance of the Jew into the abyss of *posthistoire*. In the final analysis, Lacoue-Labarthe's "caesura," as the marker of German philosophy's own unfinished engagement with an encrypted Graeco-Germanness, is a major factor in French Heideggerianism's remaining an "unconscious" philosophy.

Freudian Identification and "Fascinating Fascism"

In the first half of this chapter, we looked at some of the consequences of Lacoue-Labarthe's Heideggerian contention that philosophy has exhausted its possibilities, a metaphysical "exhaustion" that, for Lacoue-Labarthe, led horribly and logically to nothing less than the "discharge" of Europe at Auschwitz. And we are now left to ponder the implications of Lacoue-Labarthe's enigmatic claim that, at "the end of metaphysics," it is the political *(le politique)* that overdetermines the philosophical. We could summarize the allegory underwriting Lacoue-Labarthe's appropriation of the Hölderlinian "caesura" thus: it is the Jews of Auschwitz (meeting their end in German National Socialism's attempt to accede to *le politique*) who overdetermine the philosophical (that is, Heidegger's ambition for a German accession to the "historial"). The question I would pose at this point is: if French Heideggerianism is right in arguing that philosophy has exhausted its possibilities, how surprised should we be that, within the bounds of an otherwise philo-Semitic postmodernism, it is the figure of the Jew who is implicated in this exhaustion?

In the second half of this chapter, we turn to some of the coauthored work of Lacoue-Labarthe and his colleague Jean-Luc Nancy and the consequences of their claim that, like philosophy, psychoanalysis has, in effect, "exhausted" its possibilities. And once again the figure of the Jew will play a key (if highly ambiguous) role in Lacoue-Labarthe and Nancy's postmodern allegory of the "exhaustion" of psychoanalysis.

We can begin the discussion where we began in the second section of this chapter: with the concept of mimesis. Lacoue-Labarthe's use of mimesis to investigate the psychic underpinnings of German National Socialism is, in many ways, a kind of deconstructive return to Freud's concept of identification (i.e., the political subject's emotional, or "mimetic," tie to the leader as the origin of the "social bond"); it is also indicative of a recent renewed interest in France in the relationship between sociopolitics and psychoanalysis—or, as Lacoue-Labarthe and Nancy first phrased it in their essay "La Panique politique," the extent to which the political serves as the "limit" of psychoanalysis, an enigmatic claim we will examine in more detail shortly.[32]

In particular, this French "return" to Freudian identification has resulted in a renewed focus on Freud's concept of "group psychology" *(Massenpsychologie)* and its relevance, after Auschwitz, for a further understanding of the sociopsychology of fascism. The core text for this most recent French version of a "return to Freud" is *Group Psychology and the Analysis of the Ego* (1921), where Freud (himself looking back at Gustave Le Bon's 1895 *Psychologie des foules* and its study of how people behave differently when they are part of a group—a book whose concept of the leader would be exploited by Hitler and Mussolini) analyzes such institutions as the church and the army as evidence of how individuals repress their impulses in favor of a narcissistic identification with an ego-ideal. And it is in this text that Freud posits his all-important concept of *Bindung* as the psychic origin of political masses and, in its worst manifestation, of nothing less than the totalitarian impulse itself. Defined broadly, *Bindung* is the emotional tie of the subject's identification with the chosen ego ideal, the beloved leader (or the *Führer*, to use Freud's resonant term). The concept of *Bindung* (or, more precisely, *Gefühlsbindung* as the emotional tie) is the precise point at which Freud's libido theory becomes political.

Freud's *Group Psychology* and its etiology of the political subject, then, could be viewed as an uncanny anticipation of the psychological origins of German fascism. Published some years prior to German National Socialism's disastrous "cathexis" onto Hitler, Freud's study served as the forerunner of a number of significant investigations before, during, and immediately after World War II of the relationship between psychoanalysis and totalitarianism: Wilhelm Reich's *The Mass Psychology of Fascism* and its study of why the masses turned to fascism instead of communism; Georges Bataille's "The Psychological Structure of Fascism"; Erik Erikson's "Hitler's Imagery and German Youth," a study of the unresolved Oedipal conflicts of Hitler's young idolators;[33]

Adorno's "Freudian Theory and the Pattern of Fascist Propaganda" (just one of a number of studies of authoritarianism originating in the Frankfurt Institute); Hannah Arendt's *The Origins of Totalitarianism*, an account of, among other things, how the "masses" inevitably reside at the heart of totalitarianism; and, most recently in France, Claude LeFort's "L'Image du corps et le totalitarisme" (itself an expansion of Ernst Kantorowicz's *The King's Two Bodies*), and Serge Moscovici's *L'Age des foules*, which uses Freudian "group psychology" to analyze current politics.[34]

In reviewing this list over the last few decades of studies of the psychoanalytic origins of totalitarianism, it seems almost inevitable that one's thoughts would turn to the issue of Freud's own Jewish identity and the extent to which it may overdetermine any consideration of the linkage between psychoanalysis and fascism. Certainly Freud's Jewish identity is one of the grimmer ironies emerging from his attempts to theorize *Massenpsychologie;* viewing it within the framework of "group psychology," one could say that it was an inherently Nazi *Bindung* that expelled Freud from his residence in Vienna, burned his theoretical works in Berlin (as part of a public burning of Jewish-authored books organized by Goebbels in 1933), and publicly denounced the very psychoanalysis its own *Massenpsychologie* was enacting and validating.

All of which serves as a reminder that there can be no naively apolitical study of Freud's concept of identification, because identification is political to the core. In reviewing studies of totalitarianism from Reich to Moscovici, one is struck by the authors' post-Freudian readiness to associate fascism (as one of twentieth-century Europe's foremost political crises) with psychoanalysis (as one of twentieth-century Europe's foremost intellectual movements)—almost as if to imply that psychoanalysis and fascism would logically and inevitably become complicitous. At this point we should pause to consider exactly what inference we are being asked to draw from these associations between psychoanalysis and fascism. Is it that fascism is, at its political core, a psychoanalytic phenomenon inherently constituted within the psychic structures of identification? Is fascism, in short, inherently psychoanalytic? Or, even more ironically, in light of Freud's own Jewish identity, is the implication rather that psychoanalysis itself is inherently fascist?[35]

In much of the recent coauthored work of Lacoue-Labarthe and Nancy, these questions converge as a key line of inquiry for a new kind of "postmodern" psychoanalysis in the post-Holocaust. In two recent essays, "The Nazi Myth" and the much more densely deconstructive "The Unconscious Is Destructured like an Affect," Lacoue-Labarthe and Nancy return to the traditional association between psychoanalysis and fascism in an effort to demonstrate the many complexities that arise when psychoanalysis and fascism are implicated with one another. In these essays, the authors' response to the possibility of an inherently fascist psychoanalysis — that is, psychoanalysis-as-(an inherently fascist)-identification — is to factor into this association the specificity of Jewish identity by implying that the phenomenon of identification is a psychic response experienced only by Gentiles, a process of *Bindung* that is not desirable, or even psychologically possible, within Jewish experience. Though (as is characteristic of the discursive style of the French Heideggerians) they never state it explicitly, it almost seems as if Lacoue-Labarthe and Nancy's primary interest in forging their own "return to Freud" via identification is the question of the fate of the Jew within the otherwise overwhelmingly (German) Gentile psychic organization of the social bond between the masses and their leader. It is almost as if, in response to the crudely formulated and highly problematic question "Is psychoanalysis a 'Jewish' science?", Lacoue-Labarthe and Nancy, theorizing in the post-Holocaust, would instead pose the question, "Is psychoanalysis [that is, psychoanalysis-as-identification] an inherently 'Gentile' fascism?"[36]

Lacoue-Labarthe and Nancy's essay "The Nazi Myth" is one of the most recent investigations of the psychic origins of totalitarianism. This clearly written and highly readable essay constitutes a significant return to the concept of Freudian identification in order to establish it as a key political and psychoanalytic concept in need of reconsideration in the post-Holocaust.[37] In their essay, Lacoue-Labarthe and Nancy revisit the connection between the psychosocial bond *(Bindung)* and fascism, but with particular emphasis on the racial fixations of Nazi ideology as an Aryan myth necessarily constructed on an exclusion of the Jew. They argue that German totalitarianism encouraged "identificatory mechanisms" to configure itself as, specifically, a myth: "it is in the German tradition, and nowhere else, that the most rigorous reflection on the relationship of myth to the question of identification is elaborated" (296–97). In short, the result of the psychic phenomenon of *Bindung* (that is, of Germany's mimetic identification with Greece) is myth as "*the* mimetic instrument par excellence" (298). Lacoue-Labarthe and Nancy then discuss how for German National Socialism it was only a small (but sinister) step to link the formation of myth (and its "identificatory mechanisms") with race, citing in particular such scandalous works as Alfred Rosenberg's *Myth of the Twentieth Century* (1930), where race, as the bearer of myth, is celebrated for its power to consolidate individuals into a group identity. At this point we can begin to sense that what Lacoue-Labarthe and Nancy really want to argue is that myth (as "*the* mimetic instrument par excellence") is a cultural and psychic formation that is explicitly *non-Jewish*.[38] As the realization of myth, they argue, Nazism evolved into a specifically racial ideology because of the likes of Rosenberg's insistence on his privileged concept of *type* as, in Lacoue-Labarthe and Nancy's words, "an absolute, concrete, singular identity"—as, in short, "the fulfillment of the myth" itself (307). For Rosenberg, the Jew was an "antitype," the very absence of type, and thus almost by definition excluded from participation in mimetic identifications such as myth. And for Lacoue-Labarthe and Nancy, the perverse racial "logic" of German National Socialism would seem to convince us once and for all that any process of identification is not only inherently psychic, and not only inherently totalitarian, but also, by extension, inherently outside of Jewish experience. As the metaphysical "presencing" of the (Aryan) Subject-State to itself, the identificatory processes of (Nazi) myth bypass the Jew, for whom no access to the mimetic rituals of myth formation is possible.

Postmodern Psychoanalysis; or, The "Royal Road" to Jewishness

Let us return to the implications of Lacoue-Labarthe and Nancy's enigmatic claim (with which we opened this section) that the political serves as the "limit" of psychoanalysis. The complex relationship between politics (the "political," or *le politique*) and psychoanalysis was first explored in their essay "La Panique politique,"[39] and it is pursued with even greater rigor in their difficult essay "The Unconscious Is Destructured like an Affect," where the authors warn against any oversimplified attempt to "apply" psychoanalysis to politics (always specifically, and rather narrowly, defined as an "originary sociality," or the origin of the "social bond") because in the political and social realm, "psychoanalysis quickly reveals itself to be untenable, overflowing—here, psychoanalysis overflows *itself*" (191, italics in original).[40] Displaced and "overflowing," psychoanalysis, as the authors intend to argue, undoes the political as much as the political overdetermines psychoanalysis, such that the division between an "inside" and an "outside" of psychoanalysis is no longer clear. I now undertake a rigorous critique of "The Unconscious Is Destructured like an Affect," a difficult essay whose impulses, like Lacoue-Labarthe's discourse on Auschwitz, are overtly philo-Semitic—even as the essay inadvertently doubles back onto some of the traditional discursive moves of anti-Semitism. What we will come to discover is that in attempting to save psychoanalysis from claims that it is inherently fascist, Lacoue-Labarthe and Nancy must insist on returning again and again to the vexed question, "Is psychoanalysis inherently Jewish?"

Lacoue-Labarthe and Nancy begin their essay with the same question they explored in "The Nazi Myth"—whether psychoanalysis "can reinforce what is commonly called totalitarianism, or in other words, the destiny of metaphysical politics" (193). Or rather, as they ask suggestively, can psychoanalysis "point to something else" (193)? In "The Nazi Myth," Lacoue-Labarthe and Nancy seem to imply that the mimetic structures of myth formation had the effect, in Nazi Germany at least, of excluding what they portray as the non-identificatory Jew from psychoanalysis itself. In "The Unconscious Is Destructured like an Affect," however, the authors argue that in order to arrive at this ineffable "something else" they contend psychoanalysis points to, we must first attempt nothing less than a theorizing of Jewish identity itself in relationship to psychoanalysis. It is as if Lacoue-Labarthe and Nancy's goal in the essay is not still another contribution to an established line of studies from Reich to Arendt linking psychoanalysis and fascism, but rather an innovative attempt, after Auschwitz, to imagine what would constitute a distinctly Jewish process of identification—an identification that could constitute a salutary "beyond" to a totalitarian, or "metaphysical," politics whose prior effect has always been to implicate psychoanalysis in fascism. In short, their goal is to configure a (Jewish) psychoanalysis that, by definition, could provide an alternative to "identificatory mechanisms" that are inevitably complicitous with fascism.

Can there be, then, such a psychic phenomenon as a "Jewish" identification? Early in their essay, Lacoue-Labarthe and Nancy announce their intention to analyze "the singular process which is the 'identification' of the Jewish people" (193). Beginning where "The Nazi Myth" left off, they open their analysis with the following version of an anti-*Traumdeutung: "The Jewish people do not dream.* . . . They are a people who do not identify with the Father in the oneiric mode, in the mode of an immediate adhesion to the *figure* (or the fantasy, or the phantom) of the Father" (194; italics in original). The Jews are a people "who diverge (or whose 'analysis' diverges), up to a point, from the 'royal road of psychoanalysis' (that of the dream)" (194). If for Freud the dream constitutes the "royal road" to the unconscious—and if, as we have seen in "The Nazi Myth," the dream (where, among other things, one may "cathect" onto an ego ideal) is the "royal road" to (fascist) identification—then, for Lacoue-Labarthe and Nancy, the question becomes: where can we "locate" the Jew within the psychic processes of identification? Or, phrased more broadly, how can we "locate" the Jewish psyche within psychoanalysis itself?

Given the title of the conference—"La Psychanalyse est-elle une histoire juive?"—that served as the forum for their paper, it is perhaps not surprising that the authors suggest that the answer to the question of how we can locate the "royal road" to a Jewish psyche may lie in the realm of the "Jewish joke." Lacoue-Labarthe and Nancy turn to Freud's own discussion, in *Jokes and Their Relation to the Unconscious* (1905), of the *Witz* as a highly social alternative to the asocial, isolated dream, and they analyze the *Witz* as, in their summary, "a double personality, thanks to which the Jew can serve as the butt of his own joke" (194).[41] In what Lacoue-Labarthe and Nancy perceive as the inherently mimetic structure of the Freudian *Witz,* "the mocker participate[s] in the defect being mocked. In other words . . . the *Witz* is best realized by means of an identification stretching across a doubled, or collective, identity" (195). At this point, despite their own claim in "The Nazi Myth" that a collective identification is not experienced within the Jewish psyche, Lacoue-Labarthe and Nancy locate in the mimetic paradigm of the *Witz* the seeds of a "collective" Jewish personality or identity—or, in other words, "the birth of *thought* in *mimicry*" (195; italics in original). If, for Nazi Germany, myth was "*the* mimetic instrument par excellence," it seems for Lacoue-Labarthe and Nancy that the *Witz* (as "the birth of thought in mimicry") can be viewed as, in effect, "*the* identificatory mechanism par excellence" for an inherently Jewish identity.

In the strange mimesis Lacoue-Labarthe and Nancy perceive as constituting the Jewish joke, are we now to conclude that psychoanalysis *has,* in effect, become a kind of *histoire juive*? Lacoue-Labarthe and

Nancy's focus on the *Witz* as a synecdoche for the "double personality" that structures a "Jewish sociality" threatens to become overdetermined in ways the authors fail to anticipate and that call for a careful unpacking. For example, despite its philo-Semitic emphasis on the *Witz* as the psychic origin of a "collective" Jewish identity, Lacoue-Labarthe and Nancy's argument might have benefitted from a further historicizing of the *Witz* as a common anti-Semitic topos in Freud's own time. In this context, we can first consider Mortimer Ostow's analysis of Freud's interest in jokes as one of his more admittedly "Semitic" preoccupations: "It is evident that his interest in Jewish jokes arose from a desire to ascertain what a Jew is really like. Freud (1905) observed that the jokes that he quoted demonstrated that Jews are unusually inclined toward self-criticism."[42] For Freud, the *Witz* was a ritual of self-mockery that was quintessentially Jewish. But Sander Gilman has traced the transformation of Freud's interest in the joke as indicative of "what a Jew is really like" into a far more sinister appropriation of the Jewish joke as an explicitly anti-Semitic topos. Gilman quotes from Otto Weininger's immensely popular 1903 book *Sex and Character* (whose author, as Gilman points out, was ironically himself a baptized Jew), an extended investigation of the perceived "differences" between Jews and Aryans that also analyzes the category of "Jewish humor": Jews "are witty only at [their] own expense and on sexual things." In the same context, Gilman also quotes Otto Rank, who, in his essay, "The Essence of Judaism" (1905), argues that "where the religion [of the Jews] is insufficient to do this [to maintain psychic balance], Jews resort to wit; for they do not have their own 'culture.'"[43]

It is not as if Lacoue-Labarthe himself is unaware that the *Witz* was frequently deployed as an anti-Semitic topos. One need look no further than his *Heidegger, Art and Politics,* where, in a lengthy footnote, he quotes Heidegger's *Rektoratsrede* and its allusion, in a self-consciously anti-Semitic moment, to the *Witz:* "For spirit *(Geist)* is neither empty cleverness, nor the noncommittal play of wit *(Witz),* nor the endless drift of rational distinctions, and especially not world reason; spirit is primordially attuned, knowing resoluteness toward the essence of Being."[44] Unlike the concept of *Geist,* which embodied for Heidegger the spiritual foundation of German culture, the concept of the *Witz,* structured on a mocking self-parody, reveals not the essence of Being, but rather a "noncommittal" duplicity, an "endless drift" away from (German) culture. It is as if, for Heidegger, the *Witz* becomes the "royal road" that leads the nomadic, "wandering" Jew away from civilization itself.[45]

In "The Unconscious Is Destructured like an Affect," there is nothing in Lacoue-Labarthe and Nancy's ahistorical invoking of the *Witz* that indicates any awareness of the concept's charged history as an anti-Semitic topos. Nevertheless, if Freud's fascination for the *Witz* lay in its potential to reveal the essence of Jewish character ("what a Jew is really like," in Ostow's phrasing), it would seem initially that Lacoue-Labarthe and Nancy's return to the Freudian *Witz* serves as compelling evidence of their ambition to accommodate the Jew within psychoanalytic (identificatory) constructs. But as we read further, we eventually come to realize that the (Jewish) joke may be on the essay's readers, for the authors go on to warn that the *Witz* is also one of the precise points at which any theorizing of identity becomes problematic: "Perhaps one must discern here the opening of a road which would not be *royal* in any sense of the word, a path which would not only return analysis to an initial Jewishness, but which *above all* would draw analysis beyond or outside itself, and perhaps, in the same motion, beyond any identifiable 'Jewishness.' One way or the other, this path would lead *beyond the identity principle*" (195; italics in original). Characteristically, the authors are somewhat obfuscatory here—but I would unravel this passage as meaning something like the following: presumably because the psychic structure of the *Witz* is so unstable (because the *Witz* is constituted on the paradox of the mocker also participating in being mocked), then if our goal is to "locate" a Jewish psyche within psychoanalysis, the "joke" is on us, for the inherently Jewish *Witz* (the *Witz*-as-Jewish-joke) paradoxically leads us "beyond any identifiable 'Jewishness.'" If for Weininger, Rank, Heidegger, and others the *Witz* is the "royal road" to an anti-Semitic critique of Jewish identity, for Lacoue-Labarthe and Nancy it is the concept of identification (of the *Witz* as a particular kind of Jewish identification) that absolutely denies any "direct, independent, and proper access to the 'Jewish question' in Freud" (195).

At this point in their essay, Lacoue-Labarthe and Nancy make a well-perceived allusion to one of the more "symptomatic" features of Freud's *Group Psychology and the Analysis of the Ego*: the author's own admissions of failure in working through certain impasses in his theorizing of identification, and in particular that the nature of subjectivity itself is so enigmatic that we can never quite pinpoint when the psychic process of identification *originates*. But Lacoue-Labarthe and Nancy's essay begins to demonstrate its own set of "symptoms," particularly its "symptomatic" repetition compulsion to return to the question "is psychoanalysis a 'Jewish' science?" Even as they pursue their rigorous deconstruction of the "Jewish question" in Freud, the "question" I think we are still justified in posing to Lacoue-Labarthe and Nancy at this juncture in their argument is, to paraphrase (who else?) Freud himself, "what, exactly, do the authors *want* from (Freudian) identification?" Let us summarize very briefly the argument that spans the two essays we have examined so far. Arguing in "The Nazi Myth" that certain psychoanalytic processes of identification can be interpreted as leading inevitably to fascism, they seek to problematize that presumed causal relationship by offering the *Witz* as an inherently "Jewish mimesis," an identificatory process that can legitimately bring the Jew into the "fold," as it were, of identification (and, by implication, lead the Jew down the "royal road of psychoanalysis"). As an identificatory principle, the *Witz* has, for the authors, the potential to "return analysis to an initial Jewishness"—but Lacoue-Labarthe and Nancy then reason that because Freud could never successfully theorize identification, we must push *"beyond the identity principle,"* as if to argue that a focus on Jewish identity will, paradoxically, never lead us to the "Jewish question" in Freud.

Up to this point, the deconstructive labyrinths of "The Unconscious Is Destructured like an Affect" harbor a number of unintended ironies — ironies that, embedded as they are within the postmodern *jouissance,* the excess, unleashed by their analysis of the psychic process of identification, mitigate against a more complete articulation of what they want identification to be or to do. Even more significant than their failure to historicize the *Witz* as an explicitly anti-Semitic topos is the particular issue of Freud's own Jewish identity as the foremost encrypted and "symptomatic" irony of their "thinking" of psychoanalysis as an *histoire juive*. Especially if we keep in mind Freud's positing of the dream as the "royal road" to the unconscious, several questions arise at this point. Are Lacoue-Labarthe and Nancy suggesting that the reader should be attuned to the possibility (presuming their provocative claim that "the Jewish people do not dream" is valid) that the Jewish Freud ironically theorized *himself* out of the "royal road" to psychoanalysis? Is the (Jewish) "joke" on Freud for not once, but twice failing to accommodate the Jew into psychoanalysis: first through the *Witz,* which is too unstable to support an origin for identification, and second through his own admission of failure to theorize identification as the originary "social bond"? If this is their claim, the tautologies in their argument indeed become vertiginous. Are Lacoue-Labarthe and Nancy seeking a psychoanalysis whose *Dasein,* as it were, is "authentically" Jewish? Or are they subtly and implicitly exposing their own readers' quest for a psychoanalysis that is "authentically" Jewish? Are they seeking to stress the irony implicit in the Jewish Freud's inability to solve the "Jewish question" in relation to psychoanalysis? Or are they rather mocking their readers for assuming that because psychoanalysis is a kind of *histoire juive,* it *ought* to yield "direct, independent, and proper" access to the "Jewish question"? More specifically, if the *Witz,* as Lacoue-Labarthe and Nancy argue, cannot "return analysis to an initial Jewishness," and if identification *(Bindung)* fails to provide any "proper access to the 'Jewish question' in Freud," then one is left to construct the authors' own version of *l'histoire juive* thus: the Jewish founder of a (Jewish) psychoanalysis failed to locate *himself* within his own psychoanalysis. It is as if, for anyone making the premature assumption that psychoanalysis *is* a "Jewish" science, Lacoue-Labarthe and Nancy are prepared to counter with the question "how can psychoanalysis be 'Jewish' if the Jew cannot be 'located' within identification?" On the one hand, the complexity of their argument constitutes a philo-Semitic defense of Freudian psychoanalysis against charges that it is merely a "Jewish" science; but on the other hand, Lacoue-Labarthe and Nancy suggest that for anyone seeking a *beyond* to (Jewish) psychoanalysis, that process will *still* have to negotiate the "Jewish question" within psychoanalysis.

Affect and Oedipal Anxieties

As we have seen, Lacoue-Labarthe and Nancy call for a psychoanalysis that can "point to something else" that lies beyond the "identity principle." But must the "royal road" of a psychoanalysis that can lead to "something else" always double back on the figure of the Jew?

Currently in France, there is a new, post-Lacanian "return" to Freud that centers on affect, a concept that, while only partially theorized by Freud, is now increasingly held to be one of the cornerstones of psychoanalysis. In the final section of this chapter, I explore the particular dynamics of Lacoue-Labarthe and Nancy's "return" to Freudian affect (and their move away from identification) as part of their effort to configure a new kind of (Jewish) psychoanalysis. If it is identification that denies any "direct, independent, and proper access to the 'Jewish question' in Freud," then Lacoue-Labarthe and Nancy argue for affect as "the unique object of psychoanalysis" that can "return analysis to an initial Jewishness." What we must evaluate in this section are the philo-Semitic consequences of this highly complex "return" to affect, and the consequences of Lacoue-Labarthe and Nancy's new "affective logic" for the figure of the Jew in the post-Holocaust.

Let us first return to Freud ourselves in order to understand better why Freud had such difficulties in theorizing affect. The concept of affect (closely related to the enigmatic concept of *Angst* examined in chapter 2) ranks as perhaps the most difficult and inadequately theorized in the entire Freudian corpus. This difficulty hinges on the little understood yet highly significant relationship between the libidinal and the unconscious. In his essay "The Unconscious," where the concept of affect receives perhaps its most theoretical treatment, Freud emphasizes as virtually axiomatic that affect, as a physical discharge of a quantity of instinctual energy, does *not* belong to the realm of the unconscious: "In the first place, it may happen that an affective or emotional impulse is perceived, but misconstrued. Owing to the repression of its proper representative it has been forced to become connected with another idea, and is now regarded by consciousness as the manifestation of that idea. If we restore the true connection, we call the original affective impulse an 'unconscious' one. Yet its affect was never unconscious; all that had happened was that its *idea* had undergone repression."[46] At this point, Freud goes to great lengths to argue that affect is a psychic phenomenon quite different from repression. According to Freud, bodily instinct, or drive, becomes represented by a *Vorstellung* that gets repressed, while the affect attached to the drive remains manifest. Because it is the "true aim" of repression to attempt to inhibit the affect, Freud theorizes that "there are no unconscious affects as there are unconscious ideas" (178). It is important to emphasize here that Freud's insistence that the affect cannot become unconscious suggests a fundamental gap in the psychoanalytic experience between the body and representation. In order to understand this gap further, let us consider, for example, the precise relationship between affect and the hysterical body, a relationship that must be viewed as representationally overdetermined. The difficulty in interpreting hysteria is that the utterance (of pain, of loss) is replaced (or, more accurately, *dis*-placed) by the affective symptom—but a symptom that is not readily interpretable because it is so implicated in the enigmas of bodily experience.[47] There is virtually no relationship, then, between the unconscious and the corporeal (the affective). For Freud, affect is not a representational sign (because affects are never repressed); rather, it is a somatic *conversion* that continually shifts the ground of (psychic) interpretation.

Perhaps because of the interpretive difficulties that accrued from attempting to distinguish affect from repression, Freud stopped short of a fully worked out theory of affect. But in France, Freudian affect has experienced a significant revival in the recent work of Michel Henry, whose 1985 book *Généalogie de la psychanalyse* seeks a reconciliation between a philosophy of consciousness and psychoanalysis, with affect as the mediating agent.[48] Henry's project makes it clear that he opposes Lacan's emphasis on the unconscious as "linguistic" in favor of an emphasis on the unconscious as distinctly *affective*.[49] Henry proclaims that Freud's virtually forgotten concept of affect can serve as no less than the basis for an ambitious rapprochement between the discourses of philosophy and psychoanalysis, as a new way of going beyond the "metaphysics" of the subject — that is, beyond the Cartesian cogito as a moment of pure consciousness.[50]

The vexed question of the relationship between repression and affect that so troubled Freud is, in Henry's assessment, the "limit-question of psychoanalysis" (304). Working in the interstices of Freud's incompletely theorized opposition between affect and repression, Henry argues for affect (or what he sometimes refers to as "auto-affection") as the originary essence of the psyche itself: affect is the deeper foundation upon which representation (or, phrased more psychically, repression) originates. Because affect (as a kind of "presencing" of the body itself) is literally un*affected* by representation, it becomes, for Henry, the "unthought" of the history of the philosophy of consciousness. It is affect where, as he writes provocatively, "psychoanalysis finally gives up its secret. . . . For affect is not merely a drive representative. It is actually representation's foundation" (303). For Henry, then, affect is less a "psychic" state than a transcendental concept: it is because of affect that the unconscious is "nothing unconscious" at all, but the elusive escape from the language of mere representation. As a transcendental concept, affect manifests itself as a mode of self-appearance or self-immanence, a moment of feeling oneself *("se-sentir")* in feeling, a process of "auto-affection" in which the self experiences the self; Henry's affect is pure immanence, absolute subjectivity — beyond representation, beyond reduplication.

What is perhaps most significant in Henry's "return" to Freudian affect is his radical claim that consciousness and the unconscious are identical. Thus, in Henry's scheme, affect becomes constituted as a "philosophy of the unconscious" that deconstructs the opposition between consciousness and the unconscious: the affect becomes that which returns the unconscious to consciousness. As a kind of "limit" case of the philosophy of consciousness, pure affectivity offers its own mode of knowledge that experiences itself in an inescapable immediacy. For Henry, the experiencing of oneself as a self is dependent on an affect that experiences itself in an immanence so "pure" that it no longer reflects upon itself or conceives of itself (and cannot be undermined by the operations of the unconscious). It is in this sense, then, that the affect returns the unconscious to consciousness, and that the realm of the affective is beyond representation. What we begin to discover is that Henry's resuscitation of Freud's affect presents itself as nothing less than an escape from the problematics of representation itself.

Unlike Henry, whose return to affect is a means of exploring the question of whether or not there can be a philosophy of psychoanalysis, Lacoue-Labarthe and Nancy's "return" to Freudian affect in "The Unconscious Is Destructured like an Affect" is part of their ongoing investigation not of the philosophy of psychoanalysis, but of the *politics* of psychoanalysis. Much like Henry, who summarizes affect as the "limit-question of psychoanalysis," the authors also acknowledge affect as "the unique object of psychoanalysis" (197), a fundamental, bedrock principle that could serve as a new origin for psychoanalytic inquiry. But their particular interest in the affect centers on its inherently *social* properties, its usefulness for offering further insights into why Freud's concept of identification proved so difficult to theorize. In *Group Psychology*, Freud suggested an implicit link between identification and affect, referring not only to *Bindung* but also, more specifically, to *Gefühlsbindung*, the emotional tie with another that Lacoue-Labarthe and Nancy interpret as an "affective bond." As the authors argue, identification is, for Freud, "the *social* feeling"; in other words, the process of identification is initiated by/through an *affective* feeling for the other. But, as they also claim, "there is something in sociality which resists Freud's attempt to establish an identifiable theory of identification" (196). If, as Lacoue-Labarthe and Nancy state at the outset of their essay, psychoanalysis indeed "reveals itself to be untenable, overflowing," then it is because of affect, where the political always succeeds in overdetermining psychoanalysis: "With this [the concept of identification], Freud also denies himself another conclusion . . . there is no psychology of the affects, there is only a 'sociology'" (199). In other words, what Freud needed to realize was that the theorizing of identification requires a kind of "affective logic" that can destabilize the "originary" ambitions of identification (and of Freudian psychoanalysis itself).

If, for Henry, affect embodies "radical immanence" and "absolute subjectivity" (affect almost as a kind of Heideggerian "truth-event"), Lacoue-Labarthe and Nancy's project is to deconstruct affect (and the "origins" of sociality) as a kind of resistance, a *"dis*-sociation," a *désistement,* a withdrawal, a *retrait* at the heart of subjectivity. Like Henry, the authors interpret affect as "the unconscious" of consciousness itself; but in radical opposition to Henry (as well as to Freud), they make the provocative claim that "there is no subject to which an affect might appear" (199). The *Gefühlsbindung,* the emotional tie or social feeling Freud proffers as the origin of identification, has no originary capacity (what the authors refer to as the Freudian flaw of "archeophilia") because, in Lacoue-Labarthe and Nancy's "affective logic," affect (as a feeling) has no origin in an affecting, or "affectable" subject. As a "withdrawal of identity in the advent of identity" (200), Lacoue-Labarthe and Nancy's affect is not, as it is for Henry, a mode of self-immanence; rather, it is a "double identity," the "affection of an inside by an outside" (198) such that there is no clear distinction between an incorporating (or identifying) subject and an incorporated object: "If the identity of that which is called a subject does in fact have its origin in affect, in a being-affected, that is to say, in an affectable being, this identity then *alters* itself in its principle, in a pulsation of origin without origin. For to be affectable is to be always-already affected" (199).

In this "pulsation of origin without origin," Lacoue-Labarthe and Nancy locate both the constituting *and* the unraveling of the social tie in affect. And it is in this affective "pulsation of origin without origin" that the authors return to Freud and the "Jewish question" that is the essay's recurring theme. Specifically, the authors return to *Totem and Taboo,* Freud's anthropological *Ur*-narrative in which the powerful, totemic father is killed ("devoured"), only to be later "remembered" by the murderers in ritual displays of guilt and identificatory mourning. Lacoue-Labarthe and Nancy's return to the "Jewish question" occurs, in other words, at the point where, as the authors seem to imply, psychoanalysis attempts to constitute itself as most inherently "Jewish": the birth of the community is affirmed and assured when the "sons" overcome the leader-father and seal the triumph with a totemic meal as a classic illustration of Freud's ongoing fascination with the Oedipus complex and its generational clashes between fathers and sons. In Lacoue-Labarthe and Nancy's summary, "The meal is the locus of the clan's identification. . . . But the realization in practice of this 'sameness' implies the death and savage dismemberment of the totem which incarnates it" (200). For the authors, Freud failed to perceive the inherent paradox at the heart of the Oedipal totemic meal: affective attachment (to a leader-father, for example) always deconstructs itself as "the affect of a *dismemberment*" (200; italics in original). Identification is precariously constituted within this dismemberment, this "withdrawal of identity" that is manifest not as a "mode of being" (201), but as "the act of appearing disappearing" (201). A "metaphysical politics" (an identificatory, mimetic attachment to a leader) is not, in theory, possible because of affect—an affective attachment that can "appear" only as it "disappears" (or dismembers).

At stake in their critique of *Totem and Taboo* is what Lacoue-Labarthe and Nancy call "the question of the Father" (201), seemingly never far removed, for the authors, from the "Jewish question"—and a "question" that, for the authors, continually threatens to implicate psychoanalysis in fascism. "[W]ith respect to what is there dissociation? It is here that Freud, and perhaps psychoanalysis, inevitably trips itself up" (201). With the Father (the leader-father) Freud attempts to posit an originary identity, an originary cathexis, which assures "the identity of psychoanalysis" (201). But for Lacoue-Labarthe and Nancy, *Totem and Taboo* presents a flawed argument because the *désistement* at the core of affect affirms that "[t]here is no prior pact, neither symbolic nor social—for there is no subject and no Other to conclude such a pact" (201). The logic of paternal authority (of the Oedipus complex and of identification—indeed of *psychoanalysis itself*) "tips over into the abyss" (203).

In other words, for Lacoue-Labarthe and Nancy psychoanalysis becomes fully deconstructive (that is, it most fully relinquishes its originary ambitions) at the site of affect. In what I take to be their essay's most polemical claim, Lacoue-Labarthe and Nancy argue that affect "may then be that external force which, for Freud, precedes the internalized prohibition that is repression" (198). And they imply that the consequences for a Jewish identity (a "beyond" to repression?) are in-

deed significant: the absence of an originary, "always already identified" Father means that "an 'identified' sociality, that of an ethnicity,
for example [do the authors here mean Judaism?], and political sociality as such [do they here mean fascism?] can only succeed to this originary sociality" (205). If Freud had been able to theorize affect more
completely, they argue, he would have perceived that affect is the "something else" beyond "the internalized prohibition" that is the Oedipal
allegory. In short, for Lacoue-Labarthe and Nancy, one version of *l'histoire juive* of psychoanalysis is that affect does nothing less than deconstruct the prospect of "Jewishness" itself.

Now we are in a position to comprehend (if not necessarily accept)
the full force of what Lacoue-Labarthe and Nancy are attempting to
argue in this difficult and largely inaccessible essay. Their contention is
that affect (the very concept Freud found so difficult to theorize) leads
us directly to the "Jewish question" in Freudian psychoanalysis. But
affect, as the "royal road" to the Jewish question in Freud, also "tips"
psychoanalysis "over into the abyss"—the "abyss," that is, of deconstruction, the "abyss" (a metaphor not unlike the "caesura," as Lacoue-
Labarthe's privileged metaphor for Auschwitz) where psychoanalysis
overflows itself, the "abyss" where the Oedipal allegory (read "Jewishness" itself) is deconstructed by an affect that is prior to "ethnicity" and
to an "'identified' sociality." *L'histoire juive* is apparently on Freud, who,
in *Totem and Taboo,* wrongly seeks an identification, an "originary sociality" (for Jewishness?) in a nonaffective father who is never *dis*-soci-
ated, but "always already identified." For the authors, the "limit" of
psychoanalysis is the point at which Freud forgets his own concept of
affect as "the unique object of psychoanalysis."

We should not be entirely surprised, then, when we discover that at
the (political) "limit" of psychoanalysis Lacoue-Labarthe and Nancy
locate the figure of the Jew. And at this point, to conclude our chapter
where it began, it is perhaps appropriate to ponder the relationship between the authors' postmodern reconfiguring of Freudian affect and
Derrida's jewgreek, which, as we have seen, exposes French Heideggerianism as an "unconscious" philosophy. Not unlike Hegel, Lacoue-
Labarthe and Nancy are exploring the essence of an Oedipal identity
for the West. But whereas Hegel celebrates the Greek Oedipus as the
rise of Western (self)consciousness, Lacoue-Labarthe and Nancy seek
to deconstruct what they perceive as, in effect, a "jewgreek" Oedipus —
a Freudian Oedipus whose allegory of paternal authority can only lead

to the affective deconstruction of that same authority. For the authors, any attempt at a return to a "jewgreek" Oedipus will only entangle us again in the labyrinths of the "Jewish question" in psychoanalysis.

For Lacoue-Labarthe and Nancy, the deconstruction of identification through affect is the end (the "exhaustion") of psychoanalysis. But one implication of their deconstruction of identification (that is, their deconstruction of Oedipus as a powerful cultural and psychic construct) seems to be the "end" of the Jew (not unlike Lacoue-Labarthe's "caesura," in which the Jewish victim of Auschwitz is "de-structured" within a "disarticulation" of history). As we have seen, *pace* Winckelmann or Heidegger, Lacoue-Labarthe's philo-Semitic claim in *Heidegger, Art and Politics* is that Germany has no access to an originary "Greece." But at the same time, Lacoue-Labarthe and Nancy's more ambiguous claim in "The Unconscious Is Destructured like an Affect" is that Freudian psychoanalysis has no access to an originary, "Oedipal" father. In their critique of "onto-mimetology," Germany has no Greece, but neither do the Jews have an Oedipus. . . .

Perhaps conceding that their critique of mimesis is too theoretical and abstract, Lacoue-Labarthe and Nancy conclude their essay on a note of resignation, returning yet again to the concept of mimesis: "And yet *mimesis* there is, the model, the figure, must make its return; the Father must therefore *succeed*. A people and a politics must succeed" (208). Although it is affect that can lead us "beyond any identifiable 'Jewishness,'" mimesis will always intervene to lead us back to the "fascist question" in German National Socialism and to the "Jewish question" in Freud. For the authors, *l'histoire juive* is the way in which an Oedipal allegory will always intervene to provide an "origin" for Jewishness. At the end of their essay, the reader is left to ponder the following question: when French Heideggerianism renders psychoanalysis "postmodern," why is there also a compulsion to "tip" the Jew "into the abyss" of an "unconscious" philosophy? Or, to repeat a question posed at the beginning of this chapter, to what extent does a philo-Semitic, deconstructive affect suggest to us that French Heideggerianism has inadvertently served to create a Jewish-French psyche as, to echo Derrida, "the reflexive (un)consciousness of (post)modernity"?

4

After Repression: Psychoanalysis and "the jews"

Lyotard and Lévinasian Ethics

At the core of Emmanuel Lévinas's philosophy of an ethical responsibility to an Other lies his Jewish identity. And as an emigré to France from Lithuania, and as a French soldier imprisoned by the Germans during the second world war, Lévinas is at all times engaged with the relationship between *déracinement* and *la question juive*. As Judith Friedlander recounts, "During his early days in France, Lévinas took a course with Maurice Pradines on the relationship between the ethical and the political. To demonstrate how ethics could win out over politics, his professor gave the example of the Dreyfus Affair. This made a deep impression on him."[1] In other words, it was France's national trauma of the Dreyfus Affair (and of its ongoing acting out of French ambivalences about *judéité*) that served as a crucial background for Lévinas's influential "thinking" of the political through ethics — and through Judaism.

In 1935, after his earlier infatuation with the philosophy of Heidegger (under whom he studied in Freiburg in 1928–29), Lévinas began reading Franz Rosenzweig's *The Star of Redemption* (first published in 1916), a work that inspired him to begin considering the relationship between European philosophy and rabbinic Judaism. One result is that decades later, Lévinas has been at the forefront of an effort to make Judaism accessible to postmodernism;[2] it is largely because of Lévinas that the "question of the Other" *(l'Autre)* has now become a dominant mode of inquiry for Western philosophy in the post-Holocaust.

Briefly, Lévinas's project is the priority of (Judaic) ethics over (Greek) ontology — a project well known to readers of such books as *Totality and Infinity, Otherwise than Being,* and *Difficult Freedom.*[3] Lévinas seeks a justification of the ethical in philosophical terms — that is, ethics as the "difficult freedom" resulting from an encounter with the Other as the fundamentally unknowable and unthinkable. To break out of ontological categories (to break out of a Heideggerian "thinking" of Being), Lévinas seeks to "locate" a Hebrew God beyond Being, prior to ontotheology, urging us to turn to the category of an "otherwise than being" *(autrement qu'être)*, a "beyond essence." Unlike Lacan's Other of desire that serves as the "origin" of the unconscious, Lévinas's *l'Autre* eludes categories of consciousness and unconsciousness. The Other, emanating from the outside *(le dehors)*, is conceived by Lévinas as the trace of its own departure, forcing the subject to respond to something more ancient, more archaic even, than its own consciousness. The encounter with the Other decenters the subject, a process Lévinas has called the "hetero-affection" of the Infinite, leaving the subject a "hostage" *(ôtage)* to the other. The origin of ethics, then, is the subject's response to (and responsibility for) alterity, to the unknowable face *(visage)* of obligation that makes a request that can never be justified.

Of all the French Heideggerians, Jean-François Lyotard has perhaps been the most open in his admiration for Lévinas's privileging of ethics over ontology, his philosophical emphasis on the Talmudic "Do before you understand" (Lévinas's *faire avant entendre*).[4] In *Just Gaming*, which is, among other things, an extended meditation on the incommensurability of justice and ontology, Lyotard offers lengthy praise for Lévinas's privileging of the ethical "ought" over the ontological "is." Highlighting Lévinas's ethical "ought" as inherently Jewish, and inspired by his *Quatres lectures talmudiques*, Lyotard praises Lévinasian ethics in the discourse of an admiring philo-Semitism: "the absolute privileging of the pole of the addressee [as the site of obligation] . . . is to be found in Jewish thought"; "The Kant of the second *Critique* . . . is also bound to a different language game, much less 'modern' and much more 'Jewish'"; "Why the 'you must'? . . . It is quite clear that if there is a question that Judaism refuses, it is that of ontology."[5]

Attention to the philo-Semitism that informs *Just Gaming* can provide a greater appreciation of the depth of Lyotard's affinity with Lévinas, as well as offer us a first glimpse of the key relationship between the addresser and addressee that will play such an important role in *The Differend*. For Lyotard, the pole of the addressee as the site of obligation has been forgotten in Western thought; in one of his most Lévinasian moments, Lyotard argues in *Just Gaming* that the pole of the addressee "marks the place where something is prescribed to me, that is, where I am obligated before any freedom" (37). The (Jewish) pole of the addressee is the reception of the command "You must"—an affective state of "being obligated" that has no ontic derivation. All of which is to say that for Lyotard (as well as for Lévinas), obligation "is not a question of first understanding" (41).

The philo-Semitic impulses of *Just Gaming* are an anticipation of some of the central concerns of Lyotard's more recent *Heidegger and "the jews,"* whose distinctly postmodern version of *sémitophilie* renders this book perhaps one of the most overdetermined (and certainly "symptomatic") works in all of French Heideggerianism. The culmination of this chapter (as well as of my entire study of French Heideggerianism's encounter with *la question juive*) is a careful analysis of why *Heidegger and "the jews"* is so "symptomatic"—that is, why the "Jewish Question" remains encrypted within Lyotard's discourse, even in an otherwise thoughtfully and carefully worked out critique of anti-Semitism. In tracing the development of Lyotard's Lévinasian "pole of the addressee" from *The Differend* to *Heidegger and "the jews,"* I hope to provide a more complete understanding of what happens to representations of the figure of the Jew when Judaism (specifically privileged as the "origin" of ethics) becomes appropriated (and transmuted) by postmodernism. Though the ambition of *The Differend* is the articulation of a new (postmodern) ethics, Lyotard deploys the Lévinasian "Other" as an opportunity to theorize further a concept that has been a major preoccupation throughout his career—not so much a philosophical ethics, but rather a psychoanalytic affect. And, as we saw in chapter 3, when French Heideggerianism focuses on affect, anxieties about the "Jewish origins" of psychoanalysis can never be far behind.

In this chapter I focus on all that remains unresolved and problematic in Lyotard's attempt to thematize the figure of the Jew within the nexus of philosophical and psychoanalytic speculation that constitutes his version of French postmodernism. Lyotard's thoughtful appropriation of a Lévinasian ethics and the "difficult freedom" of obligation to the Other as the philosophical core of his concept of the "differend" ends up doubling back on the encrypted Jew of France's ongoing ambivalence with *judéité*. Not surprisingly, one reason is that the "royal road" (to echo Lacoue-Labarthe and Nancy via Freud) of the differend's ambition to articulate an ethical discourse of the Other feels compelled to take us first to Auschwitz.

Postmodern "Silence"

Let us begin this section where Lacoue-Labarthe and Nancy's discussion of *l'histoire juive* left off: with our own (repetition) compulsion to tell another Jewish joke. One of Lacan's favorite Jewish jokes is one told by Freud in *Jokes and Their Relation to the Unconscious*. As recounted with particular relish in his "Seminar on 'The Purloined Letter,'" Lacan cites the case of the Jew who reproaches his friend: "'Why are you lying to me?' one character shouts breathlessly. 'Yes, why do you lie to me saying you're going to Cracow so I should believe you're going to Lemberg, when in reality you *are* going to Cracow?'"[6] Lacan interprets this outburst as an apt illustration of his fundamental thesis that we are always spoken by/through the discourse of the Other. The Jew's frustration demonstrates the distinctly Lacanian irony that the truth often deceptively presents itself in the form of a lie. In the post-Holocaust, however, the joke takes on a more far-reaching resonance if we pause to consider its context within Polish geography. If we remember that Cracow is a mere forty miles from Auschwitz, then the more pertinent question for an investigation of postmodern philosophy's strange repressions of and transferences onto the Holocaust might be: why do you lie to us saying you're going to (the postmodern) "Auschwitz" so we should believe you're going to (the historical) Auschwitz (without quotation marks), when in reality you *are* only going to "Auschwitz"?

If, at that particular moment, Lacanian psychoanalysis (in the form of the Jewish joke) "locates" itself in a retracing of the road from Cracow to Lemberg and back, then much of French Heideggerianism locates itself somewhere in the indefinable space between an empirical Auschwitz and an "Auschwitz"-as-trope. Not surprisingly, Auschwitz is also a primary locus of Lyotard's ambitious attempt at a postmodern ethics. Lyotard seems overtly concerned with an empirical Auschwitz (without quotation marks) when he states factually: "Auschwitz is a city in southern Poland in the vicinity of which the Nazi camp administration installed an extermination camp in 1940."[7] But the historical, ontological "Being" of Auschwitz soon becomes destabilized in a warning about the precariousness of even trying to *name* "Auschwitz": "Is it possible to understand the linkage of name and sense without resorting to the idea of an experience? . . . [N]ames are not the realities to which they refer, but empty designators" (45, 48). For Lyotard, "Auschwitz" is less a historical event than a "para-experience" (*un né-*

gatif non niable, a "non-negatable" negative, the end of speculative discourse) that transcends historical and geographical "naming."[8]

Over the last decade, it could be argued that one of the more symptomatic efforts at a genuine mourning for a traumatic and encrypted Holocaust within philosophy has been the postmodern ethics of Lyotard. I say "symptomatic" because Lyotard's attempt to "think" the Holocaust in philosophical terms, his sense of urgency that it is time for philosophy to speak about the Holocaust, seems on occasion better understood as a psychoanalytic rather than a philosophical phenomenon. At times, it seems constituted not as a successful working through to a fuller understanding of the inexpressible trauma of the Holocaust, but rather as a kind of extended acting out in the form of a wish for a philosophy based on ethics — a philosophy that almost compulsively retains "Auschwitz" in quotation marks. When, for example, Lyotard asks, "Can 'Auschwitz' as something thought from the outside, a reference placed only 'near itself' 'for us,' be interiorized . . . and show itself to itself, know itself, in the identity of a for itself?" (89), this rhetorical question might serve as the occasion (as much as Lacoue-Labarthe's "caesura") for a reassessment of postmodern discourse and its capacity to accommodate (to *mourn*) Auschwitz as a historical event.

Lyotard's ethical project (and its unresolved transferences onto Judaism) is discussed further below. But I would like to focus first on the consequences of Lyotard's complex engagement with the Holocaust and, in particular, his appropriation of the genre of Holocaust testimony as the discursive marker of a postmodern alienation.

Elie Wiesel, for one (who, after his liberation from Buchenwald in 1945, imposed a ten-year vow of silence upon himself), talks frequently about silence after Auschwitz — silence as the impossibility of survivors' narrating fully the trauma of Auschwitz. Because of its inexpressible horror, any number of survivors have either experienced great difficulty or have refused altogether to talk about the Holocaust; their refusal to narrate is compelling evidence of their conviction that the very attempt to represent the horror of the Holocaust would only serve to diminish or trivialize that horror — to render that horror somehow more easily and falsely accessible to the imagination.

Blanchot has referred to the Holocaust as an "event without response"; but we should pause to consider how the *real* of this non-response to an unspeakable event is negotiated in radically different ways by postmodern philosophy and psychoanalysis. The concept of silence — that is, of silence as those inexplicable, unresponsive moments when communication or narration, indeed the talking cure itself, suddenly shuts down — can be viewed as fundamentally psychoanalytic. Recently, even as postmodern philosophy is seeking to constitute itself as a philosophy "after Auschwitz," psychoanalysis is increasingly turning to Holocaust survivor testimony (and its frequent punctuations by silence) for an extensive investigation of the psychic operations of trauma. Psychoanalyst Dori Laub, for example, has identified the silence in survivor testimony as a kind of paradigmatic challenge for the listener/ analyst in understanding trauma: "He or she must *listen to and hear the silence,* speaking mutely both in silence and in speech, both from behind and from within the speech. He or she must recognize, acknowledge and address that silence." If survivor testimony is riddled with silences, it is because the trauma has, in Laub's words, "not been truly witnesssed yet."⁹

For psychoanalysis, not only is silence an anticipated and inherent aspect of survivor testimony; it is also *evidential* — the necessary starting point of a projected working through to a salutary "witnessing." (In the context of survivor testimony and its efforts to preserve the integrity of eyewitness accounts, Laub's choice of the word "witnessing" here is surely not coincidental.) But one senses that, for Lyotard, silence has been over-essentialized by clinical psychoanalysis. Lyotard seeks to transform the survivors' (real) silence (the real psychic overdeterminations that accrue within Holocaust testimony) into a trope for a kind of quintessentially postmodern "silence" — that is, postmodernism's hypostatizing of the "unrepresentable" or the "unutterable" as part of its agenda to privilege the rifts and discontinuities that fragment the alienated postmodern subject. In Lyotard's postmodern discourse, "silence" is less the psychic (or psychoanalytic) marker of a traumatized memory than itself a kind of memorializing trope for the ruptures of a decentered subject.¹⁰

It is through the particular phenomenon of what he would refer to as a Holocaust "silence" that Lyotard effects a linkage between Auschwitz and his by now well-known concept of the "differend," certainly one of the more prominent and rigorous of postmodern attempts to empty discourse of content (and indeed of philosophy, or metaphysics, itself) so that a "thinking" of ethics can begin. As Lyotard defines it, the differend, as it arises in intractable disputes that cannot be settled, is "the unstable state and instant of language wherein something which

must be able to be put into phrases cannot yet be" (13). The differend
is a conflict that cannot be resolved because there is no rule of judgment. The differend occurs, for example, when a victim is unable to articulate the damage he or she has incurred: the damage incurred is ac-
companied by the loss of the means to prove the damage. The silences
of survivor testimony become, then, a kind of paradigmatic differend
for Lyotard insofar as the experiencing of trauma often means that the
horrors of Auschwitz cannot be "put into phrases."

For Lyotard, to testify is not to represent. Thus, the differend is intimately linked with the concept of a postmodern "silence" and, for that
matter, with a potential for enabling a working through or further understanding of the past on the part of the Holocaust survivor. But at this
point we must turn to a consideration of how the rigor of Lyotard's
concept of the differend also serves as the occasion for an unexpected
accommodation of other instances of "silence" and "victimization."

Lyotard's "thinking" of ethics is a scrupulous avoidance of any con-
trolling ideology: it begins by leaving everything open to question. As
if a genuine mourning for the Holocaust (by survivors or, less con-
sequentially, by postmodern philosophers) were not difficult enough,
Lyotard chooses to link his issue of Holocaust "silence" with the right-
wing Faurisson and his outrageous allegation that there never was a
master plan for a Nazi Final Solution for the Jews and that, more specifically, there were no gas chambers and no death camps. Lyotard
writes:

> Silence does not indicate which instance is denied, it signals the denial
> of one or more of the instances. The survivors remain silent, and it
> can be understood 1) that the situation in question (the case) is not
> the addressee's business (he or she lacks the competence, or he or she
> is not worthy of being spoken to about it, etc.); or 2) that it never
> took place (this is what Faurisson understands); or 3) that there is
> nothing to say about it (the situation is senseless, inexpressible); or
> 4) that it is not the survivors' business to be talking about it (they are
> not worthy, etc.). Or, several of these negations together. (14)

The differend "after Auschwitz"—Lyotard's systematic anatomizing
of the reasons for the silence of Holocaust survivors—also implicitly allows for the "victimization" of Faurisson and his insistence that there
were no gas chambers. In Lyotard's network of cause-and-effect, the
gas chambers become the "referent of a phrase," and Faurisson be-

comes a "victim" precisely because of the issue of survivor silence. Within the "judicial logic" of Lyotard's reasoning, if the survivor does not speak—if the survivor does not offer evidence (indeed proof) that Faurisson is wrong—then the accused (Faurisson) has no recourse for defending his allegation, and therefore he becomes a "victim." The only way to prove a negative, claims Lyotard, is to refute a positive: if the survivor does not offer Faurisson the opportunity of refutation (i.e., offer "proof" that gas chambers existed—a proof that can occur, by definition, only through the survivor's paradoxical death in a gas chamber), then the accused has become implicated in a differend, a "phrase" that cannot yet be put into words. The survivor's silence precludes the possibility of dispute; it has, as it were, become totalitarian.[11]

In the process of his rigorously breaking down the competing rhetorical and legal claims that constitute the overdeterminations of the differend (as "phrases in dispute"), Lyotard's "Auschwitz" finds itself located on a precarious divide between two incommensurate kinds of silence. On the one hand, "Auschwitz" is the paradigmaic differend: "The silence that surrounds the phrase, *Auschwitz was the extermination camp,* is not a state of mind, it is the sign that something remains to be phrased which is not, something which is not determined" (57; italics in original). For Lyotard, then, "Auschwitz," as a silence that cannot be phrased, serves to deconstruct psychoanalysis itself (that is, its essentializing reliance on Holocaust testimony as psychic "evidence"). "Auschwitz," a name without a referent, is not a "phrase," but rather the space of silence. As the negation of reality and of experience—as an "affirmation of nothingness" (103)—"Auschwitz" is a unique event within history because it cannot be "phrased" or represented. It is the point at which Holocaust testimony implodes into an epistemological abyss that can never "speak" the truth of its horrors. On the other hand, Lyotard's "mourning" of "Auschwitz" as the space of silence also transforms itself into an inadvertent "melancholia" for Faurisson as a victim within the differend "Auschwitz" itself has given rise to: the differend created by the silence of survivor testimony. In psychoanalysis, when the survivor is silent, it is a sign that he or she is struggling to negotiate the inexpressibility of trauma. In Lyotard's postmodern philosophy, however, when the survivor is "silent," the silence could just as readily indicate that he or she refuses to grant the listener any "authority" and, therefore, the opportunity to "speak."

It is important to emphasize here that, without question, Lyotard finds Faurisson's right-wing claims, or *non*-claims (for instance, that there were *no* gas chambers), morally repugnant. And it should be observed that throughout *The Differend,* Lyotard's writing is almost exhaustively determined to avoid any careless or inadvertent replication of the discourse of anti-Semitism. However, as Lyotard also perceives it, the ethical rigor of his postmodern philosophical project (as well as his stated goal of preventing positivist historiography from becoming such an easy target for Faurisson) demands that the differend be carefully unpacked until every voice has been heard.[12] Thus when the survivor refuses to speak, the trauma of an "after Auschwitz" has subtly shifted to a focus on Faurisson as a new kind of "victim" within the differend.

> Reciprocally, the "perfect crime" does not consist in killing the victim or the witnesses (that adds new crimes to the first one and aggravates the difficulty of effacing everything), but rather in obtaining the silence of the witnesses, the deafness of the judges, and the inconsistency (insanity) of the testimony. You neutralize the addressor, the addressee, and the sense of the testimony; then everything is as if there were no referent (no damages). If there is nobody to adduce the proof . . . then the plaintiff is dismissed, the wrong he or she complains of cannot be attested. (8)

Given that Lyotard's vertiginous discourse (where pronouns cannot readily be linked with their antecedents) problematically blurs the distinctions between plaintiff and defendant, judge and judged, victim and victimized, and addresser and addressee, how are we to assess the ethical valence of "the silence of the witnesses"? Lost in Lyotard's postmodern ethics are answers to the following questions: who, exactly, *are* his "witnesses," and how unjustifiable is their silence? What is the precise role of his "witness" within the differend? Again, we are left to wonder whether the theoretical discourse of postmodernism is a genre that can enable a genuine working through of the trauma of the Holocaust. The slippages inherent in Lyotard's vocabulary inadvertently act out a seeming condemnation of the very "witnesses" (plaintiffs? addressees?) who seek to oppose Faurisson. (To complicate matters further, Lyotard's generalizing reference to the "perfect crime" as "obtaining the silence of the witnesses" constitutes an inadvertent encrypting of the Nazis' own lexicon of a "Final Solution.") At this point, one is justified in asking, Is the (apparent?) rigor that is presumably necessary for unpacking all the potentially damaging "silences" within the differend worth all the intellectual effort? Or is Lyotard's ethical reasoning an exercise in postmodern *Trauerspiel*—a curious kind of "acting out" of legal discourse so compulsive that the Holocaust survivor and Faurisson must be forced to coexist in the strange contiguities that constitute the postmodern "differend"?

Postmodern "Affect"

In Lyotard's scheme, to doubt is to be ethical (in the "authentically" postmodern sense of the term); but, in the final analysis, we are left wondering if the differend, and its scrupulous determination to give voice to the other in one's thoughts, fully renders the spirit of Lévinas's obligation to the Other. The central questions in this section are: to what extent is there a dissonant "other" discourse underlying Lyotard's ostensible discourse of ethics? And what is at stake for the figure of the Jew in this other discourse?

For Lyotard, the differend is the site of trauma—a clear influence from Lévinas, who argues that subjectivity has its (non)origin in trauma; that is, in "a passivity of a trauma, but one that prevents its own representation, a deafening trauma, cutting the thread of consciousness that should have welcomed it in its present."[13] But for Lyotard, the trauma that results from the command "Be obligated" has not only an ethical but also a distinctly *affective* valence (as a moment that, to echo Lévinas, "prevents its own representation"); and it is this affective discourse that serves as the "other" discourse to Lyotard's deployment of a Lévinasian ethics.

In order to "listen" to Lyotard's affective discourse, let us return for a moment to his working definition of the differend. At one point Lyotard emphasizes that the differend, the state wherein something must, but cannot be put into phrases, "is signaled by what one ordinarily calls a feeling: 'One cannot find the words,' etc." (13). In the midst of Lyotard's postmodern ethics, where everything is so rigorously left open to question, it is intriguing to observe that the essentialized referent of "feeling"—of no less than affect itself—makes a sudden and unexpected appearance. A Freudian energetics (an *Affektbetrag*), as it were, intervenes as that which, again to echo Lévinas on trauma, "prevents its own representation," but also as that which structures the differend itself.

The differend (as an instance of "phrases in dispute") occurs when an experience of victimization is inarticulable. Lyotard insists that the "phrase" is not a concept, but is empty of content—and it would seem that it is affect itself that rushes in to fill the void of this nonconceptual "phrase." Amidst Lyotard's rigorous unpacking of the conflicting positions of addressers, addressees, plaintiffs, and victims, it is "feeling" that presents itself like a *deus ex machina* as one determinant of the emergence of the differend: "In the differend, something 'asks' to be put into phrases right away. . . . [T]hey must be allowed to institute idioms which do not yet exist" (13). It is crucial that we pause here to focus on two "symptoms" in Lyotard's own "phrasing" of the differend. First, we notice Lyotard struggling (within his otherwise nonaffective discourse) to find an appropriate pronoun to express the differend: the abstract, neutral "one" (as in "One cannot find the words") shifts to the inanimate "something," before finally being transformed into the distinctly human "they" (the Holocaust survivors themselves?). Second, and more important, we should note Lyotard's choice of verbs: "one *cannot* find the words"; "something *asks* to be put into phrases"; "they *must* be allowed to institute idioms" (italics added). It is as if Lyotard's differend, in other words, does not exist without an (ethical?) *urge* to do something about its "phrases in dispute." The differend is not simply a case of something that has yet to be articulated. Rather, this "something" to be articulated entails a particular "need" or compulsion that is then explained through Lyotard's own vocabulary of an ethico-affective imperative: one *cannot;* something *asks;* they *must* be allowed. "What is at stake in a literature, in a philosophy, in a politics perhaps, is to bear witness to differends by finding idioms for them" (13). Two things should be noted about this observation: Lyotard's transferential acting out of survivor testimony by calling for a "bearing witness" to differends; and the success of that "bearing witness" as dependent on the extent to which the differends (and the imperative that "something 'asks' to be put into phrases") are signaled by feelings, for instance "the feeling of pain which accompanies silence" (13). Even as Lyotard's articulation of the differend is a hyperintellected attempt to empty discourse of all content, even as the truth value of the existence of gas chambers as the privileged referent for survivor testimony disappears within the interstices of the multiple subject-positions of the differend, a "mourning" for the Holocaust would seem to make its tentative appearance at the point of affect—of the emergence of "feeling" as an ineffable "something" that "'asks' to be put into phrases," but cannot be spoken.

What is at stake in the emergence of Lyotard's "affective" discourse from the (ethical) differend? Despite his lengthy discussion of Auschwitz as a phrase empty of content and a concept beyond the logic of an "event," the Holocaust continues to exert its own "affective" pull on Lyotard. And what we come to discover is that perhaps the most compelling, if encrypted, question for Lyotard in the second half of *The Differend* is the same question that Lacoue-Labarthe's "caesura" was intended to address: is the Jew authentically "tragic"? In other words, in the second half of *The Differend,* what Lyotard may be attempting is less a postmodern philosophy of ethics than a postmodern aesthetico-psychoanalytic return to the relationship between Greek tragedy and the Jew. An urge to pose the question "Is the Jew 'tragic'?" can explain why Lyotard shifts his focus in *The Differend* not only from an ethical to an "affective" discourse, but also from the survivors of the Holocaust to the victims. This shift in focus from the survivors to the victims proves to be provocative indeed, for as Lyotard sees it, if the survivors (described previously as the site where "something 'asks' to be put into phrases") exemplify his concept of affective "need," the victims of the Holocaust *do not.* As we have seen, the (Lévinasian) pole of the addressee as the site of obligation is, for Lyotard, inherently Jewish; but the victim of Auschwitz, he claims, "is not the addressee of an obligation" (100).

Lyotard bases this enigmatic assertion not on ethico-philosophical grounds, but on what he views as the tragic requirements of achieving the "Athenian 'beautiful death'" and his analysis of the imperative *Die.* Lyotard defines the "Athenian 'beautiful death'" as the "exchange of the finite for the infinite, of the *eschaton* for the *telos:* the *Die in order not to die*" (100; italics in original). In order to accede to the "Athenian 'beautiful death,'" the imperative *Die* must be "modalized." Examples of such "modalized" imperatives are: "*Die rather than escape* (Socrates in prison), *Die rather than be enslaved* (the Paris Commune), *Die rather than be defeated* (Thermopylae, Stalingrad). A 'beautiful death' occurs when death is prescribed as an alternative to another obligation" (100; italics in original). But at "Auschwitz," claims Lyotard, the ss did not issue to its victims a "Die rather than. . . ," but simply a peremptory "Die." Thus, in Lyotard's logic, the victim of Auschwitz is not the addressee of an obligation: "'Auschwitz' is the forbiddance of the beautiful death. . . . The deportee . . . cannot be the addressee of an order to die, because one would have to be capable of giving one's life in order to carry out the order. But one cannot give a life that one doesn't have the right to have. Sacrifice is not available to the deportee, nor for that reason accession to an immortal, collective name. . . . This death must be killed, and that is what is worse than death" (100–101). Lyotard's argument that the victim's fate "worse than death" is not tragic (that is, that this fate "worse than death" is not an instance of the "Athenian 'beautiful death'") could be viewed as a powerful exposure of the senselessness and moral absurdity of the Final Solution. In support of Lyotard, we could attempt to paraphrase the difficulty of the above passage thus: if the victim (because of the juggernaut of racial extermination?) "is not the addressee of an obligation," then there can be no affective call of the other: because "sacrifice is not available to the deportee" (because there is nothing to "ask" to be put into phrases?), then murder at Auschwitz produces no "affective" moment, just an annihilating death — or, in Lyotard's words, a "death that must be killed."

But even with the benefit of such a paraphrase, it could also be observed here that in Lyotard's denial of the status of the "Athenian 'beautiful death'" to the figure of the Jew, we are edging uncomfortably closer to Heidegger's refusal to view the victims of Auschwitz as authentically tragic. And one cannot help but perceive an odd (if inadvertent) coziness between Lyotard's denial of tragic status to the victim of Auschwitz and Hegel's valorizing of Greek tragedy over the "unaesthetic" Jew (as discussed in chapter 3) who is stranded outside of world history, doomed to "horror" (Abscheu), unable to produce a genuine catharsis. In Lyotard's assertion that "sacrifice is not available to the deportee," it is difficult not to hear echoes of Hegel's claim that "the great tragedy [Trauerspiel] of the Jewish people is no Greek tragedy." In his defense, Lyotard might counter that because the "Athenian 'beautiful death'" is based on obligation (i.e., "to die rather than be defeated"), then one could make the philo-Semitic claim that Greek tragedy may be, in effect, inherently Jewish. But if this is Lyotard's conclusion, then why (in what is surely one of postmodern sémitophilie's most unsettling repetition compulsions) must the victims of Auschwitz be "killed" again?[14]

Lyotard's "Crisis of Psychoanalysis"; or, Hamlet, Moses, and the Jews

This discussion of survivors and victims of the Holocaust might seem to be the appropriate and logical moment to turn to *Heidegger and "the jews."* But, having just considered *The Differend's* linkage of Auschwitz and a Sophoclean tragic aesthetics, I would like to go backward rather than forward in Lyotard's intellectual career—back, for the time being, to Lyotard on the relationship between tragedy and psychoanalysis, and in particular to a careful consideration of three essays dating from the late 1960s to the mid-1970s: "Beyond Representation," "Jewish Oedipus," and "Figure Foreclosed." After all, Lyotard's focus in *The Differend* on the "Athenian 'beautiful death'" (and its affinities with affect) indicates that at this point we may already be much closer to psychoanalysis than to philosophy. Lyotard's repetition compulsion to "kill" the victims of Auschwitz again also signals that we are not far from Freud—and, as we have seen, when French Heideggerianism moves closer to Freud, anxieties about the "Jewish origins" of psychoanalysis are never far behind.

Lyotard's "Beyond Representation" opens with a provocative allusion to a "crisis in psychoanalysis" in France. The "crisis" in question is the notion of "applied psychoanalysis," defined by Lyotard as applying psychoanalytic concepts (such as the Oedipus Complex) to tragedy, or "the infiltration of clinical thought by tragic themes drawn from Greek and Elizabethan drama, particularly from *Oedipus Rex* and *Hamlet.*"[15] Lyotard briefly critiques the posthumously published essay "Psychopathic Characters on the Stage" (written in 1905–6), in which Freud outlines what Lyotard describes as "the genesis of psychoanalysis in terms of the problem of guilt and expiation" (156). For Freud, the birth of psychoanalysis is coincident with the birth of Greek tragedy in the sacrifice of the goat, which, in Lyotard's summary, "gives birth to socio-political drama and then to individual (psychological) drama, of which psychoanalysis is the offspring" (156). But what Lyotard objects to in Freud's psychogenesis of tragedy is that in the transition from (real) animal sacrifice to "psychological drama" (and in response to the spectator's "neurosis"), theatrical space has become "derealized." For Lyotard, the dramatic arts should not be vicarious, based on (mere) representations of a missing object.[16] Tragedy should not conceal content, but *reveal* it—in real spaces where a transgressive, disruptive libido "can play in all its ambivalence" (156). For Lyotard, "authentic" tragedy should entail affective, immediate presentation, not *re*-presentation. Authentic tragedy, as a kind of "theatre of energy," should be the affective site of *aletheia,* disclosure.

Lyotard's privileging of an "affective" theatre is one outcome of his larger project in the 1970s to theorize the relationship between the aesthetic and the libidinal. In such works as *Discours, figure*—an extended meditation on "the politics of desire"—and *Des dispositifs pulsionnels,* Lyotard interprets desire as transgressive, a disruptive deformation of aesthetic form. And in his *Économie libidinale,* Lyotard praises Freud's Thanatos, or "death-drive" (from *Beyond the Pleasure Principle*), as a prime example of energetics or libido as anxiety and disruption.[17] If there is a "crisis in psychoanalysis" in France, then for Lyotard this crisis has occurred because "the infiltration of clinical thought by tragic themes" has for too long been dominated by an aesthetics of repression (as a form of psychic re-presentation), rather than of affect.

At this point we can begin to discern a certain ambivalence toward Freudian psychoanalysis emerging in Lyotard's work. Despite the possibility that the affective intensities of his concept of the "figural" could be viewed as his own kind of filial "return" to the Freudian unconscious, Lyotard insists that the unconscious does not merely *present* the unrepresentable, but serves as the unrepresentable "other" to representation itself. And when we move to a consideration of his complex essay "Jewish Oedipus," we discover the possibility that Lyotard's privileging of affect over repression has encrypted within it an anxiety about the "Jewish origins" of psychoanalysis. Lyotard's critique of repression in "Jewish Oedipus" is long and involved—and in order to understand fully the implications of this difficult essay and its conflicted relationship with psychoanalysis, we must first revisit some of the thorny issues involving the relationship between tragedy and the German cultural imaginary first undertaken (but never fully resolved) in the last chapter.

To provide the most appropriate background for an understanding of "Jewish Oedipus," let us return briefly to that intriguing moment in *The Post Card,* discussed in chapter 2, when Derrida speaks of two figures who "never read each other, and even less encountered each other, Freud and Heidegger, Heidegger and Freud." A return to this cultural (non)encounter itself prompts another return to one of the seemingly fundamental questions for German Idealism: how inherently "Jewish" is the fate of Oedipus, his abandonment by the gods? In his essay "Jewish Oedipus," Lyotard confronts the question directly—and, in the process of replacing representation with affect, reveals a number of anxieties about the "Jewish origins" of psychoanalysis.

In the context of the question, How inherently "Jewish" is the fate of Oedipus? (and in the context of a return to the importance of Oedipus for a German cultural imaginary), one cannot help speculating on the extent to which Heidegger's hypostatizing, in his *Introduction to Metaphysics,* of an Oedipal *Dasein* was a response to what he may have viewed as Freud's characteristically "Jewish" Oedipus: an Oedipus whose "passion for disclosure of being," as Heidegger chose to phrase it, was reinterpreted by Freudian psychoanalysis as the destiny of killing off the father as the voice of the law. Like Hegel, Heidegger celebrates the moment when the (Judaic) truth of Oedipus's patricide is sublated within the hero's final attainment of (Greek) self-consciousness.

It is as if Heidegger were seeking to counter a Freudian contention that authentic tragedy always originates in patricide. But one should not overestimate Freud's investment in Oedipus as his archetypal tragic hero; Heidegger may after all have overlooked the prospect that the "real" (Jewish) Oedipus for Freud is not Oedipus, but Hamlet. It could be argued that Freud's fascination with Hamlet serves, in its broadest scope, not only as a kind of defetishization of a Germanic preoccupation with Greece (and, specifically, of an Oedipal tragic apotheosis), but also as an emphasis on the importance, within cultural history, of the *deferral* of patricide (or of the murder of the paternal uncle) as Freud's own distinctive privileging of the "Jewish" ethical.

This is perhaps the "truth" Lyotard discovered in his essay "Jewish Oedipus," where he gets to the heart of what could be perceived as the cultural *agon* being played out between a "German" Oedipus and a Freudian Hamlet. As he asks, "In the order of representation, what is there in *Hamlet* that is not in *Oedipus?* There is non-fulfillment."[18] Positing what he calls Hamlet's "*non-fulfillment* of the paternal word" as "the modern's difference from the Greek" (and thus renewing his contention in *Discours, figure* that a work of art should dispossess the space of fulfillment), Lyotard suggests the following point-counterpoint: "Oedipus fulfills his fate of desire [i.e., the killing of Laius]; the fate of Hamlet is the non-fulfillment of desire: this chiasmus is the one that extends between what is Greek and what is Jewish, between the tragic and the ethical" (401). Thus, based on Lyotard's "chiasmus," one could argue that it is by means of the deferred murder that Freud's Hamlet reverses what we have earlier seen as the Hegelian priority of the Greek tragic over the Judaic ethical. If, for Hegel, Oedipus represents a crucial separation of Greek "authenticity" from Egyptian "Orientalism," then for Freud, Hamlet may have represented a crucial recuperation of the Jewish "ethical" over the Greek "tragic," which fails to acknowledge the centrality of the *non*response to the law within cultural history.

For Hegel (and for Heidegger, as we have seen) a Greek authenticity "originates" in the moment of Oedipus's attainment of self-consciousness (that is, his knowledge that he has fulfilled the words of the oracle). But for Freud, it is Hamlet's nonfulfillment of the paternal word that constitutes the psychic space of repression and inaugurates, as he puts it in his *Interpretation of Dreams,* a new epoch in "the secular advance of repression in the emotional life of mankind."[19] Viewed in this light, then, the psychic phenomenon of repression can perhaps be perceived as ethically superior to — more psychically complex than — (mere) self-consciousness as an earlier stage "in the emotional life of mankind." One could argue that repression as the very foundation of the discipline of psychoanalysis is perhaps as much an outcome of an *agon* within cultural history between the "Greek" tragic and the "Jewish" ethical as of Freud's "discovery" of the psychic laws of the unconscious. The essence of Freudian tragedy is not the *Dasein* of self-consciousness, but rather the after-effect (the *après-coup*) of repression, the belated realization that one's freedom is only and inevitably the tragic result of the "impossible repossession" of the Other.

Hamlet's "impossible repossession" of the Other traces the peculiar temporal logic of a Freudian *Nachträglichkeit* as the belated reactivation of an initial event that may never have taken place. The voice of the Other is something that was never originally present; it is something latent, forgotten — reconstructed as an event only later in its deferred remembrance. For Freud, nonfulfillment of the paternal word is always based on a kind of *forgetting,* an initial nonrecognition that one is possessed by the voice of the Other. One after-effect of Hamlet's "impossible repossession" of the Other is, of course, his murder of Polonius, the belated site of nonrecognition of Hamlet's patricidal desire. The repression inherent in this deferral (or, more accurately, this deferred *displacement*) of patricide occurs because Hamlet, unlike Oedipus, *forgets* his father, thereby setting up his encounter with Polonius as the return of the repressed. Repression (like the voice of the Other itself) is never fully constituted until it returns, *nachträglich,* after one has forgotten the voice of the Other.

Returning specifically to "Jewish Oedipus," we can once again discern the influence of Lévinas on Lyotard's philo-Semitic re-evaluation of theatrical experience. Lyotard's analysis of Shakespearean tragedy celebrates *Hamlet*'s presentation of "non-fulfillment" as, among other things, an example of "the properly Judaic contribution" to theatre (406). In singling out Hamlet as "the modern's difference from the Greek," Lyotard underscores what he perceives as the play's "ethical," "Jewish" dimensions by means of a heavy reliance on Lévinas's *Quatres lectures talmudiques* and *Totalité et infini.* Thus, as Lyotard argues, the ethical, Lévinasian subject "knows himself possessed by an Other who has spoken; he knows himself dispossessed of origin" (402). For the ethical, as opposed to the tragic subject, he asserts, "[i]t is necessary that the son *not fulfill* the word . . . that the son's possession by the voice be older than his liberty" (403; italics in original). If Oedipus is the (Greek, tragic) "staging of non-recognition," then Hamlet is the (ethical, Jewish) re-presentation of the "non-fulfillment" of patricidal desire. Enmeshed within a Lévinasian allegory of the son's acceptance of obligation through the voice of the father, Lyotard's Hamlet hears the father's spoken word and knows himself "dispossessed of origin" (402), denied a "reconciliatory dialectic" (403).

One result of this "dispossession of origin" is the phenomenon of Hamlet's displacement—that is, displacement from his own patricidal desire by his murderous uncle Claudius. And it is in this process of displacement (a "drift," or *dérive*) that Lyotard's Lévinasian Hamlet abuts against Freud's Hamlet in the midst of what might have been an otherwise unproblematic celebration of *Hamlet*'s "properly Judaic contribution" to theatre. Hamlet's desire to "remember" his father "un-fulfills" itself, displaces itself in compulsive representations of Claudius's would-be murder, such as his staging of the murder of Gonzago and his subsequent murder of Polonius. And the ways in which we interpret these compulsive representations psychoanalytically can, in turn, draw us closer to what exactly Lyotard means when he speaks enigmatically of "the properly Judaic contribution" in *Hamlet.* Despite Lyotard's open admiration for what he calls "Freud's genius" in his essay's introductory paragraph, it is not Freud's "secular advance of repression in the emotional history of mankind" that Lyotard's essay celebrates, but rather the Lévinasian obligation to the Other and what Lyotard sees as its potential for an "aesthetics" of nonfulfillment, wherein Hamlet's displacements constitute the transgressive, disruptive deformations of aesthetic form so widely privileged in Lyotard's aesthetic theory of the 1970s. For Freud, Hamlet's deferrals, his "dispossession of origin," signal the *après-coup* of repression. But Lyotard deploys the Lévinasian obligation to the Other to probe the lineaments not of a "repressive," but of an "affective" theatre. It is as if, for Lyotard, the psychic operation of repression is in a too comfortable compliance with aesthetic form.

"Jewish Oedipus" concludes with a brief discussion of Freud's *Moses and Monotheism,* which, as yet another renowned allegory of patricidal desire in cultural history, provides for Lyotard an appropriate final commentary on *Hamlet.* And it is in this concluding discussion that Lyotard's ambivalence toward Freudian psychoanalysis comes into sharper focus. Because both *Moses and Monotheism* and *Hamlet* are structured on similar themes of the murdered father, it is logical for Lyotard to turn to what Freud himself called his "historical novel." But something else from *Moses and Monotheism* seems to exert its ineffable pull on Lyotard. When a philo-Semitic discourse centering on a Lévinasian ethics meets Freudian psychoanalysis and its own investigation of what Freud referred to as "the nature of Judaism" *(des jüdischen Wesens),* the enigmas of Lyotard's observation of "the properly Judaic contribution" in *Hamlet* can be unpacked even further.

In his great cultural document *Moses and Monotheism* (written, not insignificantly, the year he fled Vienna in 1939), Freud goes beyond the figure of Hamlet to ponder some further implications of patricidal desire, considering such questions as: What are the psychic (and cultural) consequences when the murder of the voice of the Other is both committed *and* forgotten? How does the return of the repressed manifest itself when, Oedipus-like, the murder of the father is carried out, *and,* Hamlet-like, the father's voice is forgotten—lost in deferral? What happens, for that matter, when the *non*-response to the voice of the Other becomes an extended forgetting that spans generations? The act of forgetting a patricide is, of course, fundamental to Freud's thesis in *Totem and Taboo,* where the powerful, totemic father is killed ("devoured"), only to be later "remembered" in ritual displays of guilt and identificatory mourning. Thus, in *Totem and Taboo,* forgetting always presupposes a murder—and to murder is to forget. But what does this matrix of murder, forgetting, and the return of the repressed that is so prominent in *Totem and Taboo* have to do with the formations of cultural identity we have been discussing? Within cultural history, who is the paradigmatic hero who must be murdered in order to be forgotten? Put another way, who is the hero whose forgotten murder inaugurates the return of the repressed as a mourning ritual within cultural history? For Freud, the answer is neither Oedipus nor Hamlet, but Moses the lawgiver—Moses the prototypical (murdered) voice of the Other as its "impossible repossession."

Thus Lyotard attempts a further illustration of the forgotten patricide in a brief but no less enigmatic reference to Freud's *Moses and Monotheism:* "The truly fundamental thesis of *Moses and Monotheism* is not that of Moses' Egyptian origin. . . . The essential point for Freud is that Moses should have been assassinated, since it is in this *Agieren,* these *actings-out* (the compulsive murder of the paternal figure, repeating in non-recognition that of the primal father, thematized in *Totem and Taboo* in 1913) that the Jews escape the general movement of the first murder's recognition" (405). Lyotard's allusion to *Moses and Monotheism* is intended to emphasize the importance of the "compulsive murder" and subsequent nonrecognition of the primal father within cultural history. But rather than providing further clarification of Hamlet's "impossible repossession" of/by the Other, this insertion into the argument serves only to suggest Lyotard's anxiety about the "Jewish origins" of psychoanalysis. So significant is this insertion into the text of the essay that we should pause first to consider more fully Freud's own motives in writing this complex document.

In *Moses and Monotheism,* Freud goes so far as to argue for the forgotten (repressed) murder as an identifiable phenomenon within cultural and religious history. And it is perhaps at this point that we can begin to understand the full significance of Freud's turn, late in his career, to Moses as his third great cultural hero.[20] Let us briefly rehearse the particulars of *Moses and Monotheism,* where a monotheistic theology is constituted as the "totem and taboo" narrative of the return of the repressed. According to Freud, monotheism had existed earlier in Egypt, established as a state religion by the pharaoh Amenhotep IV (or Ikhnaton). However, it lasted only for the seventeen years of his reign, after which it was completely eradicated. The Egyptian Moses preserved Ikhnaton's monotheism when he made himself the head of an oppressed Semitic tribe then residing in Egypt. But the members of this Semitic tribe revolted against the monotheistic doctrine of Moses, killing their leader and, more significantly, repressing the memory of his murder.[21] Even after the later (belated) resurgence of monotheism among the Hebrews, the memory of Moses' murder remained repressed. Thus, for Freud, Judaism "originated" in the forgotten slaying of its founder: a monotheistic Judaism required the *forgotten* patricide in order to constitute an origin for itself. Even when Moses was finally "remembered" by the Hebrews, the remembrance occurred only through the displacement of his identity onto another "Moses," a Midianite Moses who had never been in Egypt. Thus the stage was set for the origin of Judaism as nothing less than the return of the repressed itself. A monotheistic Judaism was possible only *nachträglich*, only after the murder of Moses was forgotten—born from a rupture that reemerged belatedly as a not-fully-acknowledged atonement.[22]

"[I]t was one man," argues Freud, "the man Moses, who created the Jews" (136). It was essential for Freud that this man *("der mann")* Moses be an Egyptian; and we must now turn to the issue of what precisely was at stake for Freud in his insistence on the Egyptian origins of Moses.[23] What can we infer from Freud's contention that Moses was "an Egyptian when a people needed to make him into a Jew"? (16). Freud was attacked for denying the Hebraic origins of Moses, a fulfillment of Freud's own prophecy in a letter to his son Ernst that "Jewry will be very offended."[24] But if Freud's insistence on the Egyptian origins of Moses was an affront to European Jewry during the darkest moment of its history, it was perhaps also, viewed from his perspective, a much-desired cultural and historical reinforcement of psychoanalysis itself. It could be argued that late in his career Freud was prepared to "renounce" the Jewish origins of Moses as the controversial, but necessary trade-off for securing repression (or, more accurately, the return of the repressed) as not just the origin of Judaism, but also, by extension, as nothing less than an identifiable cultural, as well as psychic, phenomenon—a phenomenon with observable *effects* within cultural history. Freud's denial of the Jewish origins of Moses, then, could be viewed as a kind of "sacrificial" move seeking to guarantee the centrality of repression (as opposed to the *Dasein* of a Hegelian/Heideggerian Oedipus?) within cultural history. As Freud argues, "my hypothesis that Moses was not a Jew, but an Egyptian creates a new enigma" (31). In referring to his hypothesis of Moses' Egyptian origins as an "enigma," Freud seems almost to be deliberately countering Hegel's argument that the cultural superiority of a Greek self-consciousness is constituted at the moment of Oedipus's solving the riddle (or what Hegel called the "unconscious symbolics") of the Sphinx. For Freud, a "solution" will always be confronted by another riddle (such as the "enigmatic" origins of Moses) — a riddle that elicits not self-consciousness, but repression as its only possible response.

As opposed to an Oedipal "disclosure of being" (as Heidegger would have conceived of it), Freud reintroduces an "Egyptian enigma," whereby the inherently "Jewish" fact of repression is predicated on an Egyptian origin. Freud's "enigma" is that in order for Judaism to have had an "origin," it must have been constituted as a belated response — specifically as deferred guilt over the murder of the never-fully-mourned leader. A monotheistic Judaism was "created" belatedly, only when the Midianite Moses was established as a kind of metonymic displacement of the "real" (murdered) Moses. Moses must be made an Egyptian so that the Jews can constitute their origin as the (belated) attempt to repress the voice of the Other that was, in some sense, never initially present. Thus the even greater enigma posed by *Moses and Monotheism* is that a "Jewish" Moses can be constituted only after the "Egyptian" Moses has been forgotten. Put simply, Freud wanted an *Egyptian* Moses because he needed a *repressed* Moses. If, for Hegel, Egypt (the "Oriental," Egyptian Sphinx) must be overcome through the attainment of self-consciousness, for Freud Egypt (that is, an "Egyptian" Moses) must be *restored* in order to constitute the return of the repressed not just as a psychic, but also as a cultural and historical phenomenon.

In sum, this hypothesis of the Egyptian origins of Moses (though he feared it would make "Jewry . . . very offended") was crucial to Freud's theory of repression as one of the founding principles of psychoanalysis. And in the conclusion to Lyotard's essay "Jewish Oedipus," what the author himself may have "repressed" (not, perhaps, unlike Hegel's rejection of the "unconscious symbolics" of the Egyptian Sphinx) is that the "enigma" of Moses' Egyptian origins was essential for Freud *not just* as the (belated) "origin" of Judaism, but as the belated origin of repression as nothing less than a transcultural phenomenon that could guarantee the validity of psychoanalysis as an emergent discipline. Near the end of his essay, Lyotard offers Freud's Moses as a useful prototype for the (murdered) voice of the Other that can contribute to a further understanding of the psychic allegory of *Hamlet*. But it is not insignificant that he glosses over the centrality of Moses' Egyptian origins for Freudian psychoanalysis — in the process implicitly undermining Freud's ambition in *Moses and Monotheism* to configure a psychoanalysis based on transcultural repression. Lyotard's glossing over is expressed as a moment of denegation: "The truly fundamental thesis of *Moses and Monotheism* is not that of Moses' Egyptian origin," but rather his assassination by his followers. Given Freud's clear indication that Moses' Egyptian origins may *indeed* have been the "fundamental thesis" of *Moses and Monotheism* (to the point that he was willing to risk an "offended Jewry"), we should further ponder the significance of Lyotard's denegation. It is as if, in "Jewish Oedipus," Lyotard overlooks Freud's ambitious move to posit a transcultural repression so that he can make a hasty return to the privileged topic of his earlier essay "Beyond Representation"—the "crisis of psychoanalysis" in France. Thus Lyotard quickly turns from Moses back to Hamlet's "un-fulfillment of desire" as the psychic space of representation: "The complex function of representation in Shakespearean tragedy must be tied to the dimension of non-fulfillment, that is to say to the properly Judaic contribution" (406). In such works as *Discours, figure,* Lyotard claims that true art should seek to dispossess the space of fulfillment. But in "Jewish Oedipus," where "the dimension of non-fulfillment" is explicitly linked with "the properly Judaic contribution" to tragedy, we may have reached the "political unconscious" of Lyotard's complex network of aesthetics, repression, and the figure of the Jew: his most polemical point in this abrupt return to *Hamlet* may be to argue that it is repression (as the "dimension of non-fulfillment") that is "the [im]properly Judaic contribution" to psychoanalysis. And in such a scheme, repression threatens to become no longer valorized as a transcultural (or trans-*aesthetic*) phenomenon, but rather historicized as the origin of (Jewish) psychoanalysis.

Thus, by the conclusion of his essay, Lyotard's denegating avoidance of the centrality for Freud of Moses' Egyptian origins gets displaced by an anxiety over the "Jewish origins" of psychoanalysis. It comes as no surprise, then, when (in an otherwise not entirely logical transition in his argument), Lyotard quotes from Freud's famous 1918 letter to his Swiss friend Oskar Pfister (a letter that is perhaps the "primal scene" of Freud's *own* anxieties about the "Jewish origins" of psychoanalysis): "Quite by the way, why did none of the devout create psychoanalysis? Why did one have to wait for a completely godless Jew?"[25] Why, Freud speculates, did psychoanalysis have to wait to be "created" by a Jew? As we have seen, it is possible to argue that *Moses and Monotheism* was written to provide an answer to that very question. But for Lyotard, Freud's speculation about why it was a Jew who "created" psychoanalysis leads not to the hypothesis of the Egyptian origins of Moses, but rather to the (in Lyotard's opinion, potentially compromising) relationship between modern drama and repression: "It was necessary to wait for it [the origin of psychoanalysis] to be a Jew because it had to be someone for whom religious reconciliation ('sublimation') be prohibited, for whom re-presentation itself, art, was unable to fill the Greek function of truth; it was necessary *to wait,* because it was necessary that this someone belong to a people for whom the beginning is the end of Oedipus and the end of theatre" (411; italics in original). In other words, psychoanalysis had to wait to be "created" by someone (a Jew) whose dramaturgy of repression would mean "the end of Oedipus" as "the Greek function of truth."

As in "Beyond Representation," what is at stake in Lyotard's "Jewish Oedipus" (with the concept of a "Jewish Oedipus" now revealing itself as Lyotard's own version of the Derridean "jewgreek") is the anxiety of a "crisis in psychoanalysis" in France. The "crisis" in question is that theatre has become a kind of "derealized" allegory of repression that can be revitalized only through the drama of *affect* as immediate presentation *(Darstellung).* For Lyotard it is not necessary to *wait* (as in "waiting" for Hamlet to recognize his own patricidal desire, or "waiting" for the origin of psychoanalysis) in order for affect (libido, desire) to manifest itself. If, for Lyotard, there is a "crisis in psychoanalysis" in France, it is because what he describes as "the infiltration of clinical thought by tragic themes" has for too long been dominated by repression, rather than affect. In the final analysis, one wonders if Lyotard's privileging of affect over repression may be a subtler way of confessing anxiety that psychoanalysis as a drama of deferral—a "waiting game," a waiting for the "dimension of non-fulfillment"—can only, in the end, reveal its inherently "Jewish" origins.

If we remember from the opening of this chapter that at least one influence on Lyotard's privileging of affect is Lévinas's concept of trauma, then we can conclude this section on Lyotard's "crisis in psychoanalysis" by reviewing some of the strange consequences that accrue when Judaism is made "accessible" to postmodernism, before then moving to a third essay by Lyotard, "Figure Foreclosed." As we have seen, Lévinas argues that subjectivity has its (non)origin in a trauma that "prevents its own representation," such that in the wake of trauma, after the Other has issued the command "Be obligated," all that is left is the trace of the Other's departure: the subject is now "hostage" to the Other. But for Lyotard, the trauma that results from the command "Be obligated" has not just an ethical, but also an affective imperative, such that he seems intrigued not so much with the *après-coup* as with the *coup* of trauma. For Lyotard, a "theatrics" of trauma would "prevent its own representation": it would constitute the theatre of shock, disruption, formlessness. Extrapolating from Lévinas's privileging of ethics over ontology, and of the Talmudic "Do before you understand," Lyotard argues (in *Just Gaming*) that obligation "is not a question of first understanding": in "Jewish Oedipus," *Hamlet* represents "the end of theatre" because the protagonist *forgets* (represses) the affective immediacy of trauma and patricidal desire. For Lyotard, Hamlet is quintessentially "Lévinasian" in "knowing himself dispossessed of origin." But also for Lyotard, Hamlet may be too much like Moses' followers in his forgetting to recognize his patricidal desire. Relying on a Lévinasian concept of trauma that "prevents its own representation" as a means of privileging the theatrics of his own immanent affect, Lyotard seemingly nuances Hamlet's version of "difficult freedom" as too Freudian in its aesthetic form—that is, not "properly" traumatized, shocked, *affect*-ed.

And what of the (forgotten) figure of Moses within this context of the affective immediacy of patricidal desire? In the final analysis, is he also incompletely *affect*-ed? If it has seemed too speculative here to speak of Lyotard's anxiety over the "Jewish" origins of psychoanalysis, let us now move to a third essay, "Figure Foreclosed," where Lyotard's call, in "Beyond Representation" and "Jewish Oedipus," for an aesthetics of affect (over a re-presentational repression) resurfaces as an explicit engagement with the "Jewish" origins of psychoanalysis—in the form of a sustained analysis of *Moses and Monotheism* we could interpret as picking up where "Jewish Oedipus" leaves off. In his analysis Lyotard refuses Judaism (a topic broached by way of Freudian psychoanalysis) the status even of a religion of "repression"; the result is that the figure of the Jew is even further distanced from Lyotard's privileged concept of affect.

In "Figure Foreclosed," Lyotard foregrounds Freud's own ambivalence about the "Jewish" origins of psychoanalysis in *Moses and Monotheism* (for instance, Freud's intention to ponder the psychic origins of Judaism) when he claims that "it is indeed Freudian psychoanalysis which Freud is psychoanalysing in *Moses*."[26] Thus Lyotard announces his intention to draw up "an accurate clinical picture of the Jewish religion" (94) — in effect, a psychoanalyzing of Freud's psychoanalyzing of psychoanalysis itself, a project he hopes can provide a clearer insight into the relationship between psychoanalysis and Judaism. In Lyotard's assessment, Judaism is not just an "obsessional neurosis" (as Freud himself characterized religious observance); rather, it suffers from the pathology of psychosis itself: Judaism is the religion not of repression, but of foreclosure *(Verwerfung)*. Psychoanalysis inherits from Judaism a "symptomatic" overestimation of the figure of the father, and thus, because Judaism is "a religion exclusively centered on the father, it is an obstacle to the full development of rationality" (70). In Judaism, claims Lyotard, castration is foreclosed, the possibility of female mediation is excluded, and a disastrous overestimation of the father occurs. The result of these foreclosures is, as we have seen, the phenomenon of the forgotten patricide: "If castration becomes the object of foreclosure . . . , then it is impossible to admit to having killed God, and it is as though the murder had never taken place" (96). (In retrospect, in "Jewish Oedipus" we can see that Lyotard's Hamlet had already inhabited an obscure threshold between neurosis and psychosis. Whereas, early in his essay, Hamlet is merely "neurotic" [399], by the essay's conclusion Lyotard describes the play as structured "by a parricidal or an incestuous compulsion foreclosed" [409–10].) For Lyotard, Judaism (at least, the Judaism configured in *Moses and Monotheism*) is where the psychic operation of forgetting becomes, in effect, psychotic. In Heidegger's reading of Oedipus, patricide eventually yields to (Greek) self-consciousness, (Greek) "authenticity." But in Lyotard's reading of Moses' murder by his Jewish followers, the forgotten patricide becomes nothing less than the origin of cultural psychosis. For that matter, Lyotard concludes his essay with a diagnosis of Freud's own Jewishness as "symptomatic": "is it not because Freud himself is a product of that peculiarly Jewish predominance of the father that he failed to recognize these indices as an invitation to elaborate a very different construction [of Judaism]?" (106).

Moreover, in "Figure Foreclosed," where Judaism is conceived as the religion not of repression but of psychosis, the Jews become distanced more than ever from Lyotard's privileged concept of affect. Specifically, Lyotard interprets the figure of the Jew as the result of an initially affective moment that degenerates into guilt. Lyotard's privileging of affect is influenced by Lévinas's concept of trauma as an "arepresentational" *coup* in the wake of the command "Be obligated." In "Figure Fore-closed," Lyotard uses Lévinas's *Quatres lectures talmudiques* as, in his own summary, "a great wealth of information" (94) for his hypothesis that, in the figure of the Jew, psychosis and guilt are linked: "God gives no sign and no means of fulfillment. He chooses the Jewish people . . . [but] what is chosen is not a fulfillment, a place, or an earthly origin, but a discursive position. God gives nothing" (97). For Lyotard, the Jews, as the "chosen people," seem "chosen" only for the "discursive po-sition" of guilt: "Guilt is an essential feature of the Mosaic religion" (99); and the "Judaic ego," as he phrases it, "is guilty of never having come to terms with the law" (101)—which is why the "Judaic ego" in-habits an obscure psychic threshold between guilt (obligation to the law) and psychosis (the foreclosure of castration). For Lyotard, the Lévinasian, traumatic immediacy of an "affection" by the other of obligation fades imperceptibly into the after-effect of guilt. And thus in Lyotard's argument, Lévinasian ethics (not without some irony) be-comes the means for a privileging of affect over Jewish guilt. Because "God gives nothing" to the Jews, for Lyotard the cultural history of Ju-daism enacts the "fall" into guilt and psychosis.

Borch-Jacobsen's "The Unconscious, Nonetheless"

With Lyotard's analysis of Moses and "the Jews" in "Figure Foreclosed," we have almost arrived at the threshold of *Heidegger and "the jews."* But before we cross this threshold, let us return to one of the central con-cerns of our last chapter: the "crisis of psychoanalysis" in France when it attempts to revisit affect as one of the cornerstones of psychoanalysis.

If French Heideggerianism continues to demonstrate anxieties about the "Jewish origins" of psychoanalysis, it may be because affect is, ironically, the "return of the repressed" in recent French efforts to configure a postmodern psychoanalysis. Lyotard's privileging of an affective immediacy and immanence over the delays, displacements, and deferrals of repression can begin to sound all too familiar if we also remember Michel Henry's *Généalogie de la psychanalyse* and its post-Lacanian return to affect as the "limit-question of psychoanalysis." As we have seen, Henry, working in the interstices of Freud's incompletely theorized opposition between affect and repression, also perceives a kind of "crisis of psychoanalysis" in France, a "crisis" that has for too long ignored pure affectivity as the origin of the psyche itself. Before moving to *Heidegger and "the jews"* (as perhaps one of the most over-determined outcomes of current French philo-Semitic discourse), I turn to Mikkel Borch-Jacobsen's *The Emotional Tie* and its rigorous critique, in a chapter intriguingly titled "The Unconscious, Nonetheless," of Henry's return to affect—a critique I feel provides a crucial background for a further understanding of what is at stake when Lyotard moves from (uppercase) "Judaism" to the lowercase "jews" as part of his own return to affect.

In the complex juncture of philosophy and psychoanalysis that constitutes so much of his writing, Borch-Jacobsen readily acknowledges his indebtedness to French Heideggerianism, namely the work of Lacoue-Labarthe and Nancy. Like them, Borch-Jacobsen insists, in his *The Emotional Tie*, on a return to Freud's *Group Psychology and the Analysis of the Ego* as "an ineluctable text" for any understanding of the intersection between politics and the psyche. And also like Lacoue-Labarthe and Nancy, Borch-Jacobsen argues that Freud's theory of identification and the social bond "causes it to overflow the political framework in which Freud tries to hold it."[27] Despite Freud's attempts to posit a subject at the origin of the Political, the Freudian field of *Gefühlsbindung*, claims Borch-Jacobsen, is highly unstable—primarily because Freud oscillated between *Gefühlsbindung* as a nonlibidinal, primary bond of identification (in which the subject wants to *be* someone) and as a libidinal object bond (in which the subject wants to *have* someone). In Borch-Jacobsen's view, the result of Freud's impasse is that we must further problematize his subject as the "origin" of the Political.

In chapter 3 we saw that for Lacoue-Labarthe and Nancy it is Freud's forgotten concept of affect (as it is for Lyotard) that can serve as the "royal road" to a reassessment of the origin of the political subject in Freud. But despite his indebtedness to their work, Borch-Jacobsen is seemingly not so eager to follow this affective "royal road" to the Political. In *The Emotional Tie*, Borch-Jacobsen praises Henry's and Lacoue-Labarthe and Nancy's returns to Freudian affect, but he insists that such returns should proceed with caution: they should be contingent on a detailed consideration of *why* Freud encountered such difficulties in theorizing the difference between affect and repression. Without such an understanding, implies Borch-Jacobsen, it is simply too easy to appropriate affect for one's own political and philosophical agenda—and this premature ease of appropriation may be the *real* "crisis of psychoanalysis" in France.

Henry views the ambiguous relationship between Freudian repression and affect as nothing less than the "limit-question of psychoanalysis." *Pace* Lacan, for Henry the unconscious is not the "fading" of the subject in aphanisis; rather, it is an auto-affective "feeling-oneself" *("se-sentir")* — a "feeling oneself" *in feeling* as a kind of (anti-Heideggerian) Being that never withdraws from itself. In his chapter "The Unconscious, Nonetheless," Borch-Jacobsen supports Henry's opposition to Lacan insofar as, in his view, French psychoanalysis, for too long limited to linguistics and to the itinerary of the signifier, has become "bloodless" (146). But Borch-Jacobsen is also highly ambivalent about Henry's "return" to Freudian affect, particularly his insistence on defining affect as "the unconsciousness of pure consciousness itself"; in other words, by means of his premise that an affect is never unconscious, Henry has done nothing less than collapse the distinction between consciousness and the unconscious. As we shall see, Borch-Jacobsen is concerned that, in the process, Henry has created a "psychoanalysis" that deconstructs psychoanalysis itself.

Henry argues that a "major error of Freudianism" (again, the underlying anxiety of insuring that psychoanalysis in France is indeed *French*) is Freud's contention that an instinct is known only by its manifesting itself as an affective state. In "The Unconscious," Freud argues that the instinct, or drive, is represented by a *Vorstellung*, which itself gets repressed. As Henry interprets it, this process of displacement from instinct to affect means that the unconscious, "originally representation's other, now contains representation" (298). Henry (like Lyotard) wants not an affect of displacement, but an affect of immanence that *presents* the drive immediately, without mediation and without representation. In a lengthy and carefully crafted critique of *Généalogie de la psychanalyse*, Borch-Jacobsen argues that Henry has allowed himself the freedom to make this interpretive move because of Freud's provocative but easily misunderstood axiom from his essay "The Unconscious" that "there are no unconscious affects" — meaning, as Borch-Jacobsen cautions, not that the affect is never unconscious, but rather that because the representation (the *Vorstellung*) of the drive to which the affect was originally attached gets *repressed,* we are left with affect as what Henry otherwise describes as "the unconsciousness of pure consciousness itself." As Borch-Jacobsen points out, "From then on, it is easy for Henry to challenge as artificial and 'speculative' the distinction between the drive and the affect supposed to represent it" (139). Henry's too liberal interpretation of Freud's axiom is that affect is a kind of pure and immediate consciousness such that, in his radical conclusion, "the unconscious does not exist" (384).

But Borch-Jacobsen reminds us of "the unconscious, nonetheless," and he does so through a return to *The Ego and the Id* as a key text for understanding some of the fundamental, non-negotiable principles of repression as a psychic operation. Specifically, Borch-Jacobsen refers to the beginning of *The Ego and the Id,* where Freud argues that the neurotic has no knowledge, no "con-science," of his or her own repression. This non-knowledge of one's own repression, in Borch-Jacobsen's view, does not mean "*reabsorption* of the unconscious into consciousness," but rather that the unconscious "invades consciousness itself" (142). The unconscious "invades" consciousness, such that the affect "exists only as accomplished, according to a 'wish fulfillment' that knows no delay . . . between the so-called 'wish' and its execution" (145). Thus affect is not an immediate process of "feeling oneself," but is rather the neurotic's indirect process of "not knowing oneself": affect is the neurotic's unconsciousness of his or her own resistance. What Henry fails to see is that the unconscious does not *want* to be discovered; thus, "consciousness" originates not in the immanence of affect, but in the neurotic's refusal (like Hamlet) to remember the *real cause* of the affect. As Borch-Jacobsen reminds us, because for Freud affect is an obstacle to the becoming conscious of what has been repressed, it is a misinterpretation to insist, as Henry does, on an "opposition" between consciousness and the unconscious. *Pace* Henry, who claims that affect is the experiencing of oneself in a pure "ipseity," or the affection of self by the self, Borch-Jacobsen emphasizes the unknown, indeed unknowable, dimension of affect: the affect (a nervous laugh, a cough, a sigh) is visible and accomplished, but the neurotic does not *feel* the affect and does not even *know* that he or she is experiencing an affect. The seeming "immanence" of affect (the fact that the affect exists "only as accomplished") is the ruse of repression. As what Borch-Jacobsen calls "the peculiar *cogito* of the unconscious" (145), the affect "is not experienced by the subject . . . and yet it acts, it exercises its cruel effects" (148). In the final analysis, it is a matter of "the unconscious, nonetheless."

"The Jews" — or, Lyotard's "Affect, Nonetheless"

For Borch-Jacobsen, any close scrutiny of an originary affect will always already be a powerful reminder of the *effects* of "the unconscious, nonetheless." Borch-Jacobsen's critique of Henry's "immanent" affect is grounded in the axiom that affect is merely the "cruel *effect*" of repression. With the caveat of "the unconscious, nonetheless" echoing in our minds, let us finally turn to *Heidegger and "the jews"* and the ways in which Borch-Jacobsen's critique of Henry can shed further light on how Lyotard chooses to configure his concept of "the jews." Lyotard's concept of "the jews" is the point at which psychoanalysis, philosophy, and the conflicting impulses of French philo-Semitism converge with the most complexity in the post-Holocaust "discourse of the Jew." And the concept of "the jews" is not unlike Henry's interpretation of affect as an immanent process of "feeling oneself feeling." Like Henry, Lyotard, in an effort to theorize an affect that is not dependent on representation, "forgets" the psychic process of repression itself. Moreover, encrypted within his enigmatic concept of "the jews" is Lyotard's earlier engagement with the "Jewish origins" of psychoanalysis. Thus, "the jews" might best be interpreted as Lyotard's desire for the "jewish" origins of psychoanalysis — that is, a (more properly French Heideggerian, postmodern) psychoanalysis whose cornerstone is not the deferrals of repression (or, for that matter, the foreclosures of psychosis), but rather the immanence of affect.

In this sense, then, it is almost as if Lyotard seeks to atone for his earlier essay "Figure Foreclosed" and its thesis that Judaism is the religion of psychosis. We will remember that in this essay, Lyotard's (decidedly uppercase) Jews embodied a religion of foreclosure where guilt (brought on by the forgotten patricide) lost its affective immediacy, threatening to become "psychotic." As I mentioned in an earlier note, Lyotard came to regret the potential misunderstandings embedded in his "diagnosis" of Judaism as psychotic. Thus in *Heidegger and "the jews,"* where Moses' Jewish followers modulate into the more tropic "jews" of postmodern alienation — a concept that, Lyotard insists, "is neither a figure nor a political (Zionism), religious (Judaism), or philosophical (Jewish philosophy) subject that I put forward under this name" (3) — Jewish "forgetting" becomes valorized not as the cause of guilt, but rather as the privileged site of affect itself. The concept of "the jews," then, can be interpreted as an explicitly philo-Semitic reconfiguration of, among other things, the "Jewish Question" within psychoanalysis.

Moreover, in its broadest scope, *Heidegger and "the jews"* is an inherently psychoanalytic endeavor insofar as it constitutes Lyotard's elliptical attempt to "mourn" Heidegger's involvement with German National Socialism. And, for that matter, Lyotard's concept of "the jews," in addition to serving as a memorial to Jewish trauma "after Auschwitz," also exposes the limitations of (Heideggerian) philosophy itself: somewhere between *The Differend* and *Heidegger and "the jews,"* the affect of the differend (and its implied ethical "urge") has modulated into the lower case "jews" as a refutation of Heidegger. But the lower case "jews" also serve as a continuation of Lyotard's ongoing and highly complex engagement with Freudian repression.

In *Heidegger and "the jews,"* Lyotard's central concern shifts from *The Differend*'s "unphraseable" to the "unrepresentable" as the basis for a postmodern mnemonics. Not unlike Lyotard's earlier concept of *figure* as that which can be neither remembered nor forgotten, "the jews" are a deconstruction of memory itself, of memory as that which can only paradoxically result in forgetting—and, by implication, a critique of histories that "forget" by presenting themselves too confidently as memorializing narratives. Thus the ethical imperative implicit in Lyotard's characterization of the differend as an affective something that *must* "be allowed to institute idioms" reappears in *Heidegger and "the jews,"* with the ethical verb "must" (and its influences via Kant and Lévinas) bodied forth in the form of the lower case "jews" as his central trope for the failure of memory.

As we saw in chapter 2, Derrida, in his *Mémoires: For Paul de Man,* analyzes the psychoanalytic concept of mourning (or, more accurately, what he calls "true mourning") as that which must become aware of its own impossibility. For Lyotard, the lower case "jews" are just such a Derridean site of "true mourning" that always already knows it has "forgotten." As the memory of what cannot be represented, as a tradition "where the forgotten remembers that it is forgotten,"[28] Lyotard's "jews" are a reminder to the reader that both memory and forgetting are elusive categories. In an explicit protest against Western anti-Semitism, Lyotard argues that "the jews" are "the irremissable in the West's movement of remission and pardon. They cannot be domesticated . . . they cannot be integrated, converted, or expelled" (22). For Lyotard, what keeps "the jews" in a perpetual state of exile is the Law—the legal

Other to whose ethical imperative there can be no adequate response. As the heir to his earlier concept of the Lévinasian "pole of the addressee," Lyotard's "jews" are obligated before the Law: they are a "simple people . . . taken hostage by a voice" (21). If the "jews" cannot be "interpreted, converted, or expelled," it is because their imposed silence before the Law renders them not (as in "Figure Foreclosed") "guilty," but rather (like the Law itself) "unrepresentable." Unlike the (upper case) Jews of his "Figure Foreclosed," who were rendered (merely) guilty by obligation, Lyotard's (lower case) "jews," because they are the intractable fact of obligation before the Law, become the site of ethics itself—that is, the ethical as a "thinking" of the forgotten (a kind of Derridean "true mourning") that should replace Heideggerian Being, or ontology.

As Lyotard argues, the West "represses" what "the jews" always already "remember that they have forgotten": the West's repression of "the jews." It then post-dates the more authentic (the more *archaic*) affective space of "the jews" as a thinking of the forgotten—that is, the traumatizing fact of obligation. Lyotard implies the following irony: even as Heidegger critiques the West's forgetting of Being, so also does the philosopher himself "forget" that the "forgotten" is not Being but the (Kantian, Lévinasian) fact of obligation before the Law. In the quasi-psychoanalytic discourse of Lyotard's postmodernism, then, ontology is founded on a "repression" of ethics, of the "older" truth of affect as the (forgotten) fact of obligation. The lower case "jews" become a trope for an "archaic" affect that allows Lyotard to argue that ethics (as his own version of *l'histoire juive*) is superior to ontology. It is as if Lyotard is claiming that "in the beginning" was affect. But it is not only German philosophy that Lyotard (like all French Heideggerians) would like to transform into something more "authentically French": it may also be (Freudian) psychoanalysis.[29]

"The jews" are an inherently psychoanalytic concept not just because they trace the lineaments of a postmodern memory. "The jews" are not just the embodiment of "ethics" (as the unforgettable obligation before the Law), but also the embodiment of "affect" itself. As Lyotard asserts, "with 'the jews,' it is a question of something like the unconscious affect of which the Occident does not want any knowledge" (26). For Lyotard, affect originates in trauma (the traumatizing fact of obligation before the Law); and his portrayal of "the jews" as "taken hostage by a voice" has been largely influenced by Lévinas's trauma that "prevents its own representation" (as well as Kant's portrayal of the Jewish God as unapproachable and radically other). Hence one of Lyotard's major arguments in *Heidegger and "the jews,"* renewing his aesthetic preoccupations of the 1970s, is that "the jews" are a "forgetting that thwarts all representation" (5).

At this point, we can be reminded of Michel Henry's interpretation of affect as a process of "feeling oneself feeling" (not to mention being reminded of the "crisis" of French psychoanalysis when it attempts its "returns" to Freudian affect). Much like Henry's affect (which he interprets as the very foundation of representation), Lyotard's "jews" embody what he calls an unconscious without "representational formations" (12). In order to arrive at an unconscious without "representational formations," an unconscious as pure *Darstellung* that does not belong to the realm of representation (or, for that matter, repression), Lyotard (unlike Henry, who engages in an overt polemic against Freud) openly embraces Freudian psychoanalysis as an ally for further configuring his affective "jews," turning in particular to Freud's elusive concept of *Nachträglichkeit* and its theorizing of psychical trauma. It is perhaps inevitable that Freud's *Nachträglichkeit* and its unconscious temporality that inhabits an obscure threshold between a "too early" and a "too late" would be appropriated by a postmodern imaginary that is seeking a "return" to trauma. But Lyotard's engagement with Freud's enigmatic concept results in a "forgetting" of repression as the cornerstone of Freudian psychoanalysis—a "forgetting" that, even as it attempts a kind of postmodern psychoanalysis (a quest, as it were, to uncover the "jewish" origins of psychoanalysis), traces its own version of a "crisis in psychoanalysis" in France.

Let us turn to Freud in order to determine exactly how Lyotard chooses to approach the concept of the unconscious differently. Freud first discusses *Nachträglichkeit* as the "origin" of psychical trauma in his *Project for a Scientific Psychology:* "we invariably find that memory is repressed which has only become a trauma by *deferred action.*"[30] The unconscious temporality of *Nachträglichkeit* problematizes the status of the traumatic event as originary; thus, Freud argues that the trauma is constituted as such only in belated activations of the event (such as narrations or dreams). The event "occurs" (and the traumatized subject reconstitutes its "meaning") only *retroactively,* through deferral. The curious temporal logic of *Nachträglichkeit* enacts a dialectic between forgetting and a latency that insures that the trauma will emerge—if only in deferral: the trauma, where shock is replaced by the (affective) symptom, exists only as always already repressed.

Lyotard appropriates Freud's *Nachträglichkeit* as an opportunity to imagine "an originary repressed that is unrepresentable" (15). But unlike Freud, who suggests that the "originary" event may never have taken place, Lyotard emphasizes an initial moment of traumatic shock during which the subject experiences an originary "excitation," or disturbance — a shock that cannot be articulated or synthesized: "It is thus a shock, since it 'affects' a system, but a shock of which the shocked is unaware, and which the apparatus (the mind) cannot register in accordance with and in its internal physics" (12). The subject is "affect"-ed, but the mind does not comprehend because the subject is not prepared to deal with the disturbance. In the space of this disarticulation, claims Lyotard, is affect. The subject experiences a shock, an affect of which he or she is unaware. But the important point for Lyotard (and here we are at the heart of his reconfiguration of *Nachträglichkeit*) is that *something has occurred* in this moment of trauma: a pure existence of affect as a "presencing" of its own presence — or, in this case (to echo Borch-Jacobsen), the *affect*, nonetheless. Freud emphasizes that the (affective) symptom exists only as always already repressed. But Lyotard captures the shock of this unrepresentable moment in a freeze frame. The traumatic shock is no longer that which is constituted in/by/through deferral (that is, it is no longer *après-coup*); rather, it is a pure event (or *coup*) unto itself: "This excitation need not be 'forgotten,' repressed according to representational procedures, nor through *acting out*. . . . Its 'excess' (of quantity, of intensity) exceeds the excess that gives rise . . . to the unconscious and the preconscious" (12). In Lyotard's affective "excess" that "exceeds the excess of the unconscious," the *après-coup* of Lévinas's trauma as a subjectivity anterior to itself has modulated, almost imperceptibly (though no less significantly), into a moment *before repression,* and Lyotard has reinterpreted Freudian *Nachträglichkeit* to theorize "the jews" as a moment before the affective immediacy of trauma is forgotten.

In this moment of an "excess" that "exceeds the excess of the unconscious," we would do well to remember Borch-Jacobsen's caveat of "the unconscious, nonetheless." Though seemingly in agreement with Freud, Lyotard's interpretation of *Nachträglichkeit* tends to elide the crucial point for Freud that it is the drama of deferral that insures the trauma will be re-presented later *without the subject recognizing it.* For

Freud, it is important to bear in mind that the "originary" affect exists as always already represented (as always already *repressed*), not as an excitation that, in Lyotard's conception, "need not be 'forgotten.'"[31] In *Studies in Hysteria,* Freud reemphasizes the temporal enigmas of *Nachträglichkeit* first outlined in his *Project for a Scientific Psychology*:

> But the causal relation between the determining psychical trauma and the hysterical phenomenon [the symptom] is not of a kind implying that the trauma merely acts like an *agent provocateur* in releasing the symptom, which thereafter leads an independent existence. . . . We must presume rather that the psychical trauma — or more precisely the memory of the trauma (what is traumatic, properly speaking, is not the event which we incorrectly call the psychical trauma, but the memory) — acts like a foreign body which long after its entry must be continued to be regarded as an agent that is still at work.[32]

To foreground "the unconscious, nonetheless" is to remember that trauma is always already a memory: it is not an *agent provocateur* leading to the symptom, but the (after)effect of memory playing itself out in deferral. For Freud, it is impossible to talk about a trauma without also talking about the symptom that *represents the memory* of the trauma.[33] Trauma, in other words, is involved in a play of "deceit": after the traumatic "first" event, the symptom appears (retroactively) as the sign of the neurotic's non-"con-science" of his or her own repression. After all, as Borch-Jacobsen reminds us in his critique of Henry, the unconscious does not *want* to be discovered.

The affect, nonetheless . . . ? This would appear to be the goal of Lyotard's appropriation of Freud's *Nachträglichkeit*. As we have seen, for Lyotard, "the jews" are "something like the unconscious affect of which the Occident does not want any knowledge." If the Occident "does not want any knowledge of 'the jews,'" then it could be argued that Lyotard "does not want any knowledge" of the possibility that the unconscious does not *want* to be discovered: he wants no "knowledge" of repression — deferral, delay, waiting. With the "unconscious affect" of "the jews," we now find ourselves repositioned within the affective aesthetics of "Beyond Representation" and "Jewish Oedipus," where Lyotard calls for a dramaturgy in which (unlike Hamlet's "non-fulfillment of his patricidal desire" that anticipates the "origin" of Freudian psychoanalysis as something for which it was necessary to *wait*) one does not have to "wait" for desire to manifest itself. Lyotard's critique in "Jewish Oedipus" of an "infiltration of clinical thought by tragic themes," which have for too long been dominated by (Freudian? Jewish?) repression rather than affect, results, in *Heidegger and "the jews,"* in an attempt to overcome Freud's "foreign body" (as the deferred memory of trauma) and its reminder that the unconscious does not *want* to be discovered. In short, in *Heidegger and "the jews,"* where an affective "excess" in turn "exceeds the excess that gives rise to the unconscious," Lyotard seeks to overcome "the unconscious, nonetheless." If the Occident "does not want any knowledge" of affect (as Lyotard's own "jewish" origins for psychoanalysis), it could also be said that Lyotard "does not want any knowledge" of repression as the "Jewish" origin of psychoanalysis—which for Lyotard is, after all, the *real* reason there is a "crisis of psychoanalysis" in France.

Postmodern "Sublime"

Somewhere in the ineffable (and itself *nachträglich*?) space between the upper case "Jews" and the lower case "jews"[34] is the space of French philo-Semitism's own trauma as it participates in the ongoing French pastime of "imagining the Jew." In *Heidegger and "the jews,"* what we come to discover is that for philo-Semitism no less than for anti-Semitism, the figure of the Jew serves as an excess that cannot be represented, the site of a traumatic incomprehensibility. And now the pertinent question becomes: to what extent is Lyotard's current postmodern "discourse of 'the jews'" less an ethico-philosophical than an aesthetic project? To what extent are Lyotard's lower case "jews" to be interpreted not so much as a "sublime object of ideology," but rather as a kind of "ideological object of the sublime"?[35] Certainly one of Lyotard's central preoccupations throughout his career has been the Kantian sublime as a kind of "aesthetics of shock." In his essay "The Sublime and the Avant-Garde," where his project is to revitalize the (modernist) aesthetics of the avant-garde for a postmodern era, Lyotard alludes to Kant's designation of the sublime as *dargestellt* (something that cannot be shown or represented). The sublime is a kind of "excess" of representation whose aesthetics are indeterminate: Lyotard's sublime is, much like Lacan's *plus-de-jouir*, "a pleasure mixed with pain, a pleasure that comes from pain."[36]

Because of this paradoxical "pleasure that comes from pain," it is only a small step for Lyotard to configure the lower case "jews" as a new version of the Kantian sublime. As its own kind of traumatic "excess" that resists representation, the "unconscious affect" of "the jews" can perhaps best be interpreted as a quasi-psychoanalytic occasion for Lyotard to resume his discourse of the sublime in a new, post-Holocaust idiom. Hence, it is not entirely surprising when, in *Heidegger and "the jews,"* Lyotard writes, "The sublime such as Kant analyzes it in *Critique of Judgment* offers . . . some traits analogous to those of the unconscious affect" (31). For Lyotard, we are engulfed by the sublime only when there is an excess the mind cannot handle: "That is why the sublime has no consideration for form, why it is an 'unform'" (32) — that is, an aesthetic version of an "unconscious affect." What we discover, then, is that Lyotard's insistence on "the jews" as the "unrepresentable" may have less to do with a "mourning" for Western anti-Semitism than with his ongoing celebration of the sublime as that which refuses to let itself be inscribed in the "aesthetic memory" of the West. As an "unform," as an "absence" of form, "the jews" have all along been pointing to "the aesthetics of shock" that constitutes Lyotard's sublime.

In his philo-Semitic configuring of "the jews," Lyotard has clearly been influenced by Kant's and Lévinas's Jewish God as the unapproachable, unrepresentable, and radical other. But in the final analysis, we are left wondering if in Lyotard's philo-Semitic discourse of "the jews" as a sublime "unform" (much as in the philo-Semitic concept of Lacoue-Labarthe's "caesura"), we can detect an encrypted anxiety that deserves investigation. If there *is* an incomplete working through in Lyotard's discourse of "the jews," is it because "the jews" are more Hegelian than Kantian? And if this is the case, what is the inadvertent outcome of Lyotard's persistent forging of such an intimate link between psychoanalysis and "the jews"? As we have seen throughout this study, post-Holocaust engagements with *la question juive* virtually always lead to an aesthetic meditation on the relationship between tragedy and Judaism (a meditation that serves as one of *the* constitutive repetition compulsions of French philo-Semitism). And thus, almost predictably, in *Heidegger and "the jews"* Lyotard renews his contention, earlier elaborated in *The Differend,* that the Jews are excluded from the fulfillment of an "Athenian 'beautiful death.'" At one point he remarks that "unconscious affect does not give rise to tragedy. 'The jews' are not tragic. They are not heroes. It is not by chance that [Elie] Wiesel's 'testimony' is that of a child" (28). Here it is important to observe that in the midst of his philo-Semitic and affective expressions of sympathy for the suffering of the young Wiesel in Auschwitz and Buchenwald, Lyotard's discourse of "the jews"—who are now (despite his earlier insistence that "the jews" are not a "nation," a "politics," or a "religion") synonymous with the real, historical Jews of the Holocaust—ends up recapitulating a neo-Hegelian aesthetics that has encrypted within it an exclusion of the Jew. At the point at which Lyotard's "aesthetics of shock" meets the Holocaust, the result is a Hegelian *Abscheu,* or non-tragic "horror."

This postmodern linkage of Lyotard's "aesthetics of shock" and Hegelian *Abscheu* has, in turn, some major consequences for any study of the encrypted anxieties of the "Jewish origins" of psychoanalysis. Lyotard's reconfiguration of the Freudian unconscious—which is necessary, as we have seen, for the *Dasein* of his affect to become manifest—has been inadvertently anticipated by Hegel's rejection of the "unconscious symbolics" of Egyptian "riddles." When in his *Phenomenology of Spirit* Hegel conceives of the Jew as "the insurmountable cleavage [*Kluft*] between the being of God and the being of men," he both anticipates and forecloses on the "origins" of psychoanalysis in repression; for, in Hegel's view, Jewish experience is "unhappy consciousness"—an (un)consciousness that is "inwardly divided in two, disunited consciousness" (158). Let us give Derrida, who, more than any figure in French postmodernism, has been consistently attuned to the encryptedness of *la question juive* in Western philosophy, the last word here. Hegel's foreclosure of the "discovery" of psychoanalysis (that is, the "discovery" that one's consciousness is always already divided by an unconscious) may be the "truth" of so much of Derrida's commentary on Hegel in *Glas.* If, for Hegel, the Jew is the failure of dialectic, if he is the loss of union and reconciliation, then, as Derrida suggests, the consequences for the later appropriation of psychoanalysis within French postmodernism are significant. Derrida poses a simple but resonant question: "Can repression be thought according to the dialectic?" (191). The answer to this question may already be encrypted in his title, *Glas*—"knell," "death knell," a tolling for the "end of metaphysics," to be sure, but maybe also a tolling for what Derrida hopes will be the end of "the end of philosophy's" resistance to repression.

Or should we give Borch-Jacobsen the last word here? In the midst of a critique of Lacan and his too persistent reliance on Hegelian dialectic as a premature resolution of the tensions between Freud's processes of primary and secondary identification, Borch-Jacobsen slips in a parenthetic remark, the significance of which, at the conclusion of my study, should be fully apparent: "(dialectic, as everyone knows, leaves piles of corpses behind)."[37] In response to the "crisis" of psychoanalysis in France (and in a decidedly post-Holocaust era that is enmeshed in an ongoing struggle to mourn the piles of corpses left behind by the "Final Solution"), we would do well to remember "the unconscious, nonetheless."

Afterword:
Back to the Future of
Psychoanalysis

Freud's Jewish Identity . . . Nonetheless

A recurring theme throughout this book has been the cultural phenomenon of a not fully worked through mourning in the French post-Holocaust and its ongoing ambivalence toward *judéité* as one of the key ideological bases of postmodernism. When the discourse of postmodernism turns to psychoanalysis for much of its polemical energy, it enacts a kind of *Trauerspiel* that has encrypted within it France's ongoing "inability to mourn" the Holocaust. Furthermore, this ambivalence toward *judéité* becomes perhaps most "symptomatic" at the point of French *sémitophilie*'s many persistent returns to the vexed question of the "Jewish origins" of psychoanalysis. In recent years, a number of French intellectuals have felt compelled to return, in particular, to *Moses and Monotheism* and the enigmas posed by Freud's renunciation of Moses' (and his own?) Jewishness — almost as if Freud's experiment in what he himself referred to as his "historical novel" had become earmarked as *the* canonical text of Freudian psychoanalysis.

For example, we can consider René Girard's analysis of how sacrifice (and, in his words, "the metamorphosis of reciprocal violence into generative violence by means of the murder of *somebody*") becomes thematized in both *Totem and Taboo* and *Moses and Monotheism*. Or we can turn to Jean-Joseph Goux's analysis of guilt in *Moses and Monotheism* and what he calls "the *jouissance* of sublimation" characterizing the act of murdering the father. Or we can think of Michel de Certeau, who views *Moses and Monotheism* as the paradigmatic text where "[t]he genesis of the historical figure of the Jew and the genesis of Freudian writing always intervene."[1]

What Seth Wolitz has referred to as France's preoccupation with "imagining the Jew" is compellingly demonstrated in these responses to *Moses and Monotheism*. Thus, much recent French intellectual thought

has become so engaged with *Moses and Monotheism,* so insistent on returning to it as the primal scene of the question of the "Jewish origins"
of psychoanalysis, that we could argue for Freud's text as a major contributor to the emergence of a Jewish-French psyche as the reflexive
(un)consciousness of (post)modernity. Moreover, we could argue that
it is French Heideggerianism in particular where these transferences
onto *Moses and Monotheism* have become the most overdetermined. For
example, as we saw in chapter 4, Lyotard's otherwise philo-Semitic concept of "the jews" has encrypted within it his ambivalent discussion of
Moses and Monotheism in such essays as "Jewish Oedipus" and "Figure
Foreclosed." Because of its status as an "encrypted" or "unconscious"
philosophy (an issue explored in the opening pages of chapter 3),
French Heideggerianism may be a particularly precarious discourse in
which to probe the issue of Freud's Jewish identity and his complex
motives for writing this "historical novel." In this afterword, I pick up
where my discussion of *Moses and Monotheism* left off, focusing on the
status of *Moses and Monotheism* "after Auschwitz" and the ways in which
some current responses to *Moses and Monotheism,* most notably by
Lacoue-Labarthe, Nancy, and Derrida, have positioned Freud's document at the complex juncture of psychoanalysis, postmodernism, and
the "Jewish question" after Auschwitz. Echoing René Major's posing
of "A Question, How indeed can one psychoanalyze after Auschwitz?,"
my afterword poses the question, How indeed can one talk about *Moses
and Monotheism* after Auschwitz? How, in other words, can so much
current postmodernism continue to fashion itself as a (pseudo)psycho-
analytic discourse while continuing not to acknowledge the melancholia encrypted in its compulsive "discourse of the Jew"?

In this context, then, we can move to a discussion of Lacoue-
Labarthe and Nancy's essay, "From Where Is Psychoanalysis Possible?"
(a sequel to their essay "The Unconscious Is Destructured like an
Affect") as the philo-Semitic, but nevertheless "symptomatic" site of
their version of a return to *Moses and Monotheism.*[2]

First, let us briefly rehearse the particulars of Lacoue-Labarthe and
Nancy's argument in "The Unconscious Is Destructured like an Affect,"
which is, in its broadest scope, a theorizing of Jewish identity in relationship to psychoanalysis. They argue that "the Jewish people do not
dream": they do not identify with the Father because (Jewish) identification with the Father is precariously constituted within the Father's
own dismemberment. For Lacoue-Labarthe and Nancy, Jewishness,

which they summarize as the *retrait* at the heart of subjectivity, is the deconstruction of psychoanalysis itself.

The authors' complex linkage between what they call the "exhaustion" of psychoanalysis and the figure of the Jew is renewed in their sequel essay, "From Where Is Psychoanalysis Possible?," a discussion of Freud's *Moses and Monotheism* that investigates the figure of the Jew as residing at the heart of psychoanalysis and its "discontents," and constitutes a rigorous renewal of their earlier focus on the "Jewish origins" of psychoanalysis. If the practice of deconstruction is, in its broadest scope, a critique of origins, then for Lacoue-Labarthe and Nancy, their project of deconstructing psychoanalysis necessarily involves a pushing against the question of the "Jewish origins" of psychoanalysis. "From where is psychoanalysis possible?" ask Lacoue-Labarthe and Nancy in their essay's title. In order to investigate this question further, Lacoue-Labarthe and Nancy (like Lyotard) turn to another question—Freud's famous question to Pfister: why did it have to be an atheist Jew who invented psychoanalysis? Thus Freud's own interrogation of the Jewish origins of psychoanalysis becomes, for Lacoue-Labarthe and Nancy, *the* "Jewish question" par excellence. From where is psychoanalysis possible? Their answer: "From where can it [psychoanalysis] construct itself and carry out its functions, if not from the space of Judaism. . . ?" (41). But their contention is that psychoanalysis also reaches its "limit" at the posing of another question: is psychoanalysis a "Jewish" science? Despite the well-known fact of Freud's own Jewish identity, the answer to this question, the authors suggest, does not readily present itself.

For Lacoue-Labarthe and Nancy, perhaps the most crucial text in the entire Freudian corpus is *Moses and Monotheism,* a historical account of the Jewish people that renders psychoanalysis, at its core, "an ethnology"—but one that "is struck from the outset with its own impossibility" (40). The authors claim the lesson of Freud's Egyptian Moses is that "the proper of the Jewish people is not properly Jewish" (42). For Lacoue-Labarthe and Nancy, this irony is the ultimate manifestation of one of the privileged topics of their earlier essay, "The Unconscious Is Destructured like an Affect"—the Jewish *Witz: Moses and Monotheism* is a "Jewish story" only insofar as it can "originate" with an *Egyptian* Moses.

For the authors, then, *Moses and Monotheism* is a sustained enactment of "the problematic of origin: the origin of the Jewish people" (45). In Judaism, recognition of the Father is belated, thus upsetting the logic of the origin. The origin of Judaism is the murder of Moses, and the identity of the Jewish people is constituted within his forgotten murder: "The Jews *themselves* did not kill Moses, for the simple reason that they did not preexist him; but those who killed Moses became the Jews" (49; italics in original). Jewish identity, therefore, does not really constitute an "identity": "because of this lack of subject, the Jews are carriers of the revelation that a social formation or political institution, whatever it may be (a people or a nation, to stay within Freud's terrain) is never capable of fulfilling itself as a subject" (50). At this point, we can recall Lacoue-Labarthe's earlier critique of mimesis in such essays as "Hölderlin and the Greeks," where he argues that the "logic" of mimesis points to an instability (a *désistement*) in any positing of identity by critiquing the ambition of German Idealism to revive an ancient Greece: "Greece itself does not exist. . . . The Greeks' proper is inimitable because it never took place." Even as, *pace* Winckelmann, there is no essential "Greekness," so also for Freud is there no essential or originary Jewishness.

For Lacoue-Labarthe and Nancy, the Jewish religion is precariously founded on the "return of the repressed": Moses the founder is killed, and the Jews are left with guilt—or, in an argument not dissimilar to the one in Lyotard's "Figure Foreclosed"—a "failure of recognition" that Jewish identity is "the paradoxically constitutive dis-sociation of human sociality" (55). The Jews "have remained religious, and the *re-ligio* is the very instance of identification and of identity" (55; italics in original). And with this observation, Lacoue-Labarthe and Nancy return to Freud's question to Pfister in an attempt to get to the heart of why, to paraphrase Freud, it was left to an *atheist* Jew to go beyond religion to the "founding" of psychoanalysis. For the authors, only an atheistic Freud could have perceived the "return of the repressed" as the *désistement* at the heart of Jewish identity. Psychoanalysis is (paradoxically) a *Jewish* science because Freud "did not let his own Jewish identity go unquestioned" (55): psychoanalysis "originates" in Freud's own perception of the *désistement* haunting Jewishness.

For the authors, Freud's attempt in *Moses and Monotheism* to theorize Jewish identity is why psychoanalysis is "impossible." But despite their deconstruction of psychoanalysis through a deconstructing of Freud's own "Jewish identity," and despite their implicit problematizing of any premature proclamation that psychoanalysis is indeed a "Jewish" science, Lacoue-Labarthe and Nancy choose, rather enigmatically, to conclude their essay with another question: "It remains, however, to ask what it means *to found*—a science, a practice, a school" (55; italics in original). Can the scientific domain effectively be dependent on something like an ethnic identity? The final sentence of their essay poses the question: "And just why did the figure of Moses haunt Freud to such a point?" (55).

The uncertain questioning of the essay's conclusion functions as a confession of the authors' concern that deconstructive discourse may *not*, after all, be the best way to probe for an answer to the question, Is psychoanalysis a "Jewish" science? Their conclusion points to a concern that deconstruction is not capable of telling us that the question may, in fact, be badly posed. Despite the deconstructive ease with which Lacoue-Labarthe and Nancy render Freud a kind of "*Juif désœuvré*" whose effacement of Moses' own Jewish origins marks the beginning of psychoanalysis as a "science," it is as if the authors, in their inconclusive conclusion, suspect that their tracing of the "exhaustion" of psychoanalysis has nevertheless not at all succeeded in evacuating the importance of Moses for Freud, has not at all succeeded in dispelling the fact that Freud's atheism still could not resist the enigmas of Moses. The authors' philo-Semitic ambition to defuse once and for all the provocative charge of the question "Is psychoanalysis a 'Jewish' science?," despite according with Freud's own strategic denials throughout his career that psychoanalysis possessed a Jewish "essence," still returns their essay squarely to the "question" of Freud's Jewish identity as an (auto)biographical intractability that their deconstructive *tour de force* cannot fully negotiate, but only abut against. The authors are still haunted by the question of "what it means *to found*": their deconstruction, in other words, cannot *dis*-originate the fact of Freud's Jewishness. Although their essay is constituted by a deconstructive *jouissance* unleashed by the paradox of Freud's desire in *Moses and Monotheism* to have an Egyptian Moses, it falters at the realization that the very subject matter of *Moses and Monotheism* was also prompted by Freud's return, late in his career, to Judaism. Despite their declaration of the "impossibility" of psychoanalysis, is it not the case that locating the origin of psychoanalysis within a Freudian identification with Moses may still be distinctly "possible"? Is psychoanalysis not a matter of Freud's Jewish identity . . . nonetheless?

Throughout his career, Lacoue-Labarthe in particular has characteristically used deconstruction to dismantle questions that can only lead to what he views as premature and misleading answers because the questions are badly posed. As discussed in chapter 3, Lacoue-Labarthe's sustained project in *Heidegger, Art and Politics,* for example, is to demonstrate how a question such as "Was Heidegger a Nazi?" is crudely phrased, and how its answer can only be approached deconstructively. Throughout their careers, both Lacoue-Labarthe and Nancy have argued that deconstruction must (almost heroically) intervene to "listen" properly to the question and prompt subtler rephrasings. In the case of what has seemingly become *the* constitutive question for an emergent Jewish-French psyche ("Is psychoanalysis a 'Jewish' science?"), Lacoue-Labarthe and Nancy seem to suggest that perhaps a better rephrasing of the question (given deconstruction's focus on the problematics of origin) might be "Can Judaism be a 'founding moment' for science?" But in their inconclusive conclusion to "From Where Is Psychoanalysis Possible?" the authors cannot get past another "originary" question: what is a "science"?

The Future of Psychoanalysis

Can the question "What is a 'science'?" lend itself to a deconstructive probing? The uncertain conclusion of Lacoue-Labarthe and Nancy's essay can return us yet again to Derrida and, in particular, his lengthy essay "Archive Fever," an extended meditation on *Moses and Monotheism,* written as if his overarching ambition were to pronounce the last word on this recent French compulsion to return to Freud's "historical novel" as the primal scene of the "Jewish question" in psychoanalysis. A central theme of Derrida's essay is the concept of the archive—in particular, psychoanalysis as a "general science" of the archive, psychoanalysis as a "science" insofar as it encompasses "everything that can happen to the economy of memory."[3] Thus Derrida's essay uncannily resumes Lacoue-Labarthe and Nancy's concluding question of "what it means *to found*—a science." Derrida chooses to approach the question temporally, such that his essay is also constituted as an extended meditation on the future, and on the complex ways in which the "origin" of psychoanalysis (or, more synecdochically, the "Freudian archive") is inexplicably bound up with its future: "What is at issue here is nothing less than the future, if there is such a thing: the future of psychoanalysis in its relationship to the future of science" (16). Picking up where Lacoue-Labarthe and Nancy left off, Derrida frames the question of the "origin" of psychoanalysis as an epistemological conundrum: how can we recognize the "origin" of psychoanalysis when we do not yet know what it will have been in the future?

We shall return to this question later. But Derrida, before further pursuit of this provocative linkage of psychoanalysis and the "question" of the future, cannot resist briefly reverting to the more familiar "question" of its past. Although, as he argues, traditionally a science "should be *intrinsically* independent of the singular archive of [its] history" (32; italics in original), in the case of psychoanalysis the archival question of its "Jewish origins" will ineluctably arise, like a repressed ghost, from the past. In what we could argue as French postmodernism's most rigorous attempt to probe the question of the origin, Derrida proposes, in effect, a prior "origin" for psychoanalysis, suggesting that we turn not to Sigmund Freud as its founder, but rather to the "arch-patriarch" Jakob Freud, Sigmund's father. If by the end of "From Where Is Psychoanalysis Possible?" Lacoue-Labarthe and Nancy's deconstruction of Jewish identity (as is typical of so much French philo-Semitic discourse) results in the real Jew being transformed into a privileged trope or signifier for the destabilized postmodern subject in a theoretical system that nevertheless persists in defining the Jew from without, then we could view Derrida's singling out of the importance of Jakob Freud for the "origins" of psychoanalysis as a move to return French Heideggerianism to the subject of real, historical Jews. And thus, in an attempt to accept the challenge of Lacoue-Labarthe and Nancy's question of "what it means *to found*," Derrida proposes the "founding" act of psychoanalysis as occurring in Vienna, in 1891, at the moment when the father Jakob presents the son Sigmund with an edition of the Ludwig Philippsohn Bible, inscribed with the father's Hebrew handwriting, on the occasion of his son's thirty-fifth birthday. Moreover, the significance of Jakob's gift of the bilingual Philippsohn Bible (with its extensive German commentary) is the possibility that its presentation as a gift should be viewed as, more accurately, a *re*-presentation, since Jakob had first given this copy of the Bible to Sigmund when the latter was just a child.

Derrida narrates that he was moved to identify this father's gift to the son as the "origin" of psychoanalysis after reading Yosef Hayim Yerushalmi's recent book *Freud's Moses: Judaism Terminable and Interminable* (referred to several times in the notes to chapter 4), an analysis of *Moses and Monotheism* whose final pages focus on the importance of

Freud's Philippsohn Bible in any consideration of his engagement with the figure of Moses throughout his career.[4] And indeed, after reading Yerushalmi's discussion one is led to conclude that the Philippsohn Bible, even more than *Moses and Monotheism,* could productively be viewed as *the* canonical text of psychoanalysis. With the presentation of this paternal gift, an "archive" originates at the moment Freud the son is ceremoniously reminded of his Jewish origins.

Viewed in the context of the Philippsohn Bible, Freud's very decision to undertake such a project as *Moses and Monotheism* becomes interpreted by Yerushalmi as the staging of an obedience to the father in the form of a return to the Bible — and for that matter, to Judaism itself. Because of Jakob (not the "tropic" Jew of so much French postmodern discourse, but a real, historical figure concerned about his son's disavowals of his own Jewish identity), Sigmund is reminded of his connection to Judaism; despite the son's disavowals, the father's gift of the Philippsohn Bible is a reminder that he cannot so readily cease being Jewish.

It is at this point that Derrida too announces a "gift": in his words, his essay "will thus naturally be dedicated" to Yerushalmi, whose narrative of Freud's receipt of the Philippsohn Bible may have served to recall Derrida to his *own* Jewish identity.

What Derrida finds most engaging about the final pages of Yerushalmi's analysis of *Moses and Monotheism* is the fact that they are structured as an apostrophe to the "ghost" of Freud himself, addressed with unabashed veneration as "Dear and most highly esteemed Prof. Freud." Yerushalmi's direct appeal to Freud in these final pages is nothing less than a kind of *mise en scène* designed to induce Freud to confess his Judaism. In Derrida's summary, Yerushalmi (in his own gesture of gift-giving) "wants also to give back to Freud his own competence, his own capacity to receive and thus to read the [father's] Hebrew inscription" in the Philippsohn Bible (28). Disturbed by such episodes in Freud's life as his courtship of Martha Bernays, during which, in his account, Freud "virtually bludgeons Martha into abandoning the Jewish rituals of her upbringing if she is to be his wife" (11), Yerushalmi, in Derrida's words, "clearly wants this [confession] to come from *Freud's mouth.* Freud must also say, in his own name . . . that psychoanalysis should honor itself for being a Jewish science. A performative by which he would as much determine science, psychoanalytic science, as the essence of Jewishness, if not of Judaism" (33; italics in original). Thus

Yerushalmi turns to the fate of psychoanalysis in the future: "Professor Freud, at this point I find it futile to ask whether, genetically or structurally, psychoanalysis is really a Jewish science; that we shall know, if it is at all knowable, only when much future work has been done. Much will depend, of course, on how the very terms *Jewish* and *science* are defined. Right now, leaving the semantic and epistemological questions aside, I want only to know whether *you* ultimately came to believe it to be so" (quoted in Derrida, 35; italics in original). From this specter of the "once and future Freud," Yerushalmi wants to know, in other words, if (in the future) Freud will have believed Judaism indeed to be "interminable." And regardless of how this specter of the "once and future Freud" might choose to answer such a question, in Derrida's estimation Yerushalmi also knows that any meditation on the question of the "Jewish origins" of psychoanalysis is ultimately tied to the future. Derrida glosses Yerushalmi's words thus: "if we want to know what this [the Freudian archive] will have meant, we will only know in the times to come" (27). For Yerushalmi and Derrida, then, the "origin" of psychoanalysis resides in the future — a future that will retroactively reveal psychoanalysis as a "Jewish science," but only if Freud "confesses" his Jewish identity.

Among other things, Yerushalmi wants the returning ghost of Freud to announce that psychoanalysis *is* (will have been?) a "Jewish science" as perhaps the only way the question of the "Jewish origins" of psychoanalysis can be finally laid to rest. As Derrida writes of Yerushalmi's goal,

> it is a thesis with a rather particular status — and a paradoxical movement: it posits not so much what *is* as what *will have been* and *ought to or should be in the future,* namely that psychoanalysis should in the future have been a Jewish science . . . in a sense, admittedly, which is radically different from that of the anti-Semitic denunciation, but which would bring to light, one more time, and according to a very Freudian gesture in its style and tradition, the truth that could be carried by the anti-Semitic unconscious. (32; italics in original)

Perhaps the ghost of Freud, appearing in the future, long after the "founding" of psychoanalysis (in the gift of the Philippsohn Bible?), *will* return to confess his Judaism. And if he does, such a pronouncement will undoubtedly, for both Yerushalmi and Derrida, project the temporal dimensions of the question to the future: psychoanalysis *"should be in the future"* a "Jewish" science—but only if Freud can resolve the issue of his Jewish identity.

Amidst Derrida's return to the "Jewish question" in Freud via Yerushalmi (his own meditation on a "Judaism interminable" and its relation to the future of psychoanalysis), we can discern an unmistakable "apocalyptic tone," a renewal of the messianic impulses of earlier essays such as "Of an Apocalyptic Tone Recently Adopted in Philosophy." His essay "Archive Fever" speaks to the "past" of French Heideggerian discourse insofar as it is preoccupied, like so much Heideggerian thought, with deconstructing traditional concepts of "eventhood" (in this case, the "origins" of psychoanalysis). But he also speaks to the "future" of French Heideggerianism (as well as of psychoanalysis) when he approaches the "Jewish origins" of psychoanalysis as not so much a "metaphysical" question, but a teleological one. Thus Derrida invites us to view the question of the "origins" of psychoanalysis as an eschaton, a moment that exists outside our lived consciousness.

Perhaps more importantly (and now I believe we are at the core of the chief polemical point in Derrida's essay), the question of the origins of psychoanalysis is also a moment that *will have been* (in the future) best approached outside the lived (un)consciousness of both anti-Semitism and philo-Semitism. Yerushalmi seeks to imagine a future in which the question "Is psychoanalysis a Jewish science?" has been (will have been) purged once and for all of the anti-Semitism that has traditionally haunted its very posing. But at present, the posing of this question inescapably signals, to echo Derrida, the "truth that could be carried by the anti-Semitic unconscious." Indeed, after reading "Archive Fever" one is left with the melancholic possibility that such a question may never be able to free itself from its anti-Semitic baggage—that an anti-Semitic unconscious will never be capable of nuancing the question "Is psychoanalysis a 'Jewish' science?" in light of the complexities of Freud's Jewish identity. For that matter "Archive Fever" (uncannily picking up, as it does, where Lacoue-Labarthe and Nancy's "From Where Is Psychoanalysis Possible?" leaves off) may be suggesting that a *philo*-Semitic (un)conscious, despite its complex and often right-minded problematizing of Freud's own questioning of his Jewish origins, is equally incapable of probing for an answer to the question; a philo-Semitic probing of the "Jewish origins" of psychoanalysis can only, in the end, double back on the impulses of an "anti-Semitic unconscious."[5] Yerushalmi insists that if psychoanalysis is indeed a "Jewish" science, then such a declaration must be spoken by Freud *and by Freud only*. And thus Yerushalmi's insistence, among other things, serves to remove the question of the "Jewish origins" of psychoanalysis altogether from the domain of the Gentile cultural imaginary, particularly when it perceives such a question as leading not to a consideration of the future of psychoanalysis, but to a polemic on the philosophical "exhaustion" of psychoanalysis.

I would now like to attempt to draw some general conclusions about where the last few pages of this afterword can be positioned vis-à-vis the framework of my book as a whole. Phrased broadly, what can we conclude from these close readings of Lacoue-Labarthe and Nancy's and Derrida's "returns" to *Moses and Monotheism* in the post-Holocaust? I would argue that Lacoue-Labarthe and Nancy's essay, in the process of portending the "exhaustion" of psychoanalysis, constitutes a cryptonymy not unlike the concept first theorized by Abraham and Torok: it is less a document on some putative last stage in the history of psychoanalysis than a symptom of an ongoing French "inability to mourn" in the post-Holocaust. Their theorizing of Jewish identity in relationship to psychoanalysis (where the "end" of philosophy also links up with the "end" of psychoanalysis) leads to a discursive overdetermination "after Auschwitz"—an argument so densely deconstructive that the final result is a cryptonymy where an "inability to mourn" cannot fully represent itself to/for itself, but rather performs a compulsive return to the question of the "Jewish origins" of psychoanalysis. Though their essay makes brief mention of Nazi anti-Semitism as the historical backdrop of Freud's writing *Moses and Monotheism,* the historical specificity of the Holocaust quickly becomes dispersed within the labyrinth of the authors' deconstructions of psychoanalysis (and of Jewish identity itself).

In this context, then, it is worthwhile to consider their essay in relationship to, say, Lacoue-Labarthe's conception of the Holocaust as a "caesura" (in such works as *Heidegger, Art and Politics*) that "disarticulates" history. One wonders to what extent Lacoue-Labarthe's concept of the "caesura," where the historical specificity of the Jewish victim at Auschwitz modulates into the more theoretical "nullity of the immediate," repeats itself compulsively (unconsciously?) in Lacoue-Labarthe and Nancy's conception of Jewishness as the deconstructive "disarticulation" of psychoanalysis itself. Thus, we can also be reminded of the "tropic" Auschwitz of Lyotard's differend (formulated after his own ambivalent forays into *Moses and Monotheism*) that modulates into his concept of "the jews" as the theoretical core of a new postmodern "sublime." In such a scheme, the Jew as, seemingly, *the* privileged trope of French Heideggerianism points to a still unresolved discourse on Auschwitz in the French post-Holocaust. And in such a scheme, French Heideggerianism, whose historical roots are implicated (however remotely) in Heidegger's infamous silence on Auschwitz, is destined to remain an "unconscious philosophy," insuring that the Holocaust remains an ongoing crisis in postmodern discourse.

Moreover, what can we conclude from Derrida's difficult "Archive Fever"—as difficult as Lacoue-Labarthe and Nancy's treatment of *Moses and Monotheism* from a stylistic point of view, but much more inclined to avoid some of the more hermetic impulses of deconstruction in his acknowledging of Jewishness as an essence? A recurring theme throughout my book has been the complexities of tracking a Derridean "subjectivity" within postmodernism. On the one hand, in such works as *De l'esprit,* for example, we see a Derrida so committed to a defense of Heidegger that a critique of Heidegger's Nazi affiliations is only tacit at best. But in "Archive Fever" we see a Derrida who, despite his earlier claim that "I do not work or think within a living Jewish tradition" (*Dialogues with Contemporary Continental Thinkers,* 107), is obviously willing to be less circumspect about his own Jewishness. In "Archive Fever" Derrida, in the wake of decades of speculation about the "Jewish origins" of psychoanalysis in the post-Holocaust, wants "to give back to Freud his own competence, his own capacity to receive and thus to read the Hebrew inscription" in the Philippsohn Bible. In other words, as we have seen, Derrida wants to give back to Freud the authority to pronounce the last word on the essence of Jewish identity and its complex relationship to psychoanalysis. At the core of an emergent Jewish-French psyche within postmodernism, then, lies Derrida, who both willingly participates in the cryptonymy of French Heideggerian discourse, and yet, in "Archive Fever," emerges from this postmodern crypt to critique the repetition compulsions behind its recurring interrogation of the "Jewish origins" of psychoanalysis.

These observations (as well as my earlier analysis of "Archive Fever" and its claims that a philo-Semitic probing of the "Jewish origins" of psychoanalysis can only, in the end, double back on the impulses of an "anti-Semitic unconscious") lead me to some final thoughts about my book's methodology, specifically its own frequent reliance on decon-

structive discourse—its deconstructing of deconstructors such as Lyotard, Lacoue-Labarthe, and Nancy—in order to perform sustained,
close readings of these authors. (The deconstructive discourse of Derrida has, I hope, been presented as a special case requiring separate consideration.) It can certainly be argued that my book's subject matter
can itself be judged as vulnerable to the same kind of critique. As Barbara Johnson has written of the project of deconstruction, "any discourse that is based on the questioning of boundary lines must never
stop questioning its own."[6] Heeding this warning, I am aware that a
danger in critiquing a discourse fraught with repetition compulsions is
that one's own discourse can begin to rehearse these very same compulsions. In its broadest scope, my book has been an extended negative
critique of French postmodernism's current attempts to "think" the
Holocaust in philosophical terms, as well as a critique of the ways in
which French postmodernism's philo-Semitic impulse inadvertently
and ironically tends to replicate the very anti-Semitism it is seeking to
redress and expose. At the conclusion of my book, it is my responsibility to at least confront, if not resolve, the question of whether or not my
immanent critique of deconstructive discourse compounds French
postmodernism's own tendency to "trope" away from the specificity of
Jewish experience—whether or not my discourse inadvertently constitutes its own "crypt" that traces the same labyrinthine flaws of the discourse I am critiquing. Obviously I can only hope that the benefits of
undertaking such close readings outweigh the risks. In defense of my
immanent critique of certain key figures of French postmodernism, my
belief throughout my book has been that any critique of a discourse
(particularly a discourse as hermetically dense as deconstruction) is
best conducted in the terms laid down by that discourse: to fail to answer the challenge of deconstruction by carefully critiquing it from
within is to leave the rigor of the discourse unchallenged—and, if only
implicitly, to allow its message to linger. Although, to be sure, my negative critique has offered no alternative as to what *would* constitute a discourse adequate to talking about Auschwitz, I hope it has allowed us to
recognize further what does *not* constitute a salutary discourse after
Auschwitz. More specifically, the purpose of my afterword has been,
among other things, to demonstrate that French postmodernism's
many symptomatic returns to the question of the "Jewish origins" of
psychoanalysis merely constitute a kind of *Trauerspiel* that encrypts but
does not fully confront the trauma of the Holocaust.

Afterword

Any further conversation on the "Jewish origins" of psychoanalysis might be, as Derrida via Yerushalmi contends, best taken out of the realm of a Gentile cultural imaginary and put into the mouth of the "once and future Freud." Despite the salutary impulses of philo-Semitism that are serving as the foundation of so much psychoanalytic discourse in the post-Holocaust, the goal for the future of psychoanalysis after Auschwitz should be the posing of questions that can stand outside the repetition compulsions of both an anti-Semitic and a philo-Semitic (un)conscious.

Notes

1. Mourning and Melancholia in the French Post-Holocaust

1. Cornelius Castoriadis has provided one such apocalyptic account of the demise of psychoanalysis. Though by no means a "postmodernist" himself, Castoriadis speaks to the fate of psychoanalysis in a postmodern era when he argues provocatively, "The history of psychoanalysis is not finished—although it is *possible* that it may finish sooner than we think." *Crossroads in the Labyrinth*, trans. Kate Soper and Martin H. Ryle (Cambridge MA: The MIT Press, 1984), 103.

2. "Theses on the Philosophy of History," in *Illuminations*, ed. Hannah Arendt, trans. Harry Zohn (New York: Schocken, 1969), 257, 258.

3. "Of an Apocalyptic Tone Recently Adopted in Philosophy," trans. John P. Leavey, *Oxford Literary Review* 6, no. 2 (1984): 3–37; published in France as *D'un ton apocalyptique adopté naguère en philosophie* (Paris: Galilée, 1983). For more on the implications for postmodernism of Derrida's "apocalyptic tone," see Herman Rapaport, "Anticipations of Apocalypse," in *Heidegger and Derrida: Reflections on Time and Language* (Lincoln: University of Nebraska Press, 1989).

4. "The Apocalyptic Imagination and the Inability to Mourn," in *Force Fields: Between Intellectual History and Cultural Critique* (New York and London: Routledge, 1993). In this context, see also Klaus R. Scherpe, "Dramatization and De-dramatization of 'the End': The Apocalyptic Consciousness of Modernity and Post-Modernity," trans. Brent O. Peterson, *Cultural Critique* 5 (1986–87): 95–129.

5. *The Philosophical Discourse of Modernity: Twelve Lectures*, trans. Frederick Lawrence (Cambridge MA: The MIT Press, 1987), 408.

6. *Stranded Objects: Mourning, Memory, and Film in Postwar Germany* (Ithaca NY: Cornell University Press, 1990), 9.

7. "The End of Innovation? Contemporary Historical Consciousness and the 'End of History,'" *SubStance* 62/63, special issue "Thought & Novation" ed. Judith Schlanger (1990), 33. In this context, see also Lutz Niethammer, *Posthistoire: Has History Come to an End?* trans. Patrick Camiller (New York: Verso, 1992).

8. *The Complete Letters of Sigmund Freud to Wilhelm Fliess, 1887–1904*, trans. and ed. Jeffrey Moussaieff Masson (Cambridge MA: Harvard University Press, 1985), 208; italics in original.

9. "Monument and Memory in a Postmodern Age," *Yale Journal of Criticism* 6, no. 2, Special issue of collected papers from the Tenth Anniversary Conference of the Fortunoff Video Archive for Holocaust Testimonies at Yale University on "The Future of Memory" (1993), 251.

10. For more on the precarious relationship between trauma and the possibility of a nonreferential history, see Cathy Caruth, *Unclaimed Experience: Trauma, Narrative, and History* (Baltimore: Johns Hopkins University Press, 1995).

11. Quoted in Primo Levi, *The Drowned and the Saved*, trans. Raymond Rosenthal (New York: Vintage International, 1989), 11.

12. *The Jewish Return into History: Reflections in the Age of Auschwitz and a New Jerusalem* (New York: Schocken, 1978), 19–24.

13. *Les assassins de la mémoire: "Un Eichmann de papier" et autres essais sur le révisionnisme* (Paris: Editions la Découverte, 1987); *Assassins of Memory: Essays on the Denial of the Holocaust*, trans. Jeffrey Mehlman (New York: Columbia University Press, 1992). Vidal-Naquet implicitly links his study of revisionist "assassinations" of memory with psychoanalysis when he describes his essay as inherently "melancholic" (*Assassins of Memory*, 140). In this context, we might also note the perverse irony of Faurisson himself choosing to frame his Holocaust "revision" in terms of memory, as demonstrated in his book's title, *Mémoire en défense: Contre ceux qui m'accusent de falsifier l'histoire: la question des chambres à gaz* (Paris: La Vieille Taupe, 1980).

14. The English text of the film is Claude Lanzmann, *Shoah: An Oral History of the Holocaust* (New York: Pantheon Books, 1985). The French edition, with a preface by Simone de Beauvoir, is *Shoah* (Paris: Fayard, 1985). For an intriguing analysis of Lanzmann's *Shoah* as miming the temporality of psychoanalysis, see Shoshana Felman, "The Obscenity of Understanding: An Evening with Claude Lanzmann," *American Imago* 48, no.4 (1991): 473–95. Felman argues that "both the film and psychoanalysis institute a quest for memory. . . . The production of the film, like psychoanalysis, takes time and occurs slowly. . . . The film and psychoanalysis both work through gaps in understanding and at the limit of understanding" (476–77). For a deeply moving study of the relationship between memory and oral testimonies on the Holocaust, see Lawrence L. Langer, *Holocaust Testimonies: The Ruins of Memory* (New Haven: Yale University Press, 1991). In this context, see also James E. Young, *The Texture of Memory: Holocaust Memorials and Meaning* (New Haven: Yale University Press, 1993); Shoshana Felman and Dori Laub, M.D., eds., *Testimony: Crises of Witnessing in Literature, Psychoanalysis, and History* (New York and London: Routledge, 1992); and Geoffrey

Hartman, ed., *Holocaust Remembrance: The Shape of Memory* (Cambridge MA and London: Basil Blackwell, 1994).

15. For an extended study of this commandment within Jewish thought, see Yosef Hayim Yerushalmi, *Zakhor: Jewish History and Jewish Memory* (New York: Schocken, 1982). For an account of how the acquisition of memory is largely dependent on membership in religious or national groups, see Maurice Halbwachs, *On Collective Memory,* ed. and trans. Lewis Coser (Chicago: University of Chicago Press, 1992).

16. "Repression," in *The Standard Edition of the Complete Psychological Works of Sigmund Freud* [hereafter *Standard Edition*], ed. James Strachey (London: Hogarth Press, 1953–74), 14:153.

17. *Negative Dialectics,* trans. E. B. Ashton (New York: Continuum, 1983), 361. Here Adorno also makes the claim that "all post-Auschwitz culture, including its urgent critique, is garbage" (356). *Negative Dialectics* was first published in 1944, the year the United States (where Adorno was living at the time) first learned of the death camps.

18. "Journals, Politics: Notes on Paul de Man's Wartime Journalism," trans. Susan Bernstein, Peter Burgard, Jonathan Hess, Eva Guelen, and Timothy Walters, in *Responses: On Paul de Man's Wartime Journalism,* ed. Werner Hamacher, Neil Hertz, and Thomas Keenan (Lincoln: University of Nebraska Press, 1989), 458.

19. "Our Clandestine Companion," in *Face to Face with Levinas,* ed. Richard A. Cohen, trans. David Allison (Albany NY: State University of New York Press, 1986), 50.

20. *The Inability to Mourn: Principles of Collective Behavior,* trans. Beverley R. Placzek (New York: Grove Press, 1975); published in Germany as *Die Unfähigkeit zu trauern: Grundlagen kollektiven Verhaltens* (Munich: Piper, 1967). Alexander Mitscherlich, a former director of the Sigmund Freud Institute, was indebted to the Frankfurt School's earlier studies of social psychology. A precursor of the Mitscherlich book is Karl Jaspers's 1947 *Die Schuldfrage: Von der politischen Haftung Deutschlands* (Munich: R. Piper, 1987), a study of German postwar guilt. For a particularly bizarre example of how easily and perversely perpetrators can choose to view themselves as victims, we can look at Jung's consideration of a collective German melancholia: "A whole nation . . . [was] swept into the blood-drenched madness of a war of extermination. No one knew what was happening to him, least of all the Germans, who allowed themselves to be driven to the slaughterhouse by their leading psychopaths like hypnotized sheep" ("After the Catastrophe," trans. R. F. C. Hull, in *Civilization in Transition* [Princeton: Princeton University Press, 1964], 212). This passage demonstrates a weirdly ironic ambiguity in

which the German Gentile perpetrators are portrayed as Jewish victims, "driven to the slaughterhouse" by their "leading psychopaths" cruelly masquerading as ego ideals.

21. "Was bedeutet: Aufarbeitung der Vergangenheit," in *Gesammelte Schriften*, vol. 10, pt. 2 (Frankfurt-am-Main: Suhrkamp, 1977): 555–72; "What Does Coming to Terms with the Past Mean?" trans. Timothy Bahti and Geoffrey Hartman, in *Bitburg in Moral and Political Perspective*, ed. Geoffrey Hartman (Bloomington: Indiana University Press, 1986).

22. *The New Conservatism: Cultural Criticism and the Historians' Debate*, ed. and trans. Shierry Weber Nicholsen, with an introduction by Richard Wolin (Cambridge MA: The MIT Press, 1989), 229–30.

23. "Journals, Politics," 459. For a reflection on what he calls the "fundamental opposition" between memory (as a "bond tying us to the eternal present") and history (as the problematic reconstruction "of what is no longer"), see Pierra Nora, "Between Memory and History: *Les lieux de mémoire*," *Representations* 26 (1989): 7–20. This essay was excerpted from Nora's magisterial three-volume study of memorial historiography, *Les lieux de mémoire* (Paris: Gallimard, 1984–1992).

24. The literature on the *Historikerstreit* is large and growing, and I will not attempt to provide a comprehensive bibliography here. For some helpful overviews in English, see Ian Kershaw's chapter "Living with the Nazi Past: The '*Historikerstreit*' and After," in *The Nazi Dictatorship: Problems and Perspectives of Interpretation* (London: Edward Arnold, 1985); Saul Friedländer, "West Germany and the Burden of the Past: The Ongoing Debate," *Jerusalem Quarterly* 42 (1987); Anson Rabinbach, "German Historians Debate the Nazi Past," *Dissent* (1988); Richard J. Evans, *In Hitler's Shadow: West German Historians and the Attempt to Escape from the Nazi Past* (New York: Pantheon Books, 1989). See also the special issue of *New German Critique* 44 (1988).

25. "History and Psychoanalysis," *Critical Inquiry* 13, no. 2 (1987): 228; reprinted in LaCapra, *Soundings in Critical Theory* (Ithaca NY: Cornell University Press, 1989).

26. "Representing the Holocaust: Reflections on the Historians' Debate," in *Probing the Limits of Representation: Nazism and the "Final Solution,"* ed. Saul Friedländer (Cambridge: Harvard University Press, 1992). A version of this essay also appears in LaCapra, *Representing the Holocaust: History, Theory, Trauma* (Ithaca NY: Cornell University Press, 1994). In this context, see also Friedländer, "Historical Writing and the Memory of the Holocaust," in *Writing and the Holocaust*, ed. Berel Lang (New York: Holmes and Meier, 1988); Friedländer, "Trauma, Transference and 'Working Through,'" *History and Memory* 4, no. 1 (1992): 39–59;

and LaCapra, "The Return of the Historically Repressed," in his *Representing the Holocaust.*

27. "On Death-Work in Freud, in the Self, in Culture," trans. Susan D. Cohen, in *Psychoanalysis, Creativity, and Literature: A French-American Inquiry,* ed. Alan Roland (New York: Columbia University Press, 1978), 85.

28. Eric Santner argues astutely that because much of the theoretical discourse of postmodernism mitigates against any attempt to locate the historical specificity of the Holocaust, we are now (dis)located in an era that is marked "under the double sign of the postmodern and the post-Holocaust" (Santner, *Stranded Objects,* 8).

29. Santner, *Stranded Objects,* 6.

30. For a definitive study of the activities of the Frankfurt School before and during the war, see Martin Jay's chapter "The Institut's Analysis of Nazism," in *The Dialectical Imagination: A History of the Frankfurt School and the Institute of Social Research, 1923–1950* (Boston: Little Brown, 1973). For a more specific treatment of the Frankfurt School's analysis of anti-Semitism and the "Jewish Question," see Jay, "The Jews and the Frankfurt School: Critical Theory's Analysis of Anti-Semitism," *New German Critique* 19 (1980): 137–49. Much of my discussion in this section is indebted to Jay's valuable studies.

31. "On the Jewish Question," in *Early Texts,* ed. and trans. David McLellan (New York: Barnes and Noble, 1971). Marx's essay was influenced by Ludwig Börne and his socioeconomic critiques of Judaism in the early 1800s. As Paul Lawrence Rose points out, Börne coined the term *Judentümlichkeit* to describe what he perceived as a "Jewification" of bourgeois capitalist society. Rose, *German Question/Jewish Question: Revolutionary Antisemitism from Kant to Wagner* (Princeton: Princeton University Press, 1990), 157. The ironic fact of Börne's own Jewish identity is perhaps best demonstrated in his document, *Candid Remarks on the New Order for the Abode and Protection of the Jewry of Frankfurt* (1801), where he identifies the "Jewish disease" *(Krankheit)* of "an excessive nervous energy *[Hypersthenie]* in the desire for trade and profit" (quoted in Rose, 144). Börne's essay could be read as one of the earliest glimpses within an emerging modernism of the psychoanalytic complexities of the phenomenon of "Jewish self-hatred" and its complicity with anti-Semitism's stereotype of the "neurotic" Jew of capitalism.

32. As Jay writes, "In their faithfulness to Marx's own attitude towards anti-Semitism, Horkheimer and his colleagues conformed to a pattern that many observers have noted: the more radical the Marxist, the less interested in the specificity of the Jewish question" ("The Jews and the Frankfurt School," 138).

33. Jay, "The Jews and the Frankfurt School," 140. Adorno's *The Authoritarian Personality* (written in collaboration with Betty Aron, Maria Hertz Levenson, and William Morrow [New York: Norton, 1969]), a sociological study of the extent to which individuals are predisposed to racism and fascism, also emphasized anti-Semitism.

34. *Dialectic of Enlightenment*, trans. John Cumming (1944; New York: Continuum, 1989). *Dialectic of Enlightenment* was written in the United States in 1944 and first published in Amsterdam in 1947 with the added essay "Elements of Anti-Semitism." For another originary link between anti-Semitism and psychoanalysis, see Ernest Jones, "The Psychology of the Jewish Question," a contribution to a 1945 symposium entitled "Gentile and Jew," published in his *Essays in Applied Psychoanalysis*, vol. 1 (New York: International Universities Press, 1964). For perhaps the most prominent postwar analysis of anti-Semitism, see Hannah Arendt's chapter, "Antisemitism as an Outrage to Common Sense," in *The Origins of Totalitarianism* (New York: Harcourt Brace & Co., 1973), where she critiques the "scapegoat theory" that anyone can serve at any time as a scapegoat. Such a theory, she argues, occludes the specificity of the history of anti-Semitism and the grim regularity with which the Jew has historically been chosen as scapegoat.

35. Horkheimer and Adorno, *Dialectic of Enlightenment*, 187.

36. "Imagining the Jew in France: From 1945 to the Present," *Yale French Studies* 85 (1994): 119.

37. Among the many studies on the history of the Jew in eighteenth- and nineteenth-century France, see in particular Arthur Hertzberg, *The French Enlightenment and the Jews: The Origins of Modern Anti-Semitism* (New York: Columbia University Press, 1968); Bernard Blumenkranz and Albert Soboul, eds., *Les Juifs et la révolution française* (Toulouse: Privat, 1976); and Jay R. Berkowitz, *The Shaping of Jewish Identity in Nineteenth-Century France* (Detroit MI: Wayne State University Press, 1989).

38. Edouard Drumont, *La France juive* (Paris: Marpont-Flammarion, 1886). The definitive study of French anticapitalist representations of the Jew is generally considered to be Pierre Birnbaum, *Le peuple et les gros: Histoire d'un myth* (Paris: Grasset, 1979).

39. For a definitive study of the infamous Dreyfus affair, see Michael R. Marrus, *Les Juifs de France à l'époque de l'affaire Dreyfus* (Paris: Calmann-Lévy, 1972). For an important study of *fin-de-siècle* anti-Semitism in France, see Zeev Sternhell, *La droite révolutionnaire, 1885–1914: Les origines françaises du fascisme* (Paris: Seuil, 1978).

40. For three excellent studies of French fascist aesthetics, see Jeffrey Mehlman, *Legacies of Anti-Semitism in France* (Minneapolis: University

of Minnesota Press, 1983); Alice Yaeger Kaplan, *Reproductions of Banality: Fascism, Literature, and French Intellectual Life* (Minneapolis: University of Minnesota Press, 1986); and David Carroll, *French Literary Fascism: Nationalism, Anti-Semitism, and the Ideology of Culture* (Princeton: Princeton University Press, 1995). See also Robert Soucy, *Fascist Intellectual: Drieu La Rochelle* (Berkeley: University of California Press, 1979); Zeev Sternhell, *Ni droite ni gauche: L'idéologie fasciste en France* (Paris: Seuil, 1983), trans. David Maisel, *Neither Right nor Left: Fascist Ideology in France* (Berkeley: University of California Press, 1986); and Diane Rubenstein's chapter "Language and Authority," in her *What's Left? The Ecole Normale Supérieure and the Right* (Madison: University of Wisconsin Press, 1990).

41. Georges Montandon, *Comment reconnaître le Juif?* (Paris: Nouvelles éditions françaises, 1940).

42. The briefest sampling of the growing bibliography on Vichy France should include Pascal Ory, *Les collaborateurs, 1940–1945* (Paris: Seuil, 1976); Robert O. Paxton, *Vichy France: Old Guard and New Order* (New York: Norton, 1975); Michael R. Marrus and Robert O. Paxton, *Vichy et les Juifs* (Paris: Calmann-Lévy, 1981), published in English as *Vichy France and the Jews* (New York: Schocken, 1981); Pierre Vidal-Naquet, "Les Juifs de France et l'assimilation" in *Les Juifs, la mémoire, et le présent,* vol. 1 (Paris: Maspero, 1981); Serge Klarsfeld, *Vichy-Auschwitz: Le rôle de Vichy dans la solution finale de la question juive en France—1942* (Paris: Fayard, 1983); Richard I. Cohen, *The Burden of Conscience: French Jewry's Response to the Holocaust* (Bloomington: Indiana University Press, 1987); Jacques Adler, *The Jews of Paris and the Final Solution: Communal Response and Internal Conflicts, 1940–1944* (New York: Oxford University Press, 1987); Henri Rousso, *Le syndrome de Vichy* (Paris, 1987); translated as *The Vichy Syndrome: History and Memory in France since 1944,* trans. Arthur Goldhammer (Cambridge: Harvard University Press, 1991); Annette Wieviorka, *Déportation et génocide: Entre la mémoire et l'oubli* (Paris: Plon, 1992); André Kaspi, *Les Juifs pendant l'Occupation* (Paris: Les Belles-Lettres, 1992); Tony Judt, "Resistance and Revenge: The Semantics of Commitment in the Aftermath of Liberation," in *Past Imperfect: French Intellectuals, 1944–1956* (Berkeley: University of California Press, 1992); published in France as *Passé imparfait: Les intellectuels en France, 1944–1956* (Paris: Librairie Arthème Fayard, 1992); Susan Zuccotti, *Betrayal in France: The Holocaust, the French, and the Jews* (New York: Basic Books, 1993); and Steven Ungar, "Vichy as Paradigm of Contested Memory," in *Scandal and Aftereffect: Blanchot and France since 1930* (Minneapolis: University of Minnesota Press, 1995).

Two recent documentary films on Vichy, following on the heels of Marcel Ophuls's *Le chagrin et la pitié* (1971), are Jean Marboeuf's *Pétain* and Claude Chabrol's *L'œil de Vichy*.

43. For a compelling account of the complexities of the Barbie trial, see Alain Finkielkraut's *L'avenir d'une négation: Réflexion sur la question du génocide* (Paris: Seuil, 1982), published in English as *Remembering in Vain: The Klaus Barbie Trial and Crimes Against Humanity* (New York: Columbia University Press, 1992).

44. Vidal-Naquet, *Assassins of Memory*, 91.

45. "From Individual to Collectivity: The Rebirth of the 'Jewish Nation' in France," in *The Jews in Modern France,* ed. Frances Malino and Bernard Wasserstein (Hanover NH and London: University Press of New England, 1985), 248. For a fuller treatment of this thesis, see Trigano, *La République et les Juifs* (Paris: Gallimard, 1982).

46. Trigano, "From Individual to Collectivity," 250, 253, italics in original.

47. Wolitz, "Imagining the Jew in France," 134.

48. "Qu'est-ce qu'un collaborateur?," republished in Jean-Paul Sartre, *Situations* (Paris: Gallimard, 1976), 3:43–62. For an intriguing recent discussion of the gender resonances of this essay (i.e., Sartre's claim that the collaborator is a "failed male"), see Carroll, *French Literary Fascism,* 149–52.

49. *Réflexions sur la Question Juive* (Paris: Paul Morihien, 1946); *Anti-Semite and Jew,* trans. George J. Becker (New York: Schocken Books, 1976). For a recent critique of Sartre's *Anti-Semite and Jew* as an inadvertent "reification of race" that robs the Jew of agency and subjectivity, see Lawrence D. Kritzman, "Critical Reflections: Self-Portraiture and the Representation of Jewish Identity in French," in *Auschwitz and After: Race, Culture, and "the Jewish Question" in France,* ed. Lawrence D. Kritzman (New York and London: Routledge, 1995), 99–102.

50. Sartre, *Anti-Semite and Jew,* 60, 16, italics in original.

51. See, for example, such works as *Le livre des questions* (Paris: Gallimard, 1963), published in English as *The Book of Questions,* trans. Rosmarie Waldrop (Middletown CT: Wesleyan University Press, 1976); *Du désert au livre: Entretiens avec Marcel Cohen* (Paris: Pierre Belfond, 1980); *Le livre des marges II: Dans la double dépendance du dit* (Montpellier: Fata Morgana, 1984). Derrida has written an important essay on Jabès, "Edmond Jabès and the Question of the Book," in *Writing and Difference,* trans. Alan Bass (Chicago: University of Chicago Press, 1978). For two excellent studies on Jabès in English, see Richard Stamelman, *Lost beyond Telling: Representations of Death and Absence in Modern French Poetry* (Ithaca NY: Cornell University Press, 1990), and Warren F. Motte Jr.,

Questioning Edmond Jabès (Lincoln: University of Nebraska Press, 1990). The quotation is from "L'étranger d'Edmond Jabès," interview with André Velter, *Le Monde,* April 1989, 18; quoted in Richard Stamelman, "The Strangeness of the Other and the Otherness of the Stranger: Edmond Jabès," *Yale French Studies* 82 (1993): 121. In a similar vein, in his memoir *Souvenirs obscur d'un Juif polonais né en France,* Pierre Goldman, former member of the Communist resistance in France, writes, "To be or not to be French, that was never the question. I didn't think to ask it. I believe I always knew that I was simply a Polish Jew born in France." Quoted in Judith Friedlander, *Vilna on the Seine: Jewish Intellectuals in France since 1968* (New Haven: Yale University Press, 1990), 35. For more on the experience of Polish Jews in France, see Jonathan Boyarin, *Polish Jews in Paris: The Ethnography of Memory* (Bloomington: Indiana University Press, 1991). For more reflections on the colonized North African (in this case, Tunisian) Jew in France, see Albert Memmi, *Portrait d'un Juif* (Paris: Gallimard, 1962), published in English as *Portrait of a Jew,* trans. Elisabeth Abbott (London: Eyre and Spottiswoode, 1963); and *La libération du Juif* (Paris: Gallimard, 1966), published in English as *The Liberation of the Jew,* trans. Judy Hyun (New York: The Orion Press, 1966).

52. *Le Juif imaginaire* (Paris: Seuil, 1980); published in English as *The Imaginary Jew,* trans. Kevin O'Neil and David Suchoff (Lincoln: University of Nebraska Press, 1994). For a brief biography of Finkielkraut, see Friedlander, *Vilna on the Seine,* 91ff. For a compelling and provocative discussion of the inherent paradox of Finkielkraut's *Juif imaginaire,* i.e., its inhabiting of an obscure threshold between *une judéité baladeuse* (or "roaming" Jewishness) and its rootedness in Jewish memory, see Nathalie Rachlin, "Alain Finkielkraut and the Politics of Cultural Identity," *SubStance* 76/77 (1995): 73–92.

53. Peter Gay's *A Godless Jew: Freud, Atheism, and the Making of Psychoanalysis* (New Haven: Yale University Press, 1987) and Steven Marcus's *Freud and the Culture of Psychoanalysis* (New York: Norton, 1987) are two important studies seeking to downplay the Jewish origins of psychoanalysis. Key studies seeking to highlight the significance of Freud's Jewish identity for psychoanalysis include David Bakan, *Sigmund Freud and the Jewish Mystical Tradition* (London: Free Association Books, 1990); John Murray Cuddihy, *The Ordeal of Civility: Freud, Marx, Lévi-Strauss, and the Jewish Struggle with Modernity* (New York: Basic Books, 1974); Marthe Robert, *D'Œdipe à Moïse: Freud et la conscience juive* (Paris: Calmann-Lévy, 1974); published in English as *From Oedipus to Moses: Freud's Jewish Identity,* trans. R. Manheim (Garden City NY: An-

chor Books, 1976); and Dennis B. Klein, *Jewish Origins of the Psychoanalytic Movement* (Chicago: University of Chicago Press, 1985). For a recent reconsideration of the controversy concerning Freud's Jewish identity, see Ivar Oxaal, "The Jewish Origins of Psychoanalysis Reconsidered," in *Freud in Exile: Psychoanalysis and Its Vicissitudes,* ed. Edward Timms and Naomi Segal (New Haven: Yale University Press, 1988), 37–54. It is also worth noting that in the introduction to their collection of essays, *Psychoanalysis in France* (New York: International Universities Press, 1980), co-editors Serge Lebovici and Daniel Widlöcher make a point of contextualizing French psychoanalysis within the "Jewish Question" of the cultural origins of psychoanalysis: "Resistance to the dissemination of Freudian theory in France is longstanding" (vii).

54. Jeffrey Mehlman, "Translator's Foreword," in Elisabeth Roudinesco, *Jacques Lacan & Co.: A History of Psychoanalysis in France, 1925–1985,* trans. Mehlman (Chicago: University of Chicago Press, 1990), xii; first published in France as *La bataille de cent ans: Histoire de la psychanalyse en France,* vol. 1: *1885–1939* (Paris: Ramsay, 1982) and vol. 2: *1925–1985* (Paris: Seuil, 1986). For a useful overview of the aversion of early French psychoanalysis to "Freudianism," see David Macey's chapter "Retrospective," in his *Lacan in Contexts* (London and New York: Verso, 1988).

55. For the precise details of Lacan's appointment to the SPP, see Roudinesco, *Jacques Lacan & Co.,* 297–320. In this context, we can discern the disciplinary tensions behind Loewenstein's insistence that "[t]here are no specifically 'Jewish' deviations in the evolution of the oedipus complex or of the castration complex, nor any 'Jewish' mode of development of the libido" (Loewenstein, *Christians and Jews: A Psychoanalytic Study* [New York: International Universities Press, 1951], 109).

56. "Translator's Foreword," in Roudinesco, *Jacques Lacan & Co.,* xiii.

57. There is no small irony to Pichon's attempt to "Gallicize" the SPP, for in 1953 the Société Française de Psychanalyse established itself as a rival organization to the SPP. As Roudinesco writes, the underlying orientation of the SFP was more "Christian" and "Gallic" (read non-Jewish), as opposed to the prevailing sentiment that the SPP was dominated by the exiled members of the Austro-Hungarian (and, presumably, more "Freudian") psychoanalytic diaspora (262–63). The SFP's split from the SPP strikes one as a particularly vivid demonstration of French anxiety about "Freudianism."

58. By the outbreak of World War II, the dreaded specter of "Freudianism" seemed particularly entrenched in the cultural imaginary of French psychoanalysis. In 1940, in the scholarly realm, far removed from Pi-

chon's power politics but no less entangled in the "Jewish Question" than the circumstances of Lacan's appointment to the SPP, Angelo Hesnard, one of the founders of the SPP, wrote a treatise with a negative focus on what he referred to as Freud's "Hebraism" (later published as *Freud dans la société d'après guerre* [Geneva, Lausanne: Mont Blanc, 1946]). Hesnard's openly French Nationalist leanings made him a key contributor to the prewar efforts of French psychoanalysis to conceive of itself as exclusively non-Jewish. For more on the younger Hesnard's anti-Freudianism, see Jean-Pierre Mordier, *Les débats de la psychanalyse en France, 1895–1926* (Paris: Maspero, 1981).

59. The subject of Lacan and the "Jewish Question" is too complex and lengthy to attempt to resolve here. It is a subject that Roudinesco, to her credit, confronts directly, noting that Lacan had a brief friendship with the fascist writer Pierre Drieu la Rochelle (110), and that in the early 1950s he was, like so many French intellectuals, fascinated with Heideggerian philosophy. But it may also be important to bear in mind that he was married to the Jewish Sylvie Maklès (Bataille), and he remained friends with Sacha Nacht and other Jewish psychoanalysts (despite being embroiled over the years in some bitter disputes with Nacht, primarily over such controversies as his "variable length" sessions with patients). As Roudinesco makes clear, Lacan "would never adopt as his own the ideals of 'Frenchness' in whose name Pichon had 'traded' him for a foreigner" (123).

In recent years there has been increased interest not so much in the details of Lacan's biography as in the influence of Jewish thought on Lacan's theories. For example, in his essay "The 'floating signifier': From Lévi-Strauss to Lacan," the second half of which is a commentary on a series of fragments from an interview with Lacan later published as "Radiophonie" in *Scilicet* 2/3 (Paris, 1970), Jeffrey Mehlman briefly discusses "Lacan's choice of Midrash, that perpetuation of the Law, as the exegetic tradition in which Freud might be inscribed" (in *Yale French Studies* 48 [1975]: 33). In an intriguing if somewhat speculative essay, "Judaism in the Life and Work of Jacques Lacan: A Preliminary Study" (trans. Noah Guynn, *Yale French Studies* 85 [1994]), Gérard Haddad, a former analysand of Lacan and author of *L'enfant illégitime: Sources talmudiques de la psychanalyse* (Paris: Hachette, 1981), focuses on "the apparently marginal yet essential question of Lacan's relationship to Judaism" (202). Haddad makes a case for a strong "Judaic" influence on Lacan based on Lacan's enthusiastic reading of Elie Benamozegh's *Israël et l'humanité* (1914), a work of Kabbalistic inspiration. Haddad also makes the intriguing claim that Lacan's concept of the "objet a," one of the cornerstones of his theory of desire, was conceived, in a 1963 seminar, in a moment of reflection on Judaism.

60. *Cryptonymie: Le verbier de l'Homme aux loups,* preceded by "Fors" by Jacques Derrida (Paris: Aubier-Flammarion, 1976); published in English as *The Wolf Man's Magic Word: A Cryptonymy,* trans. Nicholas Rand, foreword by Jacques Derrida (Minneapolis: University of Minnesota Press, 1986). It was Abraham and Torok who introduced the details of the Wolf Man to France, although Lacan does include a discussion of the Wolf Man when analyzing the relationship between the real and fantasy in *The Four Fundamental Concepts of Psycho-Analysis,* trans. Alan Sheridan (New York: Norton, 1981), 41. For more on the concept of the *fantôme* and cryptic incorporation, see Abraham and Torok, "Notules sur le 'fantôme,'" in *L'écorce et le noyau* (Paris: Aubier-Flammarion, 1987). For some excellent commentary on Abraham and Torok in English, see Peggy Kamuf, "Abraham's Wake," *Diacritics* 9, no. 1 (1979): 32–43; Nicholas Rand's translator's introduction to *The Wolf Man's Magic Word,* "Toward a Cryptonymy of Literature"; and Esther Rashkin, "Tools for a New Psychoanalytic Literary Criticism: The Work of Abraham and Torok," *Diacritics* (1988): 31–52.

61. For a brief account of Abraham's difficulties within the SPP, see Roudinesco, 600–602.

62. Jacques Derrida, "Fors: The Anglish Words of Nicolas Abraham and Maria Torok," trans. Barbara Johnson, *Georgia Review* 31, no. 1 (1977), 67; also reprinted in English in *The Wolf Man's Magic Word: A Cryptonymy,* trans. Nicholas Rand (Minneapolis: University of Minnesota Press, 1986). In his essay, Derrida also describes his friendship with Abraham as a "dialogue that went on for almost twenty years between us, along various paths—parallel, tangential, intersecting" (90).

63. "The Purveyor of Truth," in *The Post Card: From Socrates to Freud and Beyond,* trans. Alan Bass (Chicago: University of Chicago Press, 1987), 413; published in France as "Le facteur de la vérité," in *La carte postale: De Socrate à Freud et au-delà* (Paris: Aubier-Flammarion, 1976). "Le facteur de la vérité" first appeared in *Poétique* 21 (1975).

64. *Of Grammatology,* trans. Gayatri Chakravorty Spivak (Baltimore MD: Johns Hopkins University Press, 1976); published in France as *De la grammatologie* (Paris: Les Éditions de Minuit, 1967).

65. *Writing and Difference,* trans. Alan Bass (Chicago: University of Chicago Press, 1978); published in France as *L'écriture et la différance* (Paris: Seuil, 1967).

66. *The Post Card,* 265; italics in original. Here Derrida is playing off *The Ego and the Id,* where Freud argues that philosophers cannot under-

stand consciousness: "To most people who have been educated in philosophy, the idea of anything psychical which is not also conscious is so inconceivable that it seems to them absurd and refutable simply by logic" (*Standard Edition*, 19:13). Not surprisingly, Stephen Melville has concluded that "psychoanalysis has become one of the most insistent references in Derrida's writing. The interest deconstruction takes in psychoanalysis is permanent and complex" (Melville, *Philosophy Beside Itself: On Deconstruction and Modernism* [Minneapolis: University of Minnesota Press, 1986], 85).

67. Geoffrey Bennington and Jacques Derrida, *Jacques Derrida* (Paris: Seuil, 1991); published in English as *Jacques Derrida*, trans. Geoffrey Bennington (Chicago: University of Chicago Press, 1993), 134–35. In a recent essay, Jill Robbins describes Derrida's *Circumfession* as "something *like* a Jewish autobiography" that consciously invites comparisons with the *Confessions* of Augustine, who also came from Algeria (Robbins, "Circumcising Confession: Derrida, Autobiography, Judaism," *Diacritics* 25, no. 4 [1995], 24; italics in original).

68. The imagery of Abraham and Torok's cryptonymy—and the ghosts of the Holocaust—are surely embedded in the elliptical observation on history in Derrida's recent book *The Gift of Death*. In a chapter entitled "Secrets of European Responsibility," an essay on the Czech philosopher Jan Patocka, a compatriot of Vaclav Havel, Derrida writes, "history never effaces what it buries; it always keeps within itself the secret of whatever it encrypts, the secret of its secret" (Derrida, *The Gift of Death*, trans. David Wills [Chicago: University of Chicago Press, 1995], 21; published in France as "Donner la mort," in *L'éthique du don, Jacques Derrida et la pensée du don*, ed. Jean-Michel Rabaté and Michael Wetzel [Paris: Transition, 1992]).

69. Suchoff, *The Imaginary Jew*, xvii.

70. Quoted from an unpublished document given to Elisabeth Roudinesco by Major in Roudinesco, *Jacques Lacan & Co.*, 613. In this context, it is worth noting that Major was a strong supporter of Abraham and Torok and that, also in 1984 (as noted by Roudinesco), he introduced into France an anthology of German writings on psychoanalysis under Nazism: J.-L. Evrard, *Les années brunes*, Vert et Noir (Paris: Éd. Confrontation, 1984).

71. Kojève, *Introduction to the Reading of Hegel* (New York and London: Basic Books, 1969), 76. For a definitive summary of Kojève's seminars on Hegel in the thirties, see Vincent Descombes, *Modern French Philosophy*, trans. L. Scott-Fox and J. M. Harding (New York: Cambridge University Press, 1980), 10–47; originally published in France as *Le*

même et l'autre (Paris: Minuit, 1979). See also Michael Roth's *Knowing and History: Appropriations of Hegel in France* (Ithaca NY: Cornell University Press, 1988).

Given Lacan's presence as a student in Kojève's seminars, it is not surprising that a certain Hegelian-Kojèvian genealogy can be detected in Lacanian psychoanalysis. For Kojève, desire could only be satisfied in death; and it is, of course, Kojève's Hegelian interpretation of desire that has so deeply informed the "desire" that serves as the renowned cornerstone of Lacanian psychoanalysis. At one point, Lacan argues, "the reality of the subject's own death is an unimaginable object, and the analyst, like anyone else, can know nothing about it unless he is a being promised to death" (Lacan, *Écrits: A Selection,* trans. Alan Sheridan [New York: Norton, 1977], 348–49). Of Lacan's intellectual development in the 1930s, Mikkel Borch-Jacobsen argues, "In reality, Lacan was searching through Freud only for what would serve to confirm 'facts' that he had already interpreted in para-Hegelian terms" (Borch-Jacobsen, *Lacan: The Absolute Master,* trans. Douglas Brick [Stanford: Stanford University Press, 1991], 28).

72. See, for example, his *L'arrêt de mort* (Paris: Gallimard, 1948); published in English as *Death Sentence,* trans. Lydia Davis (Barrytown NY: Station Hill Press, 1978). In this context, we can consider Bataille's assertion, amidst a celebration of the theme of excess in his *L'érotisme* (Paris: Union générale d'éditions, 1965), that we should not fear facing the inconceivable beyond death (published in English as *Death and Sensuality,* trans. Mary Dalwood [San Francisco: City Lights, 1986]).

73. Bataille, *Œuvres complètes: Écrits posthumes, 1922–1940,* vol. 2 (Paris: Gallimard, 1988). Bataille's essay on the death camps, "Réflexions sur le bourreau et la victime: S.S. et déportés" (first published in *Critique* in 1947) has been translated as "Reflections on the Executioner and the Victim," trans. Elizabeth Rottenberg, *Yale French Studies* 79 (1991): 15–19. Bataille writes ambiguously of the systematic extermination of the Jews: "This negation of humanity is barely less degrading than is that of the executioner. The executioner demeans himself, demeans his victim" (17). Here, Bataille is to be credited (unlike Heidegger) with a postwar sensitivity to Nazi atrocities toward the Jews. But in the process he also rather uncannily anticipates the Mitscherlichs' study of postwar guilt, and in particular their observation of how readily the nonvictims ambiguously shifted their object of interest from the victims to the perpetrators.

74. *The Inoperative Community,* ed. Peter Connor, trans. Peter Connor, Lisa Garbus, Michael Holland, and Simona Sawhney, (Minneapolis: Uni-

versity of Minnesota Press, 1991), 1; originally published in France as *La communauté désœuvrée* (Paris: Christian Bourgois, 1986). Another key influence on Nancy's concept of "community" is Blanchot's *The Unavowable Community*, trans. Pierre Joris (Barrytown NY: Station Hill Press, 1988), published in France as *La communauté inavouable* (Paris: Minuit, 1983). For some valuable observations on the influence on Nancy of Blanchot's concept of *désœuvrement*, see Fynsk's foreword to *The Inoperative Community*, p. xvii. For more of Nancy's reflections on Bataille's "thinking" of sacrifice—and his opening observation that "[c]ontemporary reflection on sacrifice cannot *not* be haunted by the thought of Bataille" (20)—see his essay "The Unsacrificeable," trans. Richard Livingston, *Yale French Studies* 79 (1991): 20–38.

75. In this context, we can be reminded of Adorno's own linkage, in *Negative Dialectics,* of Auschwitz and a "metaphysics" of death whereby "Auschwitz confirmed the philosopheme of pure identity as death" (362).

76. As if the encryptedness of *la question juive* in Nancy's concept of *la communauté désœuvrée* were not complicated enough, the psychogenesis of Nancy's postmodern *Trauerspiel* becomes even more overdetermined when we consider the fascist implications of some of the writings of Nancy's major influences, Bataille and Blanchot. The question of Bataille's concept of "community" and his preoccupation at times with the "fascist question" is only recently being reassessed. As early as 1937, Bataille published an essay "Nietzsche and the Fascists," defending Nietzsche against charges of fascism (in Bataille, *Visions of Excess: Selected Writings, 1927–1939*, ed. Allan Stoekl, trans. Allan Stoekl with Carl R. Lovitt and Donald M. Leslie Jr. [Minneapolis: University of Minnesota Press, 1985]). But despite his critique of fascism, speculation has persisted that Bataille's biography reveals an attraction for it, such that Allan Stoekl, for one, has felt the need for some "damage control." Stoekl opens his essay "Truman's Apotheosis: Bataille, 'Planisme,' and Headlessness" with the question, "Was Georges Bataille a fascist?" a would-be collaborator? (*Yale French Studies* 78 [1991]: 181). Stoekl's essay argues carefully that many of Bataille's writings on community constitute not support for but rather a critique of fascism. In the same collection of essays, Jean-Michel Besnier (author of *La politique de l'impossible: L'intellectuel entre révolte et engagement* [Paris, 1972]) argues that Bataille's "politics of the impossible" is a refusal of Hegelianism and a testing of Kojève's "end of history" ("Georges Bataille in the 1930's: A Politics of the Impossible," trans. Amy Reid, *Yale French Studies* 78 [1991]: 170). In this context, see also Stoekl's *Politics, Writing, Mutila-*

tion: The Cases of Bataille, Blanchot, Roussel, Leiris, and Ponge (Minneapolis: University of Minnesota Press, 1985).

We might note in this context that Blanchot denies that Bataille was a collaborator in his essay, "Les intellectuels en question," *Le débat* 29 (1984). But the matter of Blanchot's own wartime past is equally complex. The irony of Blanchot's writings on postmodern *l'oubli* is the extent to which some of the fascist implications of his earlier, interwar writings have been forgotten (or "repressed") by so many of his readers. In the early 1980s, Jeffrey Mehlman was among the first to discuss the significance of Blanchot's political writings for the interwar monthly *Combat*, writings that, reflecting the ideology of *Combat* itself, flirted with French Nationalist and fascist sentiments. For details, see Mehlman, "Blanchot at *Combat:* Of Literature and Terror," in his *Legacies of Anti-Semitism in France* (Minneapolis: University of Minnesota Press, 1983). For the most recent reassessment of the significance of Blanchot's interwar writings for the post-Holocaust (and a particularly valuable study of the displacement of Blanchot's involvement with Heidegger's writings), see Steven Ungar, *Scandal and Aftereffect: Blanchot and France since 1930* (Minneapolis: University of Minnesota Press, 1995).

77. *Letters of Sigmund Freud,* ed. Ernst Freud, trans. Tania Stern and James Stern (New York: Basic Books, 1960), 428.

78. *The Infinite Conversation,* trans. Susan Hanson (Minneapolis: University of Minnesota Press, 1992), 123–29; published in France as *L'entretien infini* (Paris: Gallimard, 1969). *The Infinite Conversation* constitutes, among other things, an extended meditation on the moral origins of Judaism.

79. *Strangers to Ourselves,* trans. Leon S. Roudiez (New York: Columbia University Press, 1991), 182–83; published in France as *Étrangers à nous-mêmes* (Paris: Fayard, 1988). In her chapter "'Ours to Jew or Die,'" on Louis-Ferdinand Céline in her *Powers of Horror,* a "thinking" of French fascism generally, and more specifically a meditation on the virulently anti-Semitic writings of Céline and his bizarrely paranoid visions of the "Jewification" of French culture, Kristeva cannot resist (amidst a listing of his crude stereotypes and anti-Semitic ravings) celebrating what she calls the "the enchantment of his style" and its "call to rhythm and joy" (*Powers of Horror: An Essay on Abjection,* trans. Leon S. Roudiez [New York: Columbia University Press, 1982], 179; published in France as *Pouvoirs de l'horreur* [Paris: Seuil, 1980]). In this essay, the boundary between the discourses of anti-Semitism and of philo-Semitism seems especially fragile and permeable. For more on the difficulties of assessing Kristeva's assessment of Céline's style, and of her focus on what she

terms "the function of the Jew in the economy of Célinian discourse," see Kaplan, *Reproductions of Banality,* 108–9, and Carroll, *French Literary Fascism,* 183–86.

80. *The Sublime Object of Ideology* (London and New York: Verso, 1989), 96–97; italics in original. See also his *For They Know What They Do: Enjoyment as a Political Factor* (London and New York: Verso, 1991).

81. In *The Imaginary Jew,* Finkielkraut perceives no small irony in French philo-Semitism's "fetishizing" of the Jew: "The image of the Jew is undergoing a kind of reversal of fortune: now he is the one who has roots, and it's the French philo-Semite, that poor wandering goy, who sees himself as deracinated and stateless" (94). For perhaps the earliest analysis of the odd convergences between philo- and anti-Semitism, see *The Jew as Pariah: Jewish Identity and Politics in the Modern Age,* ed. Ron H. Feldman (New York: Grove Press, 1978).

82. The Jewish poet and Holocaust survivor Paul Celan has become just such a privileged trope for French postmodernism. Philippe Lacoue-Labarthe (*La poésie comme expérience* [Paris: Christian Bourgois, 1986]) and Derrida (*Shibboleth: Pour Paul Celan* [Paris: Galilée, 1986]) have devoted entire books to Celan; and the last sentence of Lyotard's *Heidegger and "the jews"* reads: "'Celan' is neither the beginning nor the end of Heidegger; it is his lack: what is missing in him, what he misses, and whose lack he is lacking" (*Heidegger and "the jews,"* trans. Andreas Michel and Mark Roberts [Minneapolis: University of Minnesota Press, 1990], 94; published in France as *Heidegger et "les juifs"* [Paris: Galilée, 1988]). For more on what he calls French postmodernism's "curious interest" in Celan, see Mark M. Anderson, "The 'Impossibility' of Poetry: Celan and Heidegger in France," *New German Critique* 53 (1991): 3–18. Anderson observes astutely that Lacoue-Labarthe's book in particular "diminishes Celan's Jewishness . . . his cultural situation in eastern Europe" (17), a prime example of how the historical specificity of the real Jew (i.e., the significant cultural contexts that have shaped the Jew within Eastern and Western Europe) is elided in the discourse of French Heideggerianism. Indeed, Lacoue-Labarthe's book seems at least as preoccupied with Heidegger (with a Heideggerian reading of the other in Celan) as with Celan himself. In this context it can be argued that French Heideggerianism seems reluctant to address the specific historical processes leading to Nazi Germany's creation of the "metaphysical" (racial) Jew as an abstract concept that becomes the object of anti-Semitism. One wonders, for example, what French Heideggerianism would make of a figure such as Jean Améry (a.k.a. Hans Maier), former inmate of Auschwitz, born in Austria of a Christian

mother and a Jewish father, but raised with no sense of a Jewish identity—until Nazi Germany *made* him a Jew available for deportation (what Améry himself once defined as a "catastrophe Jew"). Until French Heideggerianism confronts in more detail the reason why the existence of the Jew has traditionally been so precarious in Europe, it is difficult to judge the discursive validity of its highly tropic, decontextualized figure of the Jew in the post-Holocaust.

83. *L'écriture du désastre* (Paris: Gallimard, 1973); published in English as *The Writing of the Disaster,* trans. Ann Smock (Lincoln: University of Nebraska Press, 1986).

84. The compulsive encrypting of Auschwitz in quotation marks reflects French Heideggerianism's fascination with the postmodern theme of "citationality." In "Signature Event Context," Derrida has argued, "Every sign, linguistic or not linguistic, spoken or written . . . in a small or large unit, can be cited, put between quotation marks." In *Margins of Philosophy,* trans. Alan Bass (Chicago: University of Chicago Press, 1982), 12.

85. One wonders if French Heideggerianism's problematic engagement with psychoanalysis isn't one of the major impulses behind the late Sarah Kofman's *Paroles suffoquées* (Paris: Galilée, 1987), a work indicating that, late in her career, Kofman (whose father was deported from Drancy to Auschwitz during the war) felt an urge to separate herself from philosophy and psychoanalysis in order to write about the Holocaust.

In this context of an encrypted Auschwitz, one wonders if it is the work of Blanchot, Lacoue-Labarthe, Lyotard, and others that is implicitly referred to by Jean Baudrillard in his essay "Necrospective": "It is because philosophy too has disappeared today (and there lies *its* problem, for how can something live if it has disappeared?) that it seeks to demonstrate that it was definitively compromised along with Heidegger, or rendered aphasic by Auschwitz" (in *The Transparency of Evil: Essays on Extreme Phenomena,* trans. James Benedict [London and New York: Verso, 1993], 90; published in France as *La transparence du mal: Essai sur les phénomènes extrêmes* [Paris: Galilée, 1990]). In his essay's "Postscript," Baudrillard implicitly accuses French Heideggerianism of being a major contributor to the French *fin de siècle*'s "necro-cultural pathos, its endless commemorations and mummifications" (93).

86. "Feu la cendre," *Des femmes* 6 (1987): 27; published in English as *Cinders,* trans. and ed. Ned Lukacher (Lincoln: University of Nebraska Press, 1991). The leitmotif of *la cendre* and themes of incineration also occur in Derrida's *Shibboleth: Pour Paul Celan. Feu la cendre* is explored

in intriguing detail by David Farrell Krell in his chapter "Of Ashes: The Promise of Memory in the Recent Thought of Jacques Derrida," in his *Of Memory, Reminiscence, and Writing: On the Verge* (Bloomington: Indiana University Press, 1990). In his commentary on Derrida's trope of the ash, Krell argues that "ash both preserves and loses the trace. Preserves it through all the heat of incineration, holocaust, immolation, and passion" (311). "Encrypted" within Krell's observation is an enigmatic lowercase "holocaust"—but the message of Krell's encrypting is clear: the Real of the Holocaust has become one of the privileged subjects of much of Derrida's recent work. More explicitly, Avital Ronell has argued that "Derrida had been listening for the murmurs of the Holocaust long before this became, for intellectuals, somewhat of a journalistic imperative" ("The Differends of Man," *Diacritics* 19, nos. 3–4 [1989], 63).

2. *Daseinsanalyse:* Derrida, Heidegger's Silence, and the Return of the Repressed

1. "Paul de Man's Silence," *Critical Inquiry* 15 (1989): 732; reprinted as "After the Apocalypse: Paul de Man and the Fall to Silence," in Felman and Laub, eds., *Testimony: Crises of Witnessing in Literature, Psychoanalysis, and History,* 120–64.
2. *The Complete Letters of Sigmund Freud to Wilhelm Fliess,* ed. Masson, 208.
3. "The Personal, the Political and the Textual: Paul de Man as Object of Transference," *History and Memory* 4, no. 1 (spring/summer 1992): 15; reprinted in LaCapra, *Representing the Holocaust.*
4. "How to Avoid Speaking: Denials," trans. Ken Frieden, in *Languages of the Unsayable: The Play of Negativity in Literature and Literary Theory,* ed. Sanford Budick and Wolfgang Iser (New York: Columbia University Press, 1989), 27; published in France as "Comment ne pas parler: Dénégations," in *Psyché: Inventions de l'autre* (Paris: Galilée, 1987), 535–95.
5. *Blindness and Insight: Essays in the Rhetoric of Contemporary Criticism* (Minneapolis: University of Minnesota Press, 1983), 157. In his essay on Blanchot (who himself wrote for the interwar monthly *Combat*) in the same volume, de Man writes, "Blanchot's recent work compels us to become aware of the full ambivalence of the power contained in the act of forgetting" (149), almost as if hinting at his awareness of Blanchot's own flirtations with fascism. For a recent reading of de Man's essays of the 1950s against the grain of his wartime journalism, see Ortwin de Graef, *Serenity in Crisis: A Preface to Paul de Man, 1939–1960* (Lincoln and London: University of Nebraska Press, 1993).

6. *Mémoires: For Paul de Man,* trans. Cecile Lindsay, Jonathan Culler, and Eduardo Cadava (New York: Columbia University Press, 1986), 22; reprinted in France as *Mémoires: Pour Paul de Man* (Paris: Galilée, 1988).

7. "On Some Motifs in Baudelaire," in *Illuminations,* trans. Zohn.

8. *The Rhetoric of Romanticism* (New York: Columbia University Press, 1984), 81.

9. *Stranded Objects: Mourning, Memory, and Film in Postwar Germany* (Ithaca NY: Cornell University Press, 1990), 20. For more on an absence of de Manian affect, see LaCapra, "The Personal, the Political and the Textual," 9–10. For de Man's tone in his writings as a "repudiat[ion] of pathos," see Marc Redfield, "De Man, Schiller, and the Politics of Reception," *Diacritics* 20, no. 3 (1990): 50–70.

10. "The Blindness of Hyperboles: The Ellipses of Insight," *Diacritics* 3, no. 2 (1973): 38.

11. "Whatever Derrida's reservations concerning Freud's 'metapsychological fable,' the fact remains that deconstruction operates upon the Freudian economy. It is not for nothing that the principal theme of grammatology is the 'repression' of writing" (David Farrell Krell, "Engorged Philosophy: A Note on Freud, Derrida, and 'Différance,'" in *Derrida and Différance,* ed. David Wood and Robert Bernasconi [Evanston IL: Northwestern University Press, 1988], 7).

12. De Man, "The Rhetoric of Blindness: Jacques Derrida's Reading of Rousseau," in *Blindness and Insight.*

13. Klein, "The Blindness of Hyperboles," 38–39. As Klein later argues, "It is precisely de Man's inability to read Derrida's re-inscription of the Freudian notion of repression, of the unconscious, that is marked in the text by the vertige that seizes his language, as what is being repressed returns to take its revenge" (41).

14. "Fascist Ideology," in Walter Laqueur, ed., *Fascism: A Reader's Guide* (Berkeley: University of California Press, 1976), 352.

15. "Like the Sound of the Sea Deep within a Shell: Paul de Man's War," trans. Peggy Kamuf, *Critical Inquiry* 14, no. 30 (1988): 621; reprinted in Werner Hamacher, Neil Hertz, and Thomas Keenan, eds., *Responses: On Paul de Man's Wartime Journalism* (Lincoln: University of Nebraska Press, 1989), 127–64.

16. This essay has been published in *Wartime Journalism, 1939–1943, by Paul de Man,* ed. Werner Hamacher, Neil Hertz, and Thomas Keenan (Lincoln: University of Nebraska Press, 1988). In "Les Juifs," one could say that de Man is consciously contributing to the desire for a modernism that is *Judenfrei,* consciously building on the paranoia of the Jew as "the other of the European." In his essay "The Monument Disfigured,"

Samuel Weber interprets de Man's article thus: "It is the Jews who intrude, deranging the 'continuity' and immanence of Western History" (*Responses*, ed. Hamacher, Hertz, and Keenan, 416).

In his essay "Conclusion: Walter Benjamin's 'The Task of the Translator,'" de Man praises Benjamin's account of translation as "a wandering, an *errance*, a kind of permanent exile if you wish, but it is not really an exile for there is no homeland" (in *The Resistance to Theory*, 92), a celebration of wandering that, in some sense, "atones" for his more youthful privileging of rootedness within a literary "tradition." In the context of de Man's essay in *Le Soir*, we can note the irony of his list of great, non-Jewish writers: Gide, Hemingway, Lawrence—and, significantly, Kafka as the Jew who inadvertently "wanders" into a list of writers that (except for Proust) de Man evidently intended as Gentile.

17. In this context, it may not be merely coincidental that appearing on the same page as de Man's "Les Juifs dans la littérature actuelle" is an article entitled "Une doctrine juive: Le Freudisme," reflecting anxieties about the "Jewish" origins of psychoanalysis at a time when the Nazis were strengthening their influence in France and Belgium.

18. Freud, *Inhibitions, Symptoms and Anxiety* (New York: W. W. Norton, 1959), 92.

19. "The Unconscious," in *Standard Edition* 14:178.

20. *The Legend of Freud* (Minneapolis: University of Minnesota Press, 1982), 50; italics in original. Weber's chapter "Metapsychology—Set Apart" is an excellent study of Freud's little-understood concept of anxiety.

21. *Standard Edition* 18:24–25.

22. Weber, *The Legend of Freud*, 59.

23. "The Temptation of Fascism and the Question of Literature: Justice, Sorrow, and Political Error (An Open Letter to Jacques Derrida)," *Cultural Critique* (1990): 59.

24. For more on what he views as Derrida's faulty separation of "vulgar" anti-Semitism and "rational" anti-Semitism in his apology for de Man, see Richard Wolin's chapter "Deconstruction at Auschwitz: Heidegger, de Man, and the New Revisionism," in his *Labyrinths: Explorations in the Critical History of Ideas* (Amherst: University of Massachusetts Press, 1995), 216–22.

25. Carroll, "The Temptation of Fascism," 48; italics in original.

26. *The Post Card*, 265; italics in original.

27. *Primal Scenes: Philosophy/Literature/Psychoanalysis* (Ithaca NY: Cornell University Press, 1986), 113. Herman Rapaport remarks on Lukacher's observation of this "violated genealogy" in his *Heidegger and Derrida*, 199–200.

28. In an interview in *Le Nouvel Observateur,* Derrida discusses the theme of an "encrypted father" in *La carte postale.* In response to the question "What was your father's name?" Derrida answers enigmatically, "He had five names. All the family names are encrypted . . . in *La carte postale,* and they are often unreadable even to those who bear them" ("An Interview with Derrida," in *Derrida and Différance,* ed. Wood and Bernasconi, 74). Significant sections of *Glas,* written at the time of his father's death, can also be read as Derrida's invoking of the "ghost" of the name of the Jewish father.

29. "The Suture of an Allusion: Lacan with Léon Bloy," in *Legacies of Anti-Semitism in France.*

30. *Being and Time,* trans. John Macquarrie and Edward Robinson (New York: Harper, 1962), 228.

31. Emmanuel Lévinas, "Admiration and Disappointment: A Conversation with Philippe Nemo," in *Martin Heidegger and National Socialism: Questions and Answers,* ed. Günther Neske and Emil Kettering, trans. Lisa Harries and Joachim Neugroschel (New York: Paragon House, 1990), 151.

32. Lyotard, *Heidegger and "the jews,"* 4.

33. Martin Heidegger, *Über de Humanismus* (Frankfurt: Vittorio Klostermann, 1981); "Letter on Humanism," trans. Frank A. Capuzzi and J. Glenn Gray, in *Martin Heidegger: Basic Writings,* ed. and trans. David Farrell Krell (New York: Harper and Row, 1977). For a recent reassessment of Heidegger's "Letter on Humanism" and its "highly charged hermeneutical and political afterlife," see Anson Rabinbach, "Heidegger's *Letter on Humanism* as Text and Event," *New German Critique* 62 (1994): 3–38.

34. Beaufret's analysis with Lacan also involves a tale of "silence." As narrated by Roudinesco, "irritated by his analyst's silence, Beaufret decided to make him speak. . . . 'Two or three days ago,' he said, 'I was in Heidegger's home in Fribourg and he spoke to me about you.' Lacan reacted immediately . . . 'What did he say to you?' The trap had worked" (in *Jacques Lacan & Co.,* 298).

35. "The Political Implications of Heidegger's Existentialism," in *The Heidegger Controversy: A Critical Reader,* ed. Richard Wolin (Cambridge MA: The MIT Press, 1993), 168. First published as "Les implications politiques de la philosophie de l'existence chez Heidegger," trans. Joseph Rovan, *Les Temps Modernes* 2, no. 14 (1946–47): 342–60.

36. *Heidegger et le Nazisme,* trans. Myriam Benarroch and Jean-Baptiste Grasset (Paris: Éditions Verdier, 1987); *Heidegger and Nazism,* ed. Joseph Margolis and Tom Rockmore, trans. Paul Burrell, Dominic

DiBernardi, and Gabriel R. Ricci (Philadelphia: Temple University Press, 1989). In the wake of this book's publication, some of the more influential studies of Heidegger's politics are Richard Wolin, *The Politics of Being: The Political Thought of Martin Heidegger* (New York: Columbia University Press, 1990); Tom Rockmore and Joseph Margolis, eds., *The Heidegger Case: On Philosophy and Politics* (Philadelphia: Temple University Press, 1992); Tom Rockmore, *On Heidegger's Nazism and Philosophy* (Berkeley: University of California Press, 1992); and Hans Sluga, *Heidegger's Crisis: Philosophy and Politics in Nazi Germany* (Cambridge: Harvard University Press, 1993).

37. *L'affaire Heidegger* as French philosophy's "return of the repressed" is also demonstrated twenty years later in 1966, when one of Heidegger's most outspoken supporters, Beaufret's student François Fédier, wrote a review essay that attacked three books critical of Heidegger, including Adorno's *Jargon of Authenticity* ("Trois attaques contre Heidegger," *Critique* 234 [November 1966]: 83–94). Fédier eventually wrote a book critical of Farias, *Heidegger: L'anatomie d'un scandale* (Paris: Robert Laffont, 1988).

38. *Martin Heidegger* (Harmondsworth and New York: Penguin, 1978), 123.

39. These quotations appeared in a special issue of *Le Nouvel Observateur* on "Heidegger et la pensée Nazie," 22–28 (January 1988). This issue also contained contributions from Derrida, Fédier, Lacoue-Labarthe, Gadamer, and Habermas. Blanchot's contribution, "Penser l'apocalypse," appeared on pp. 43–45; the quote from Lévinas appeared on p. 49. Blanchot's and Lévinas's articles, translated into English by Paula Wissing, appeared in *Critical Inquiry* 15, no. 2 (1989), as, respectively, "Thinking the Apocalypse: A Letter from Maurice Blanchot to Catherine David," 475–80, and "As If Consenting to Horror," 487. For an intriguing analysis of the "peculiarity" of Blanchot's choice of an epistolary format for the essay, as well as the letter's oddly "apologetic" tone, see Steven Ungar, *Scandal and Aftereffect,* 62–66.

40. *Ethics and Infinity: Conversations with Philippe Nemo,* trans. Richard A. Cohen (Pittsburgh PA: Duquesne University Press, 1985), 88; italics in original. Published in France as *Ethique et infini: Dialogues avec Philippe Nemo* (Paris: Arthème Fayard and Radio France, 1982). Lévinas's own response to Nazism is recounted in his essay "Reflections on the Philosophy of Hitlerism," first published in *Esprit* in 1934 and republished in an English translation by Séan Hand in *Critical Inquiry* 17 (1990): 63–71. See also his essay on the Holocaust, "Useless Suffering," trans. Richard Cohen, in *The Provocation of Levinas: Rethinking the Other,* ed.

Robert Bernasconi and David Wood (London and New York: Routledge, 1988).

41. "Heidegger's Silence," in *Martin Heidegger and National Socialism,* ed. Neske and Kettering, 147. For more on Derrida's reluctance to issue explicit and public condemnations of Heidegger's silence, see Jean-Luc Nancy's interview with Derrida in "'Il faut bien manger' ou le calcul du sujet: Entretien (avec J.-L. Nancy)," *Cahiers Confrontations* 20 (1989), 113.

42. *De l'esprit: Heidegger et la question* (Paris: Editions Galilée, 1987); published in English as *Of Spirit: Heidegger and the Question,* trans. Geoffrey Bennington and Rachel Bowlby (Chicago: University of Chicago Press, 1989). In the same year, Derrida also published a second book on Heidegger, *Psyché: Inventions de l'autre* (Paris: Galilée, 1987).

43. *The Political Ontology of Martin Heidegger,* trans. Peter Collier (Stanford: Stanford University Press, 1991), 3; originally *L'ontologie politique de Martin Heidegger* (Paris: Éditions de Minuit, 1988).

44. *What's Wrong with Postmodernism: Critical Theory and the Ends of Philosophy* (Baltimore MD: Johns Hopkins University Press, 1990), 223; italics in original.

45. For an excellent analysis of *De l'esprit* as situated in what he calls "the impossible space between languages," see Allan Stoekl, *Agonies of the Intellectual: Commitment, Subjectivity, and the Performative in the Twentieth-Century French Tradition* (Lincoln: University of Nebraska Press, 1992), 217–26.

46. "Die Frage nach der Technik," in *Vorträge und Aufsätze* (Pfullingen: Neske, 1985); "The Question Concerning Technology," trans. William Lovitt, in *The Question Concerning Technology and Other Essays* (New York and London: Garland, 1977). For a useful discussion of Heidegger's analysis of the meaning of the "Being" of technology, see Edith Wyschogrod, *Spirit in Ashes: Hegel, Heidegger, and Man-Made Mass Death* (New Haven: Yale University Press, 1985).

47. "The Question Concerning Technology," 15. Derrida's two references in *De l'esprit* to Heidegger's "Question Concerning Technology" (117 n.4, 130 n.5) address only the last line of Heidegger's essay: "For questioning is the piety of thought."

48. In John D. Caputo's deft summary, "The scandal of the silence is compounded by the scandal of the occasional discourse" (Caputo, *Demythologizing Heidegger* [Bloomington: Indiana University Press, 1993], 133).

49. *The New Constellation: The Ethical-Political Horizons of Modernity/Postmodernity* (Cambridge MA: The MIT Press, 1992), 131; italics in original.

50. Caputo, *Demythologizing Heidegger,* 144. In this context we should consider Heidegger's letter to Marcuse (20 January 1948) in response to

Marcuse's expression of horror about Jewish genocide: "if instead of 'Jews' you had written 'East Germans,' then the same holds true for one of the allies, with the difference that everything that has occurred since 1945 has become public knowledge, while the bloody terror of the Nazis in point of fact had been kept a secret from the German people" (quoted in *The Heidegger Controversy,* ed. Wolin, 163). Habermas comments on Heidegger's refusal to perceive the Jew as a victim: "Under the leveling gaze of the philosopher of Being even the extermination of the Jews seems merely an event equivalent to many others. Annihilation of Jews, expulsion of Germans—they amount to the same" ("Work and *Weltanschauung:* The Heidegger Controversy from a German Perspective," in *The New Conservatism: Cultural Criticism and the Historians' Debate,* ed. and trans. Nicholsen, 55–56).

51. We might note here that Derrida does perceive an inherent contradiction in Heidegger's antibiologistic *Geist* that troubles him. In Derrida's conception, Heidegger seeks to oppose a humanistic *Geist* to Nazi biologism; but, Derrida claims, in so doing Heidegger has "forgotten" the deconstructive lesson that terms opposing one another are also always already in complicity with one another. In the *Geist* without quotation marks, Heidegger finds himself trapped within metaphysics because biological racism and humanism, though seemingly opposed, are complicitous with one another in a "metaphysics of the subject." In Derrida's valuation, Nazism cannot be opposed to humanism—and thus, at this point (for Derrida), what Heidegger is guilty of is the "crime" of humanism. For more on Derrida's reading of Heidegger's Nazism as a humanism, see Jeffrey Mehlman's essay "Perspectives: On de Man and *Le Soir,*" in *Responses: On Paul de Man's Wartime Journalism,* 329.

52. *Heidegger et les modernes* (Paris: Éditions Grasset & Fasquelle, 1988); published in English as *Heidegger and modernity,* trans. Franklin Philip (Chicago: University of Chicago Press, 1990). One could refer here to any number of studies on the general topic of "Heidegger and modernity." I am singling out Ferry and Renaut's analysis because, themselves seeking to "rehabilitate" humanism for contemporary French philosophy, these two have chosen French Heideggerianism as their particular target, and they have specifically attacked Derrida and Lacoue-Labarthe for their claim that the Heidegger of 1933 was attracted to Nazism because he was still in the grip of "humanist" thought.

53. Dieter Thomä, "Making Off with an Exile—Heidegger and the Jews," trans. Stephen Cho and Dieter Thomä, *New German Critique* 58 (1993): 85; italics in original.

54. Derrida's linguistic shift from German to French is philosophically

significant. We should bear in mind that Heidegger had his own speculations on why he was so well-received in France, where, in his estimation, the French language could not allow for a "thinking" of Being: "I have in mind especially the inner relationship of the German language with the language of the Greeks and with their thought. This has been confirmed for me today again by the French. When they begin to think, they speak German, being sure that they could not make it with their own language" (Heidegger, "Only a God Can Save Us" ["Nur ein Gott kann uns noch retten"], trans. Maria P. Alter and John D. Caputo, in Wolin, ed., *The Heidegger Controversy*, 113; originally published in *Der Spiegel*, 31 May 1976).

55. "Die Sprache in Gedicht: Eine Erörterung von Georg Trakls Gedicht," in *Unterwegs zur Sprache* (Pfullingen: G. Neske, 1959); published in English as "Language in the Poem: A Discussion of Georg Trakl's Poetic Work," in *On the Way to Language*, trans. Peter D. Herz (New York: Harper and Row, 1971). For an argument casting doubt on Derrida's interpretation of Trakl, see Krell, "Spiriting Heidegger," in *Of Derrida, Heidegger, and Spirit*, ed. David Wood (Evanston IL: Northwestern University Press, 1993), 11–40.

56. In a footnote Derrida alludes to Helvétius's book, also entitled *De l'esprit*, which was burned at the foot of the great staircase of the Palais de Justice by order of Parlement in 1759 (115 n.4).

57. Herman Rapaport's interpretation of *De l'esprit* is particularly attuned to the ways in which Derrida reads against the grain of Jewish thought, and to the possibility of an encrypted Holocaust within Heideggerian thought. Rapaport depicts the Hebraic *ruah* as a "Jewish outcry" in the face of a *Geist* "which is not allowed to be addressed from the perspective of the Jews" (*Heidegger and Derrida: Reflections on Time and Language* [Lincoln: University of Nebraska Press, 1989], 171). In his "Perspectives: On de Man and *Le Soir*" (in *Responses: On Paul de Man's Wartime Journalism*, 334), Jeffrey Mehlman also discusses *De l'esprit*'s encrypted Holocaust. In particular, Mehlman sees great significance in Derrida's characterization of "mind aflame" as that which "does not merely *displace*, it *deports (déporte)*." In Derrida's choice of the verb *déporte*, Mehlman perceives an encrypted allusion to the deportation of the Jews to the death camps.

Interestingly, Freud makes reference to the Hebrew *ruah* in *Moses and Monotheism*. In his section entitled "The Progress in Spirituality," he writes: "If we may trust to language, it was the movement of the air that provided the image of spirituality, since the spirit borrows its name from the breath of wind (*animus, spiritus*, Hebrew *ruach* = smoke)"

(Freud, *Moses and Monotheism*, trans. Katherine Jones [New York: Vintage Books, 1967], 146).

58. As Derrida writes, "And one of the most obsessing ghosts among the philosophers of this alchemy would again be Hegel who . . . situated the passage from the philosophy of nature to the philosophy of spirit in the combustion from which, like the sublime effluvia of a fermentation, *Geist*—the gas—rises up or rises up again above the decomposing dead, to interiorize itself in the *Aufhebung*" (99).

59. "Theses on the Philosophy of History," 257.

3. *L'Histoire Juive:* Caesura, Affect, and the "Jewish Question" in Psychoanalysis

1. Susan A. Handelman, *The Slayers of Moses: The Emergence of Rabbinic Interpretation in Modern Literary Theory* (Albany: State University of New York Press, 1982), 163–78.

2. Richard Kearney, *Dialogues with Contemporary Continental Thinkers* (Manchester, U.K.: Manchester University Press, 1984), 107. For Derrida's explicit interest in his own Jewish tradition, see his essays "Edmond Jabès and the Question of the Book" and "Ellipsis" in *Writing and Difference*. But we are well reminded of Allan Megill's cogent observation that "[t]he 'thematics of the Jew' most often appears in Derrida in sublimated or disguised form" (Megill, *Prophets of Extremity: Nietzsche, Heidegger, Foucault, Derrida* [Berkeley: University of California Press, 1985], 304).

3. "Violence and Metaphysics: An Essay on the Thought of Emmanuel Lévinas," in *Writing and Difference*, 153; italics in original. For a provocative and cogent analysis of Derrida's playing off the Hebraic-Hellenic dichotomy in this essay, see Vassilis Lambropoulos, *The Rise of Eurocentrism: Anatomy of Interpretation* (Princeton NJ: Princeton University Press, 1993), 224–39.

4. "Interpretation at War: Kant, the Jew, the German," trans. Moshe Ron, *New Literary History* 22, no. 1 (1991): 39–95.

5. The failure of Cohen's attempt at a cultural rapprochement between the German and the Jew is sadly and ironically underscored by Derrida when he refers parenthetically to the death of Cohen's wife Martha in Theresienstadt at the age of eighty-two (48).

6. "Onto-Theology of National-Humanism (Prolegomena to a Hypothesis)," *Oxford Literary Review* 14, nos. 1/2 (1992): 3–23.

7. *Glas* (Paris: Galilée, 1974); English trans. by John P. Leavey Jr. and Richard Rand (Lincoln: University of Nebraska Press, 1986), 38.

8. The conference proceedings have been published as *Les fins de l'homme: À partir du travail de Jacques Derrida,* ed. Jean-Luc Nancy and Philippe Lacoue-Labarthe (Paris: Galilée, 1981). For a cogent and useful review essay of this conference, see Nancy Fraser, "The French Derrideans: Politicizing Deconstruction or Deconstructing the Political," *New German Critique* 33 (1984): 127–54.

9. "Transcendence Ends in Politics," trans. Peter Caws, in *Typography: Mimesis, Philosophy, Politics,* ed. Christopher Fynsk (Cambridge: Harvard University Press, 1989), 270. Originally published as "La transcendance finie/t dans la politique," in *Rejouer le politique* (Paris: Galilée, 1981), 177–214; collected in Lacoue-Labarthe, *L'imitation des modernes: Typographies II* (Paris: Galilée, 1986).

10. Quoted in "Hölderlin and the Greeks," trans. Judi Olson, in *Typography,* 236; originally published as "Hölderlin et les grecs," *Poétique* 43 (1980): 267–81; collected in *L'imitation des modernes,* 13–36.

11. *Heidegger, Art and Politics: The Fiction of the Political,* trans. Chris Turner (Oxford: Basil Blackwell, 1990), 76; originally published as *La fiction du politique* (Paris: Christian Bourgois, 1987).

12. "Hölderlin and the Greeks," 242, 246; italics in original.

13. See also his *Hölderlins Hymnen "Germanien" und "Der Rhein,"* Gesamtausgabe, vol. 39 (Frankfurt am Main: Klostermann, 1980). Two key German studies from the 1950s on Heidegger's return to Hölderlin are Else Buddeberg, "Heidegger und die Dichtung: Hölderlin," *Deutsche Vierteljahrschrift für Literaturwissenschaft und Geistesgeschichte* 26, no. 3 (1952): 293–330, and Beda Alleman, *Hölderlin und Heidegger* (Zurich: Atlantis Verlag, 1954). Also within the context of the post-Holocaust, it is appropriate to note Paul de Man's essay "Heidegger's Exegeses of Hölderlin" in *Blindness and Insight,* 246–66. See also Andrzej Warminski's chapter "Heidegger Reading Hölderlin," in his *Readings in Interpretation: Hölderlin, Hegel, Heidegger* (Minneapolis: University of Minnesota Press, 1987).

14. Michael E. Zimmerman, *Heidegger's Confrontation with Modernity: Technology, Politics, and Art* (Bloomington and Indianapolis: Indiana University Press, 1990), 116. Zimmerman's chapter "Hölderlin and the Saving Power of Art" provides a clear and cogent analysis of Heidegger's appropriation of Hölderlin for his "national aestheticism."

15. "Hölderlin and the Greeks," 242; italics in original. See also Lacoue-Labarthe's chapter "The Caesura of the Speculative," trans. Robert Eisenhauer, in *Typography;* originally published as "La césure du spéculatif," collected in *L'imitation des modernes,* 33–69.

16. *Heidegger, Art and Politics,* 45. In a detailed discussion of Peter Szondi's

essay "The Overcoming of Classicism" (*Überwindung des Klassizismus,* in *Hölderlin-Studien* [Frankfurt am Main: Suhrkamp, 1970]), an essay on Hölderlin's "anticlassicism," Warminski sees Lacoue-Labarthe's analysis of Hölderlinian tragedy as picking up where Szondi left off, and he critiques Lacoue-Labarthe's continuing emphasis on the concept of mimesis: "The problem with Lacoue-Labarthe's reading [of Hölderlin], we could say, is that he continues to use the discourse of mimesis, 'mimetology,' long after it has outlived its use" (*Readings in Interpretation,* 39).

17. Lacoue-Labarthe, *Heidegger, Art and Politics,* 44.

18. Hegel's depiction of the "unaesthetic" Jew is one of the recurring themes throughout Derrida's *Glas.* In Derrida's summary, for Hegel "the Jew remains stiff, on edge, taut in his opposition to maternal nature"; the Jew lacks "the spirit of beauty *(Geist der Schönheit)*"; the Jew "is a stone heart. He is insensible"—without feeling, *Empfindung* (39, 46). For a useful overview of Hegel and the subject of Judaism, see Emil Fackenheim, *Encounters between Judaism and Modern Philosophy: A Preface to Future Jewish Thought* (New York: Basic Books, 1973), 89–96, 153–69.

19. Hegel, *Early Theological Writings,* trans. T. M. Knox (Philadelphia: University of Pennsylvania Press, 1979), 265.

20. One could speculate on the extent to which the extreme scatological turn in Hegel's Judeophobia may have been influenced by some of the sentiments echoed in Martin Luther's 1543 pamphlet, *On Shem Hamphoras and the Descent of Christ,* and its attack on the Jews' presumed misreading of Scripture. Picking up with the moment "when Judas Iscariot hung himself," Luther's pathological narration, demonstrating a bizarre mix of anal and oral fixations, unfolds thus: "Perhaps the Jews had their servants there with golden pots and silver bowls to catch Judas's piss and other reliques (as they are called). Then they ate and drank the shit mixed with piss to become so sharp-eyed in interpreting the Scripture" (quoted in Sander L. Gilman, *Jewish Self-Hatred: Anti-Semitism and the Hidden Language of the Jews* [Baltimore MD: Johns Hopkins University Press, 1986], 60).

21. Nietzsche, *Beyond Good and Evil: Prelude to a Philosophy of the Future,* trans. R. J. Hollingdale (Harmondsworth, U.K.: Penguin Books), 1973.

22. *Aesthetics: Lectures on Fine Art,* vol. 1, trans. T. M. Knox (Oxford: Clarendon Press, 1975), 360.

23. *The Philosophy of History,* trans. J. Sibree (New York: Dover Publications, 1956), 220. For the definitive study of the figure of Oedipus in the

context of nineteenth-century German cultural history, see Peter Rudnytsky, *Freud and Oedipus* (New York: Columbia University Press, 1987). As Rudnytsky points out, the early anthropologist J. J. Bachofen was obviously influenced by Hegel when he wrote, in his *Mother Right,* "Oedipus marks the advance to a higher stage of existence. He is one of those great figures whose suffering and torment lead to a higher human civilization, who, themselves still rooted in the older state of things, represent the last great victim of this condition and by this same token the founder of a new era" (quoted in *Freud and Oedipus,* 189). Some fifty years ago, in his three-volume study of Greek culture, Werner Jaeger eerily echoes Hegel: "From the point of view of the present day, the Greeks constitute a fundamental advance on the great peoples of the Orient, a new stage in the development of society" (*Paideia: The Ideals of Greek Culture,* vol. 1, trans. Gilbert Highet [New York: Oxford University Press, 1939], xiv). For a detailed study of the underrating of Egyptian and Phoenician influences in ancient Greek culture (one that has occasioned much scholarly debate and controversy), see Martin Bernal, *Black Athena: The Afroasiatic Roots of Classical Civilization,* vol. 1: *The Fabrication of Ancient Greece* (New Brunswick NJ: Rutgers University Press, 1987).

24. For more on the relation in Hegel between Egypt and Greece, see Jean-Joseph Goux, *Œdipe philosophe* (*Oedipus, Philosopher,* trans. Catherine Porter [Stanford: Stanford University Press, 1993]). In his introduction, Goux asserts that, unlike André Green or Didier Anzieu, he deploys the Oedipus myth in order to interrogate (and, as he emphasizes, even "threaten") psychoanalytic experience rather than affirm it. For Goux, the Oedipus myth transcends any philosophical and psychoanalytic discourse.

25. *Early Theological Writings,* 2–5.

26. *An Introduction to Metaphysics,* trans. Ralph Manheim (New Haven: Yale University Press, 1959), 145.

27. In this context, we can also consider the resonances of Lacoue-Labarthe's depiction of Auschwitz as Europe's "discharge," where he is perhaps consciously echoing the Final Solution's slaughter of Jews through "discharge" (such as the gas vans of Chelmno), or its attempt, in the crematoria of Auschwitz, to reduce the body of the Jew to a kind of industrial waste. In his "Thinking the Apocalypse," Blanchot also deploys the metaphor of "discharge" when he critiques Heidegger's infamous analogy between a "motorized food industry" and the "manufacturing" of corpses in much the same language as Lacoue-Labarthe: "It is indeed true that at Auschwitz and elsewhere Jews were treated as

industrial waste and that they were considered to be the effluvia [*la décharge*] of Germany and Europe" (478).

28. "The Echo of the Subject," trans. Barbara Harlow, in *Typography,* 175; originally published as "L'écho du sujet," in *Le sujet de la philosophie: Typographies I* (Paris: Aubier-Flammarion, 1979), 217–303.

29. In his Seminar XI, Lacan sets forth his concept of the *tuché* as "the encounter with the real"—the encounter "in so far as it may be missed, in so far as it is esssentially the missed encounter" of a trauma (Lacan, "Tuché and Automaton," in *The Four Fundamental Concepts of Psycho-Analysis,* trans. Alan Sheridan [New York: W. W. Norton & Company, 1977], 55).

30. *Heidegger, Art and Politics,* 46.

31. I have appropriated this term from Derrida, who, in his essay "Interpretations at War," speaks openly of the *"démesure"* (or the "excess") of anti-Semitism (69). In the final analysis, given patterns of past anti-Semitic discourse in France, one is left to question the usefulness of any linkage of mimesis with the figure of the Jew. One thinks, for example, of Céline's anti-Semitic tirades in *Bagatelles pour un massacre* (1937) and *Les beaux draps* (1941): "The Jews, you know, they're all camouflaged, disguised, chameleon-like. . . . [The Jew] is mimetic" (quoted by Julia Kristeva, "'Ours to Jew or Die': Céline and the Categories of Anti-Semitism," *Powers of Horror,* 181). Between the opposing poles of Céline's anti-Semitism and Lacoue-Labarthe's philo-Semitism, it is difficult to determine why it is desirable to attempt to implicate the Jew, however positively, in any discussion of mimesis.

32. Mikkel Borch-Jacobsen is another key contributor to this recent French effort to reconsider the relevance of politics for psychoanalysis. Alluding to what he summarizes as "the confused state of psychoanalysis in France," Borch-Jacobsen has also called for a reinvestigation of the political foundations of psychoanalysis: "The image has been prevalent, especially in France since the 1950's, of a psychoanalysis purified of any political aim, and thus of a depoliticizing and desocializing psychoanalysis" (*The Emotional Tie: Psychoanalysis, Mimesis, and Affect,* trans. Douglas Brick et al. [Stanford CA: Stanford University Press, 1993], 19, 1; originally published in France as *Le lien affectif* [Paris: Aubier Montaigne, 1991]). I discuss the work of Borch-Jacobsen in more detail in chapter 4.

33. For a detailed and fascinating study of the relationship between male pre-Oedipal desire and fascist fantasy among the German counter-revolutionary *Freikorps,* see Klaus Theweleit, *Männerphantasien,* 2 vols. (Frankfurt am Main: Verlag Roter Stern, 1977–78). The English trans-

lation is *Male Fantasies,* trans. Chris Turner and Erica Carter (Minneapolis: University of Minnesota Press, 1987).

34. Wilhelm Reich, *The Mass Psychology of Fascism,* trans. Vincent R. Carfagno (New York: Farrar, Straus & Giroux, 1970); Georges Bataille, "La structure psychologique du fascisme," in *Œuvres complètes,* vol. 1 (Paris: Gallimard, 1970); Erik Erikson, "Hitler's Imagery and German Youth," *Psychiatry* 5 (1942): 475–93; Theodor Adorno, "Freudian Theory and the Pattern of Fascist Propaganda," in *Psychoanalysis and the Social Sciences,* ed. Geza Roheim (New York: International Universities Press, 1951); Hannah Arendt, *The Origins of Totalitarianism* (New York: Harcourt, Brace & World, 1966); Claude Lefort, "L'image du corps et le totalitarisme," in *L'invention démocratique* (Paris: Fayard, 1981); Serge Moscovici, *L'âge des foules* (Paris: Fayard, 1981). For an excellent study of Freud's analysis in *Group Psychology* of the leader as ego-ideal, see Michael S. Roth, *Psycho-Analysis as History: Negation and Freedom in Freud* (Ithaca NY: Cornell University Press, 1987), 148–55.

35. Borch-Jacobsen frames the problem thus: "Such is the hypothesis, the *organicist* hypothesis, which, as is immediately obvious, implies an integrally political—and why not say it?—*totalitarian* conception of the social bond, since, from the beginning, it presupposes society to be one, united, unanimous, and undivided" (Borch-Jacobsen, *The Emotional Tie,* 5).

36. The preoccupations behind such a line of inquiry are not far removed, of course, from Lacoue-Labarthe's own concern, in his *Heidegger, Art and Politics,* that Heidegger's detractors avoid drawing what the author would view as a premature conclusion that *Dasein* necessarily contains the seeds of fascism.

37. "The Nazi Myth," trans. Brian Holmes, *Critical Inquiry* 16 (1990): 291–312; originally published as "Le mythe nazi," in *Les mécanismes du fascisme* (Strasbourg: Colloque de Schiltigheim, 1980).

38. It should be noted that their argument might actually have its origins in contemporary Jewish theology. In *Das Wesen des Judentums,* Leo Baeck, a former student of Hermann Cohen, argued that because of its emphasis on ethics, Judaism foreclosed on myth. In Alexander Altmann's summary, "Myth is therefore categorically excluded from the Jewish realm. Judaism, Baeck asserts, is the only religion which has produced no mythology proper" ("Theology in Twentieth-Century German Jewry," *Leo Baeck Institute Year Book* 1 [1956], 199). Horkheimer and Adorno's *Dialectic of Enlightenment,* among other things an extended meditation on the rise of European fascism, demonstrates the extent to which enlightenment modernity is implicated in myth: "Just

as . . . myths already realize enlightenment, so enlightenment with every step becomes more deeply engulfed in myth" (11–12). For a discussion of myth as inherently "totalitarian" and "immanentist," see Nancy's chapter "Myth Interrupted," in his *The Inperative Community*.

39. "La panique politique," in *Cahiers Confrontations* 2 (Paris: Aubier, 1979). This essay was the authors' first investigation of the relationship between psychoanalysis and politics, specifically an analysis of Freudian group psychology and the extent to which the "metaphysical model of the Political" was based on group fascination for and bonding to a leader figure.

40. This essay was originally given as a talk in 1980 in Montpellier, France, at a conference titled "La psychanalyse est-elle une histoire juive?" and was published in the conference proceedings, as "Le peuple juif ne rêve pas," in *La psychanalyse est-elle une histoire juive?*, ed. Adélie Rassial and Jean-Jacques Rassial (Paris: Seuil, 1981). The English translation by Brian Holmes appears in *Michel Henry: Philosophy and Psychoanalysis*, ed. Mikkel Borch-Jacobsen, special issue, *Stanford Literature Review* 6, no. 2 (1989): 191–208.

41. In this context, I think it is appropriate to quote the English translator Brian Holmes, who, commenting on the title of the conference in which their talk first appeared, writes in a footnote: "The question itself ['Is psychoanalysis a Jewish story, joke?'] contains far more than a simple reference to Freud's *Jokes and Their Relation to the Unconscious*, for the multivalence of the French word *histoire*—which can mean 'joke,' 'story,' 'affair,' 'history,' or even possibly 'lie'—makes it into an instance of the untranslatable *Witz*, a 'joking production' which sketches the virtual field of a social, and therefore *affective*, rapport" (194 n.4).

42. Mortimer Ostow, "Judaism and Psychoanalysis," in *Judaism and Psychoanalysis*, ed. Mortimer Ostow (New York: KTAV Publishing House, 1982), 13.

43. Quoted by Sander L. Gilman, *The Jew's Body* (New York and London: Routledge, 1991), 135.

44. *Heidegger, Art and Politics*, 25 n.4.

45. In this context, it is worth noting that in *The Literary Absolute*, their study of the emergence of the concept of "literature" in German Romanticism, Lacoue-Labarthe and Nancy discuss the *Witz* as the witty "sudden idea" (not unrelated, as they point out, to the French *esprit*), knowledge that "knows itself even as it knows what it knows" (*The Literary Absolute: The Theory of Literature in German Romanticism*, trans. Philip Barnard and Cheryl Lester [Albany: State University of New York Press, 1988], 53; originally published as *L'absolu littéraire* [Paris:

Seuil, 1978]). Anticipating their discussion of the *Witz* in "The Unconscious Is Destructured like an Affect," the authors refer to the *Witz* as "the preferred genre of conversation, of *sociality*" (53). But Lacoue-Labarthe and Nancy also discuss how, for the Jena romantics, the *Witz* can be "equivocal or dangerous": "Its absolute, combinative quality is always threatened from below by its inferior, fleeting, almost formless character" (54). In this context, we can see how it would require only a small step away from the Jena romantics' interpretation of the *Witz* for Heidegger to make an anti-Semitic association between the *Witz* and the "formless," "dangerous" Jew.

46. *Standard Edition* 14:177–78.

47. Cynthia Chase comments on the uninterpretability of affect, arguing that because affect in general results from the displacement of repressed ideas, it actually *prevents* cognition" ("'Transference' as Trope and Persuasion," in *Discourse in Psychoanalysis and Literature,* ed. Shlomith Rimmon-Kenan [London and New York: Methuen, 1987], 214). Jacques-Alain Miller also argues that affect does not always speak for the Real of bodily experience: "some think [mistakenly] that what we put under the word 'affect' is a kind of direct access to the truth, that when an affect is there, *there is* truth" ("A and a in Clinical Studies," in *Acts of the Paris–New York Psychoanalytic Workshop* [New York, 1986], 27). But, as Miller contends, "affects are very strangely coded" (28). For more on the enigmas of affect and what she calls "the grammaticality of the symptom," see Monique David-Ménard, *Hysteria from Freud to Lacan,* trans. Catherine Porter (Ithaca NY: Cornell University Press, 1990), 64ff.

48. *Généalogie de la psychanalyse* (Paris: Presses Universitaires de France, 1985); published in English as *Genealogy of Psychoanaysis,* trans. Douglas Brick (Stanford CA: Stanford University Press, 1993). Henry points out that a reconciliation between a philosophy of consciousness and psychoanalysis was originally the goal of one of the earliest French works on Freud, Roland Dalbiez's *La méthode psychanalytique et la doctrine freudienne* (Paris: Desclée de Brouwer, 1936). For more on this subject, see Henry, "Phénoménologie de l'inconscience," *Communio* (May–June 1987). Henry's "return" to Dalbiez is perhaps significant in light of the latter's claim, in *La méthode psychanalytique,* that Freud's metapsychology has no systematic, philosophical consistency. For more on Dalbiez's distinction between Freudian "method" and "doctrine," see Roudinesco, *Jacques Lacan & Co.,* 59, and Macey, *Lacan in Contexts,* 29.

49. In his effort to break with Lacan, Henry points to affective response as one semiotic indicator of how one chooses to evaluate the sucess of Lacan's proposed "return to Freud": "Some go so far as to declare

without bursting out laughing that the structure of the unconscious is that of a language" (*Généalogie de la psychanalyse,* 385). In other words, an affective burst of laughter becomes the sign of an implicit affiliation with Henry's "affective" psychoanalysis over Lacan's "linguistic" psychoanalysis.

50. For more on Henry's attempts at a rapprochement between philosophy and psychoanalysis, see François Roustang, "A Philosophy for Psychoanalysis?" trans. Terry Thomas, *Stanford Literature Review* 6, no. 2 (1989): 171–90; first published in *Critique* 463 (1985.)

4. After Repression: Psychoanalysis and "the jews"

1. Friedlander, *Vilna on the Seine,* 82.
2. For a critique of this effort because of what she sees as Lévinas's misrepresentations of Judaism, see Gillian Rose's chapter "Angry Angels— Simone Weil and Emmanuel Lévinas," in her *Judaism and Modernity: Philosophical Essays* (Oxford: Blackwell, 1993).
3. *Totality and Infinity: An Essay on Exteriority,* trans. Alphonso Lingis (Pittsburgh: Duquesne University Press, 1969); *Totalité et infini: Essai sur l'extériorité* (The Hague: Martinus Nijhoff, 1961); *Otherwise than Being or Beyond Essence,* trans. Alphonso Lingis (The Hague: Martinus Nijhoff, 1981); *Autrement qu'être ou au-delà de l'essence* (The Hague: Martinus Nijhoff, 1973); *Difficult Freedom: Essays on Judaism,* trans. Séan Hand (Baltimore MD: Johns Hopkins University Press, 1990); *Difficile liberté: Essais sur le judaïsme* (Paris: Albin Michel, 1963). For a sophisticated study of Lévinas's difficult later works, see Mark C. Taylor's chapter "Infinity," in his *Altarity* (Chicago: University of Chicago Press, 1987). More recently, for a valuable discussion of how Lévinas's engagement with the Hebrew ethical tradition "must be posed in a Greek and Heideggerian language that covers it up," see Jill Robbins's chapter "Alterity and the Judaic: Reading Lévinas," in her *Prodigal Son/Elder Brother: Interpretation and Alterity in Augustine, Petrarch, Kafka, Lévinas* (Chicago: University of Chicago Press, 1991). For a recent cogent and perceptive reading of Lévinas in conjunction with Lacan's *Seminar VII: The Ethics of Psychoanalysis,* see Kenneth Reinhard, "Kant with Sade, Lacan with Lévinas," *Modern Language Notes* 110, no. 4 (1995): 785–808.
4. Derrida has also had a very complex engagement with Lévinas's ethics. For useful studies of the ethics of Derridean deconstruction and of Derrida's dialogue with Lévinasian ethics, see Simon Critchley, *The Ethics of Deconstruction: Derrida and Lévinas* (Oxford: Blackwell, 1992); Irene Harvey, *Derrida and the Economy of Différance* (Bloomington: In-

diana University Press, 1986), 169ff; and Robert Bernasconi, "Lévinas and Derrida: The Question of the Closure of Metaphysics," in *Face to Face with Lévinas,* 181–202.

5. Jean-François Lyotard and Jean-Loup Thébaud, *Just Gaming,* trans. Wlad Godzich (Minneapolis: University of Minnesota Press, 1985), 30, 37, 44, 53; originally published as *Au juste* (Paris: Christian Bourgois, 1979). See also his essay "Lévinas' Logic," trans. I. McLeod, in Richard C. Cohen, ed., *Face to Face with Lévinas* (Albany: State University of New York Press), 117–58. When philosophy offers philo-Semitic praise for the "ethical" Jew, we should always pause to consider its motives. In his *Beyond Good and Evil,* amidst a discussion of selections from Kant's *Critique of Judgement,* Nietzsche has an impulse to praise "Jewish morality": "What Europe owes to the Jews?—Many things, good and bad, and above all one thing that is at once the best and the worst: the grand style in morality, the dreadfulness and majesty of infinite demands . . . and sublimity of moral questionabilities" (*Beyond Good and Evil: Prelude to a Philosophy of the Future,* trans. R. J. Hollingdale [Harmondsworth, U.K.: Penguin Books, 1973], 161–62). A Jewish ethics of "infinite demands," for Nietzsche as "majestic" as they are "dreadful," becomes here a symptomatic site of Nietzschean ambivalence about Germany's encrypted Jewish Question.

6. Lacan, "Seminar on 'The Purloined Letter,'" trans. Jeffrey Mehlman, *Yale French Studies* 48 (1972): 49.

7. *The Differend: Phrases in Dispute,* trans. Georges Van Den Abbeele (Minneapolis: University of Minnesota Press, 1988), 44; originally published as *Le différend* (Paris: Minuit, 1983). Lyotard's observations on Auschwitz, initially entitled "Discussions: Ou, phraser 'après Auschwitz,'" were first delivered at the 1980 Cérisy colloquium on "The Ends of Man," the primary topic of which was "The End of Metaphysics." For a provocative summary of the debate following Lyotard's paper, see Avital Ronell, "The Differends of Man," *Diacritics* 19, nos. 3–4 (1989): 64–66.

8. In his *Assassins of Memory,* Vidal-Naquet cogently warns of the dangers associated with using "Auschwitz" as a synecdoche for all the death camps, claiming that carelessly conceived invocations of Auschwitz can only serve to play into the hands of "revisionists" like Faurisson and Serge Thion, who define Auschwitz simply as "a great industrial center, specializing in the production of synthetic rubber" (43). In response to Adorno's appropriation of "Auschwitz" as an instance of "negative dialectics," Vidal-Naquet writes, "Absolute negativity? Does such a concept have any meaning for a historian? . . . Auschwitz juxta-

posed an extermination camp (Birkenau), a work camp (Auschwitz I) and a factory-camp for the production of synthetic rubber (Auschwitz III Monowitz). The site of absolute negativity would rather be Treblinka or Belzec" (97). In other words, the horrors of Auschwitz-Birkenau are so easily elided by the revisionists' insistence on Auschwitz III Monowitz as the "essential" Auschwitz that Vidal-Naquet wonders if the killing centers of Treblinka or Belzec, sites of total, exclusive annihilation, would not be more appropriate "synecdoches" for the horrors of the Holocaust.

Vidal-Naquet's warnings about "synecdochalizing" Auschwitz are intended, among other things, to protect the goals of positivist historiography, a pursuit that has taken a deconstructive beating in a postmodern, post-Holocaust era. For example, the historian Hayden White, in an essay examining the status of historical knowledge as a discursive construct, subjects the Holocaust to the "politics of interpretation." White is sympathetic to Vidal-Naquet, but he feels compelled to add that "any historical object can sustain a number of equally plausible descriptions or narratives of its processes" ("The Politics of Historical Interpretation: Discipline and De-Sublimation," in *The Politics of Interpretation*, ed. W. J. T. Mitchell [Chicago: University of Chicago Press, 1982], 137). For a cogent critique of White's position, see Carlo Ginsburg, who writes: "We can conclude that if Faurisson's narrative were ever to prove *effective,* it would be regarded by White as true as well" ("Just One Witness," in *Probing the Limits of Representation,* ed. Friedländer, 93; italics in original). See also Howard Horwitz's essay, "'I Can't Remember': Skepticism, Synthetic Histories, Critical Action," *South Atlantic Quarterly* 87, no. 4 (1988): 787–820. As Horwitz argues, "In his [White's] view, historical events are inherently 'meaningless,' and historical narratives 'endow' these meaningless events with moral content. . . . [But] if no narrative or fact is more true than another, on what grounds should we prefer White's morality—his preference for holocaust history—to that of the revisionists?" (797). For a further elucidation of how, in his words, "positivist historians are at the mercy of a Faurisson if they imagine that justice consists solely in the application of cognitive rules" in the context of Lyotard's differend, see Geoffrey Bennington, *Writing the Event* (New York: Columbia University Press, 1988).

9. Shoshana Felman and Dori Laub, M.D., *Testimony: Crises of Witnessing in Literature, Psychoanalysis, and History* (New York and London: Routledge, 1992), 58, 57; italics in original. Other key studies of the Holocaust from a psychoanalytic perspective include Martin S. Bergmann

and Milton E. Jucovy, eds., *Generations of the Holocaust* (New York: Basic Books, 1982); Randolph L. Braham, ed., *The Psychological Perspectives of the Holocaust and of its Aftermath* (New York: Columbia University Press, 1988); Steven A. Luel and Paul Marcus, eds., *Psychoanalytic Reflections on the Holocaust: Selected Essays* (New York: Holocaust Awareness Institute Center for Judaic Studies, University of Denver, 1984); Robert M. Prince, *The Legacy of the Holocaust: Psychological Themes in the Second Generation* (Ann Arbor MI: UMI Research Press, 1985).

10. In this context, one could speculate on the extent to which Heidegger's infamous silence about the death camps, discussed in chapter 2, is also encrypted within Lyotard's postmodern theorizing of "silence."

11. Christopher Norris cogently summarizes the dilemma of Lyotard's position on survivor silence thus: "What he thus fails to recognize—for reasons bound up with his doctrinaire postmodernist stance—is the fact that in the great majority of cases there is no such conflict between truth-telling motives (or cognitive interests) on the one hand, and issues of ethical accountability on the other. Getting things right—or as right as one can get them by the best methods of empirical, historical or factual-documentary research—may itself be a prime responsibility in matters of ethico-political judgement" (*Uncritical Theory: Postmodernism, Intellectuals and the Gulf War* [Amherst: University of Massachusetts Press, 1992], 72).

12. In the process of wading through the sheer difficulty of Lyotard's rhetoric, the reader must be sensitive to embedded ironies in his discourse. Here Lyotard is attacking the Hegelian dialectical logic claiming that if one is a victim, one cannot bear witness: "Either you are the victim of a wrong, or you are not. If you are not, you are deceived (or lying) in testifying that you are. If you are, since you can bear witness to this wrong, it is not a wrong" (5). But the critique is, at best, tacit or embedded.

13. Lévinas, *Otherwise than Being*, 111. In this context of a trauma that "prevents its own representation," we can also consider Lévinas's essay "La signification et le sens," where he describes his concept of the face (*le visage*) as "apresentation" (*Hors sujet* [Montpellier: Fata Morgana, 1987]), 141. Lévinas's concept of "apresentation" has, as we will see, clearly influenced Lyotard.

14. In chapter 1 I quoted from Jean-Bertrand Pontalis, who has argued that the "teleological purpose [of mourning] has been said to 'kill the dead'" ("On Death-Work in Freud, in the Self, in Culture," 85)—as if to remind us that mourning "after Auschwitz" always threatens (like Lyotard's discussion of the "Athenian 'beautiful death'") to deteriorate

into a melancholic repetition compulsion that "kills," but never fully "remembers" the dead. In this context, we might also note that in *Beyond the Pleasure Principle,* which features, among other things, a theorizing of the repetition compulsion, Freud cites an episode in Tasso's epic *Gerusalemme liberata,* where Tancredi, having killed the Amazon Clorinda in battle, later attempts to cut down a tree that houses her spirit. In effect, Tancredi attempts to "kill" her *again*—for Freud as compelling an example as any of the psychic phenomenon of the repetition compulsion.

15. "Beyond Representation," preface to the French translation of Anton Ehrenzweig, *L'ordre caché de l'art* (Paris: Gallimard, 1974); English trans. Jonathan Culler, in *The Lyotard Reader,* ed. Andrew Benjamin (Oxford: Blackwell, 1989), 156. At the beginning of *The Tragic Effect* (trans. Alan Sheridan [Cambridge: Cambridge University Press, 1977], 1), André Green speaks of "a mysterious bond between psycho-analysis and the theatre," a bond that prompts his analogy between the unconscious and theatre as the "other" scene. (*The Tragic Effect* was originally published in France as *Un œil en trop: Le complexe d'Œdipe dans la tragédie* [Paris: Minuit, 1969]). But amidst this reflection on the privileged status of the theatre in Freud's thought, Green poses the question, "Should psychoanalysis still seek material for interpretation in works of art?" (18). Like Lyotard, Green argues that in studying tragedy one should consider "the role of affect" (28). See also Green's essay "The Unbinding Process," where he writes, "Affects can be communicated through silence; they can be hinted at by nonlinguistic signs. . . . But as soon as one decides to communicate by means of the spoken or written word, recourse must inevitably be made to representation" (trans. Lionel Duisit, *New Literary History* 12, no. 1 [1980]: 34; first published as "La déliaison," *Littérature* 3 [1971]: 33–52).

16. In his essay "The Scene Is Primal," Lacoue-Labarthe places Lyotard's essay within the context of *The Birth of Tragedy,* reminding us that for Nietzsche tragedy never presents, but only *re*-presents suffering ("The Scene Is Primal," trans. Karen McPherson, in *The Subject of Philosophy,* ed. Thomas Trezise, trans. Trezise, Hugh J. Silverman, Gary M. Cole, Timothy D. Bent, Karen McPherson, and Claudette Sartiliot [Minneapolis: University of Minnesota Press, 1993], 105); originally published as *Le sujet de la philosophie* (Paris: Aubier-Flammarion, 1979).

17. *Discours, figure* (Paris: Klincksieck, 1971); *Des dispositifs pulsionnels* (Paris: Christian Bourgois, 1973); *Économie libidinale* (Paris: Minuit, 1974). For excellent studies of Lyotard's "libidinal aesthetics," see David Carroll, "Aesthetic Antagonisms," in his *Paraesthetics: Foucault, Lyo-*

tard, Derrida (New York: Methuen, 1987); Peter Dews, "Jean-François Lyotard: From Perception to Desire," in his *Logics of Disintegration: Post-Structuralist Thought and the Claims of Critical Theory* (London and New York: Verso, 1987), 109–43; Bill Readings, *Introducing Lyotard: Art and Politics* (London and New York: Routledge, 1991).

18. "Jewish Oedipus," trans. Susan Hanson, *Genre* 10, no. 3 (1979): 401; "Œdipe Juif" in *Dérive à partir de Marx et Freud* (Paris: Union générale d'éditions, 1973).

19. *The Interpretation of Dreams,* trans. James Strachey (New York: Avon, 1965), 298.

20. Freud's turning to Moses late in his career might be more accurately portrayed as a *return* to Moses, as evidenced by his 1914 essay "The Moses of Michelangelo" (*Standard Edition,* 13:211–36), in which Michelangelo's enigmatic sculpture of Moses is held up as an example of suppressed fury and sublimation. For detailed treatments of the importance of the figure of Moses for Freud, see Martin S. Bergmann, "Moses and the Evolution of Freud's Jewish Identity," *Israel Annals of Psychiatry and Related Disciplines* 14 (1976): 3–26; Marthe Robert, *From Oedipus to Moses: Freud's Jewish Identity,* trans. Ralph Manheim (Garden City NY: Anchor Books, 1976); Edwin Wallace, "The Psychodynamic Determinants of *Moses and Monotheism,*" *Psychiatry* 40 (1977): 79–87; Jean-Joseph Goux, "Moses, Freud, and the Iconoclastic Prescription," in his *Symbolic Economies: After Marx and Freud,* trans. Jennifer Curtiss Gage (Ithaca NY: Cornell University Press, 1990); originally published in France as "Moïse, Freud: La prescription iconoclaste," in *Les iconoclastes* (Paris: Seuil, 1978); and most recently, Yosef Hayim Yerushalmi, *Freud's Moses: Judaism Terminable and Interminable* (New Haven: Yale University Press, 1991).

21. Here Freud acknowledges the influence on him of the Biblical scholar Ernst Sellin's book *Mose und seine Bedeutung für die israelitisch-jüdische Religionsgeschichte* (*Moses and his Significance for the History of Jewish Religion,* 1922), in which Moses is the victim of assassination by his people (*Moses and Monotheism,* trans. Katherine Jones [New York: Vintage Books, 1939], 42).

22. Rainer Nägele also discusses the concept of *Nachträglichkeit* in relationship to Freud's perception of how the Biblical Moses story is structured ("Belatedness: History After Freud and Lacan," in *Reading After Freud: Essays on Goethe, Hölderlin, Habermas, Nietzsche, Brecht, Celan, and Freud* [New York: Columbia University Press, 1987], 190–201). For a recent account of *Moses and Monotheism* as a history of deferred trauma, see Caruth, *Unclaimed Experience.*

23. For a useful discussion of how Freud's insistence on the Egyptian Moses was by no means original, see Yerushalmi, *Freud's Moses*, 4–8.

24. Quoted in Yerushalmi, *Freud's Moses*, 6.

25. Freud and Pfister, *Briefe, 1909–1939*, ed. Ernst L. Freud and Heinrich Meng (Frankfurt am Main: S. Fischer, 1963); published in English as *Psycho-Analysis and Faith: The Letters of Sigmund Freud and Oskar Pfister*, trans. Eric Mosbacher (New York: Basic Books, 1963). Quoted in Lyotard, "Jewish Oedipus," 411.

26. In *The Lyotard Reader*, ed. Benjamin, 70. Lyotard's essay was written in 1968, but was not published until sixteen years later, in *L'Écrit du Temps* 5 (winter 1984). In a preface, Lyotard explains why the publication of this essay was delayed and apologizes for much of the essay's content and its potential for being misunderstood. For a brief discussion of this essay in the context of his analysis of the links between "the traditional iconoclastic Jewish attitude toward visual representation and a powerfully antiocular impulse in postmodernism" (546), see Martin Jay, *Downcast Eyes: The Denigration of Vision in Twentieth-Century French Thought* (Berkeley: University of California Press, 1933), 574–79.

27. *The Emotional Tie: Psychoanalysis, Mimesis, and Affect*, trans. Douglas Brick et al. (Stanford CA: Stanford University Press, 1993), 2, 7; originally published as *Le lien affectif* (Paris: Aubier Montaigne, 1991). For Borch-Jacobsen's most detailed consideration of Freud's etiology of identification, see his *The Freudian Subject*, trans. Catherine Porter (Stanford CA: Stanford University Press, 1988); originally published as *Le sujet Freudien* (Paris: Flammarion, 1982).

28. *Heidegger and "the jews,"* trans. Andreas Michel and Mark Roberts (Minneapolis: University of Minnesota Press, 1990), 28; originally published as *Heidegger et "les juifs"* (Paris: Galilée, 1988).

29. In an essay *"Heidegger and 'the jews':* A Conference in Vienna and Freiburg," the text of a speech delivered after the publication of *Heidegger and "the jews,"* Lyotard is less elliptical, more openly polemical about his ambition for an authentically "French" philosophy. To provide three samplings: "[By 1938] German became a dead language for me, spoken only by the men of death, the army and the police of the Third Reich"; "Since the end of the eighteenth century, after the French Revolution and during the difficult formative period of the nation-states of Europe, there has been no important French philosophy. . . . Philosophy was German"; "The discussion of philosophical representations in the West, which have been the object of the Heideggerian anamnesis since 1934, is dedicated to leaving this affect [of "the jews"] forgotten" (in Lyotard, *Political Writings*, trans. Bill Readings and Kevin Paul

[Minneapolis: University of Minnesota Press, 1993], 135, 138, 143). This essay originally appeared as "Apropos de *Heidegger et 'les juifs,'*" in *Passagen Verlag* (1988).

30. *Standard Edition* 1:356; italics in original.
31. We might note here that it is not as if Lyotard has simply misunderstood an otherwise difficult concept. In his essay "Emma" (*Nouvelle Revue de Psychanalyse* 39 [1989]: 43–70), published a year after *Heidegger and "the jews,"* Lyotard provides a thorough explanation of *Nachträglichkeit* in his discussion of Freud's case history of Emma from *Project for a Scientific Psychology.* Among other things, Lyotard's commentary shows his full understanding of *Nachträglichkeit* as demonstrating that the subject forgets that he or she has been "affected." For a useful summation of this article, as well as a cogent comparison between Lyotard's differend and Lacan's concept of the Real as a missed encounter, see Anne Tomiche, "Rephrasing the Freudian Unconscious: Lyotard's Affect-Phrase," *Diacritics* 24, no. 1 (1994): 43–62.
32. Freud and Breuer, *Studies in Hysteria,* in *Standard Edition,* 2:6.
33. Jean Laplanche emphasizes this point when, in an extended commentary on *Nachträglichkeit,* he writes, "Neither of the two events in itself is traumatic; neither is a rush of excitation. The first one? It triggers nothing: neither excitation or reaction, nor symbolization or psychical elaboration" (*Life and Death in Psychoanalysis,* trans. Jeffrey Mehlman [Baltimore MD: Johns Hopkins University Press, 1976], 41; originally published as *Vie et mort en psychanalyse* [Paris: Flammarion, 1970]). See also Laplanche and J.-B. Pontalis's entry on "Après-coup" in their *Vocabulaire de la psychanalyse* (Paris: PUF, 1967).
34. There is an ominous irony in the trope of the lower case "jews" of which Lyotard almost certainly is not aware. In Nazi Germany, the publishing industry, in a common anti-Semitic impulse, was thought to be "infiltrated" with Jews; as a consequence, meticulous lists chronicled the "racial" affiliations of publishers by means of the designations small "a" for Aryan and small "j" for Jewish. In his essay "Ruminations of a Slow-witted Mind" (*Critical Inquiry* 17 [1990]), written in 1933, Robert Musil laments the pervasiveness of anti-Semitism and the widespread assumptions that Jewish middlemen controlled the publishing industry, offering the following sampling of a "racial" listing of publishers: "if I go over them without naming names (Fischer j [Jewish], Insel a [Aryan], DVA [Deutsche Verlagsanstalt] a, Row[ohlt] 1/2 2 [Ernst and Paul] Cassirer, j j, Diederichs a, Kiepenh[auer] a, G. Müller a, Verlag der Mar. Ges. a), the list conains more Aryans than Jews" (60). Lyotard's deployment of the lower case "jews" notwithstanding,

Musil's listing is compelling evidence that the lower case "j" was a less than neutral (and decidedly non-tropic) predictor of who would eventually be deported to the death camps.

35. I think it appropriate here to echo the title of Žižek's *The Sublime Object of Ideology*, given the author's own unresolved "discourse of the Jew," and in particular his constituting of the Jew as a kind of traumatic, incomprehensible "excess of symbolization."

36. "The Sublime and the Avant-Garde," trans. Lisa Liebmann, Geoff Bennington, and Marian Hobson, *Paragraph* 6 (1985): 9. The French text is a paper delivered by Lyotard in Cambridge, England, in March 1984.

37. Lacan, *The Absolute Master*, 34.

Afterword: Back to the Future of Psychoanalysis

1. René Girard, *Violence and the Sacred*, trans. Patrick Gregory (Baltimore MD: Johns Hopkins University Press, 1977); Jean-Joseph Goux, *Symbolic Economies: After Marx and Freud*, trans. Jennifer Curtiss Gage (Ithaca NY: Cornell University Press, 1990); Michel de Certeau, *The Writing of History*, trans. Tom Conley (New York: Columbia University Press, 1988), 312.

2. "From Where Is Psychoanalysis Possible?," trans. Brian Holmes, in "The Psychoanalytical Field," ed. Jean-Marie Apostolidès, special issue of *Stanford Literature Review* 8, nos. 1–2 (1991): 39–55.

3. "Archive Fever: A Freudian Impression," trans. Eric Prenowitz, *Diacritics* 25, no. 2 (1995): 26. This was a lecture presented in 1994 in London at an international conference titled "Memory: The Question of Archives," organized by René Major and Elisabeth Roudinesco.

4. For more on the importance of Freud's Philippsohn Bible, see William J. McGrath, *Freud's Discovery of Psychoanalysis: The Politics of Hysteria* (Ithaca NY: Cornell University Press, 1986), 46–53.

5. In this context, it is worth noting that de Certeau, in his chapter on *Moses and Monotheism*, also seems to be grappling with the complexities of this question when he writes, "Freud is Jewish, and I am not. Then what can I ultimately 'understand' about this *other* [Moses] without whom I could not be a Christian, and who evades me by being, 'behind,' the necessary figure who stays inaccessible, the repressed who returns?" (*The Writing of History*, 34; italics in original).

6. "Nothing Fails Like Success," in *A World of Difference* (Baltimore MD: Johns Hopkins University Press, 1987), 14.

*The Jews and Germany: From
the "Judeo-German Symbiosis" to
the Memory of Auschwitz*
By Enzo Traverso
Translated by Daniel Weissbort

*Richard Wagner and the
Anti-Semitic Imagination*
By Marc A. Weiner

*Undertones of Insurrection: Music,
Politics, and the Social Sphere
in the Modern German Narrative*
By Marc A. Weiner

*The Mirror and the Word:
Modernism, Literary Theory, and
Georg Trakl*
By Eric B. Williams

Index

Index